Curating Design

Curating Design

Context, Culture and Reflective Practice

DONNA LOVEDAY

BLOOMSBURY VISUAL ARTS

LONDON · NEW YORK · OXFORD · NEW DELHI · SYDNEY

BLOOMSBURY VISUAL ARTS
Bloomsbury Publishing Plc
50 Bedford Square, London, WC1B 3DP, UK
1385 Broadway, New York, NY 10018, USA
29 Earlsfort Terrace, Dublin 2, Ireland

BLOOMSBURY, BLOOMSBURY VISUAL ARTS and the Diana logo are trademarks of
Bloomsbury Publishing Plc

First published in Great Britain 2022

Cover design by Louise Dugdale
Cover image, Left: *The Revolution Woodstove*, Bits to Atoms and
Beirut Makers. 5th Istanbul Design Biennial, 2020 © Kayhan Kaygusuz.
Right: The Design Museum ©Hufton+Crow

A catalogue record for this book is available from the British Library.

Library of Congress Cataloging-in-Publication Data
Names: Loveday, Donna, author. Title: Curating design / Donna Loveday.
Description: London ; New York : Bloomsbury Visual Arts, 2022. |
Includes bibliographical references and index.
Identifiers: LCCN 2022005841 (print) | LCCN 2022005842 (ebook) |
ISBN 9781350162761 (paperback) | ISBN 9781350162778 (hardback) |
ISBN 9781350162792 (pdf) | ISBN 9781350162785 (epub)
Subjects: LCSH: Decorative arts–Museums. | Museums–Curatorship.
Classification: LCC NK450 .L68 2022 (print) | LCC NK450 (ebook) |
DDC 745.075–dc23/eng/20220412
LC record available at https://lccn.loc.gov/2022005841
LC ebook record available at https://lccn.loc.gov/2022005842

ISBN: HB: 978-1-3501-6277-8
PB: 978-1-3501-6276-1
ePDF: 978-1-3501-6279-2
eBook: 978-1-3501-6278-5

Typeset by Newgen KnowledgeWorks Pvt. Ltd., Chennai, India
Printed and bound in India

To find out more about our authors and books visit www.bloomsbury.com
and sign up for our newsletters.

Contents

Illustrations

Contributors

Renata Becerril is a design curator and critic based in Mexico City. Renata is the founding director of the international design festival, *Abierto Mexicano de Diseño*, the first of its type in Latin America. She also established and directs *Capitales*, a design consultancy and gallery. She has worked for Vitra Design Museum and curated exhibitions for the World Bank (the design section in *About Change: Art from Latin America and the Caribbean*), The London Festival of Architecture (*mAxico: Architectures from Mexico*), the Franz Mayer Museum (*Tapetes: Tapetes Anudando Historias – Enlazando Ideas*) and several exhibitions within the design festival *Abierto Mexicano de Diseño*. Renata has taught at the design university *Centro* where she was Head of Foundation Year. She has also been a guest nominator for the *Designs of the Year* exhibition at the Design Museum, London. She holds an MA in Curating Contemporary Design from Kingston University in partnership with the Design Museum, London. Renata is currently working on an urban project focused on placemaking for the government of Tampico, in the State of Tamaulipas in Mexico.

Wilhelm Finger is a founder and co-director of Double Decker, a curating and design practice which occupies a unique space in its field. The London-based studio curates artwork collections for leading hotels and cruise liners. The studio also designs visual identities and curates exhibitions and events for high-profile cultural institutions, including the Oscar Niemeyer Museum, Brazil, the Design Museum, London, the Science Museum, London and the Onassis Cultural Centre, Athens. Wilhelm has a visual design publishing practice that predates his work with Double Decker. He has worked on collaborations with some of the world's most distinctive brands such as Comme des Garçons and Palais de Tokyo. Wilhelm studied Communication Design at Central Saint Martin's, London, and holds an MA in Curating Contemporary Design from Kingston University in partnership with the Design Museum, London, where he met his creative partner Melita Skamnaki, sparking the birth of Double Decker.

Corinna Gardner is Senior Curator of Design and Digital at the Victoria & Albert Museum, London. Corinna leads the museum's Rapid Response Collecting programme and her research focuses on contemporary product and digital design and the role they play in society. She was lead curator, together with Johanna Agerman Ross, on a new gallery for twentieth- and twenty-first-century design that opened at the V&A in 2021, *Design 1900–Now*. In 2015, Corinna co-curated *All of This Belongs to You*, an exhibition about the design of public life and the role of institutions in contemporary society. Prior to joining the V&A, Corinna worked at Barbican Art Gallery, London on exhibitions including *Bauhaus: Art as Life* (2012), *OMA: Progress* (2011), Random International's *Rain Room* (2012) and Cory Arcangel's *Beat the Champ* (2011). She holds an MA in History of Design from the Royal College of Art and the V&A, London. Corinna is working towards the development and delivery of a digital design collecting strategy for the V&A. She is also working on exhibitions about design and public good, and the problem and promise of plastic in today's world.

Andrea Lipps is Associate Curator of Contemporary Design at Cooper Hewitt, Smithsonian Design Museum, New York, where she conceives, develops and organizes major award-winning exhibitions and books, most recently *Nature – Cooper Hewitt Design Triennial* (2019), *The Senses: Design beyond Vision* (2018), *Joris Laarman Lab: Design in the Digital Age* (2017) and *Beauty – Cooper Hewitt Design Triennial* (2016). Andrea is an accomplished writer and editor on contemporary design, having authored and edited numerous publications, essays and scholarly articles. Her work has appeared in the *New York Times*, *Wall Street Journal*, the *New Yorker*, *Vogue*, *WWD*, *Architectural Digest, W* and *The Financial Times*. She is a regular visiting critic, lecturer and thesis advisor. She participates on international design juries and frequently moderates and speaks at events, symposia and academic conferences. She holds an MA in Decorative Arts and Design from Parsons with the Cooper Hewitt, Smithsonian Design Museum. Andrea is currently leading the museum's efforts to build its nascent Digital Design collection.

Riya Patel is a design and architecture curator and writer. From 2015 to 2020 she was curator of The Aram Gallery in London, an independent gallery space dedicated to new and experimental design. Riya is a contributing editor at *Icon* magazine and writes for several publications including *Disegno*, *Wallpaper* and *The Independent*. She was previously senior editor at *Icon* and spent a year in Amsterdam as an editor of *Frame* magazine. Riya began her journalism career at the *Architects' Journal* and *The Architectural Review*, and holds an MArch in Architecture from Cardiff University.

Melita Skamnaki is a founder and co-director of Double Decker, a curating and design practice which occupies a unique space in its field. The London-based studio curates artwork collections for leading hotels and cruise liners. The studio also designs visual identities and curates exhibitions and events for high-profile cultural institutions, including the Oscar Niemeyer Museum, Brazil, the Design Museum, London, the Science Museum, London and the Onassis Cultural Centre, Athens. Previously Melita was a creative director at

DDB Athens, Upset and Ogilvy, Athens, overseeing accounts with Vodafone, Aegean Airlines and Action Aid. She studied Art and Design at Camberwell College of Arts, London, and holds an MA in Curating Contemporary Design from Kingston University in partnership with the Design Museum, London, where she met her creative partner Wilhelm Finger, sparking the birth of Double Decker.

Sumitra Upham is Head of Public Programmes at the Crafts Council, London. From 2017 to 2021, Sumitra was Senior Curator of Public Programmes at the Design Museum, London, where she was responsible for programming residencies and temporary projects. In 2019 she was appointed Curator of Programmes for the 5th Istanbul Design Biennial, *Empathy Re-Visited: Designs for More than One*, curated by Mariana Pestana with Billie Muraben. In 2020, she joined the Board of Trustees at Cubitt. Previously, Sumitra was associate curator at the Institute of Contemporary Arts, London, where she curated educational projects and exhibitions including *Radical Disco: Architecture and Nightlife in Italy, 1965–1975* in collaboration with Dr Catharine Rossi, *See Red Women's Workshop* and *Shout Out! UK Pirate Radio in the 1980s*. Prior to this, she was part of the exhibitions team at White Cube, London. Sumitra holds an MA in Curating Contemporary Design from Kingston University in partnership with the Design Museum, London.

Fleur Watson is Executive Director and Chief Curator for the Centre for Architecture Victoria | Open House Melbourne. From 2012 to 2020 Fleur was Curator and Industry Fellow at RMIT Design Hub Gallery where she co-directed an ambitious programme experimenting with new ways to exhibit, perform and translate the design process and creative research in active exchange with public audiences. Fleur has held senior curatorial roles in Australia and internationally, including as the founding executive curator for the Lyon Housemuseum Galleries (2018–19); invited architecture curator for the National Gallery of Victoria's survey exhibition *Melbourne Now* (2013–14); curator (architecture) for the European Capital of Culture (Maribor, Slovenia, 2012) and a contributing exhibitor for *Formations* (Australian pavilion) at the 13th Venice Architecture Biennale. She has curated a series of design festival programmes including *Unlimited: Designing for the Asia Pacific* (2010) and *State of Design Festival* (2007–9) and, in 2010, co-founded *Pin-Up Project Space*, an independent exhibition space for architecture and design (2010–14). Fleur holds an MA in Curating Contemporary Design from Kingston University in partnership with the Design Museum, London, and in 2015 completed a practice-based PhD at RMIT University. Fleur is a former editor of *Monument* magazine (2001–7), the series editor for *Editions: Australian Architectural Monographs* (Thames & Hudson) and author of the publication, *The New Curator: Exhibiting Architecture & Design* (Routledge, 2021).

Acknowledgements

This book marks the development of a curatorial practice that began some twenty-five years ago. Over that time, my thinking and practice has been shaped with the support of many people.

The book derives from a body of research undertaken for a doctoral degree at Kingston University. Special thanks go to my academic supervisors, Professor Penny Sparke and Dr Catharine Rossi for their careful guidance and for sharing many first-hand insights into the development of design as theory and practice. I would also like to thank Kingston University for the financial support that enabled me to pursue the PhD.

I am grateful to my former colleagues at the Barbican and the Design Museum, London, for giving me the opportunity to work on so many inspiring exhibitions, and where I was able to learn and hone my practice as a curator. Special thanks to staff at the Design Museum for providing access to the museum's archives during a busy transition period, in particular Tom Wilson, Head of Collections.

I have been fortunate to witness the developing practice of design curation through my roles as curator, head of Exhibitions and head of Curatorial at the Design Museum and through my role as course leader on the MA Curating Contemporary Design at Kingston University in partnership with the Design Museum. Special thanks to Professor Catherine McDermott for her encouragement and support. Thanks also to my current teaching partner, Associate Professor Jana Scholze, for her support.

I would also like to thank the editorial team at Bloomsbury especially commissioning editor, Rebecca Barden, and editorial assistant, Olivia Davies, and all those who have given kind permission for images to be used in this publication.

And finally, a big thank you to my parents for their love and support and, most importantly, to Simon for his constant and unwavering encouragement and support.

Introduction

In November 2016, London's Design Museum moved from its former location at Shad Thames in south-east London to open in its new home on Kensington High Street, west London. Housed in a landmark grade II listed modernist building from the 1960s, which had been the site of the Commonwealth Institute, the project was the culmination of a five-year construction process (Figure 0.1). Designed by John Pawson, two basement levels were excavated below the footprint of the original building increasing its floor plan to 10,000 square metres. The museum had now tripled in size from its previous premises in south-east London. The renovated building, with its distinctive copper-covered, hyperbolic paraboloid roof, offered two major temporary gallery spaces, a free permanent collection display, a restaurant overlooking Holland Park, auditorium, studios, library, archive and new learning facilities.[1] In a press release issued by the museum, Director Deyan Sudjic explained:

This project is important not just for the museum but for the investment in the creative future that it represents. The Design Museum sees design as borderless, international in scope and a vital means of understanding the world around us.

The first two exhibitions at the museum's new location in Kensington signalled an evolving curatorial strategy that was moving away from the original focus of the museum on the mass-manufactured object when it opened in 1989.

The museum's opening exhibition, *Fear and Love: Reactions to a Complex World* (24 November 2016–23 April 2017) featured eleven newly commissioned works by designers and architects dealing with pressing contemporary topics (Figure 0.2). The exhibition explored a spectrum of issues including networked sexuality, sentient robots, slow fashion and settled nomads. The exhibition

---

[1] 'The Design Museum Opens in Kensington', Design Museum: Press Release, 24 November 2016. Available at: https://designmuseum.org/new-design-museum (accessed 15 December 2018).

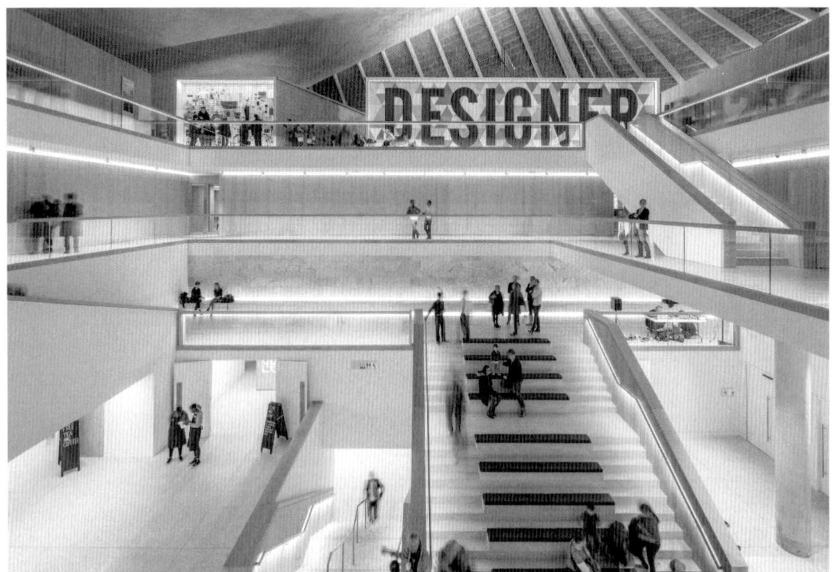

FIGURE 0.1 *Interior view, the Design Museum, London, 2016.*
© *Gareth Gardner.*

was curated by the museum's Chief Curator, Justin McGuirk, who had been appointed to the role in 2015 from his previous role as editor of *Icon* magazine.[2] The exhibition presented the proposition that design in the twenty-first century is deeply connected not just to commerce and culture, which had been a focus for the museum in its early years, but to urgent underlying political and social issues that inspire fear and love.

Through the exhibition, McGuirk argued that issues such as sustainability, climate change, anxieties over the spread of surveillance and the growth of digital technology are now central to our understanding of mass-produced objects. By inviting designers to create installations for the exhibition, the museum presented itself as a laboratory of ideas and as a place for engaging with, and understanding, how the world is changing.[3]

This position reflected a new focus for design museums globally and a more critical engagement with contemporary design practice. In the twenty-first century, the world is confronting many challenges and design is one

---

[2] Dan Howarth, 'Justin McGuirk Appointed Chief Curator at London's Design Museum', *Dezeen*, 3 August 2015. Available at: https://www.dezeen.com/2015/08/03/justin-mcguirk-appointed-chief-curator-london-design-museum (accessed 12 December 2018).

[3] *'Fear and Love: Reactions to a Complex World'*, Design Museum: Press Release, 24 November 2016–23 April 2017. Available at: https://designmuseum.org/new-design-museum (accessed 12 December 2019).

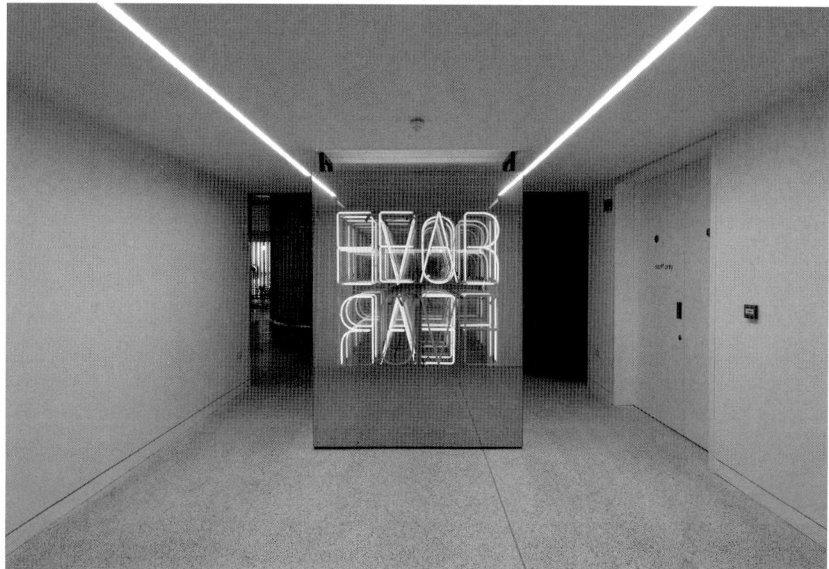

FIGURE 0.2 Fear and Love: Reactions to a Complex World, *Design Museum, London, 24 November 2016–23 April 2017. © Max Creasy / OK-RM.*

of many tools with which to address those challenges, both not only on a small scale but also at a larger, more global scale. Writing in 2016, McGuirk explained:

> I want to get away from the idea of a design museum being a place where you put objects on plinths. I want a more experiential format that allows you to think about issues, ideas and experiences … Design used to be for the user but now the user is increasingly one of the determinants of the outcome.[4]

In December 2014, following a three-year closure, the Cooper Hewitt, Smithsonian Design Museum in New York reopened. The renovated Carnegie Mansion offered 60 per cent more exhibition space with four floors of exhibition galleries and the first full-floor installation devoted to works from the museum's collection. Ten exhibitions and installations throughout the building prompted and responded to key questions at the heart of design. In a press release issued by the museum, Director Caroline Baumann commented:

---

[4]Richard Martin, 'What Are Design Museums For?', *Apollo*, 26 September 2016. Available at: https://www.apollo-magazine.com/what-are-design-museums-for/ (accessed 3 October 2019).

> The new Cooper Hewitt is a must-see and must-do destination to experience historical and contemporary design in a way like never before. The museum's dynamic exhibition programme, enhanced by interactive experiences that draw the visitor into the design process, will shape how people think about the power of design and ultimately, its capability to solve real world problems.[5]

The Design Museum in London and the Cooper Hewitt, Smithsonian Design Museum in New York are examples of a global expansion in design-focused museums. This expansion can be interpreted as a response to the growing importance of design, its increasing visibility and, as design critic Liz Farrelly has suggested, 'the authority of the museum to speak for design'.[6]

Design is a fast-changing subject. The term has come to encompass so many things in the past few decades, objects but also services, systems, experiences, the virtual and the digital. When the Design Museum opened in London in 1989, it was the first in the UK of a new type of specialist museum focusing on the collection, study and exhibition of design. At the time of its opening, it was one of a small number of high-profile design and applied arts museums internationally, which included the Museum of Modern Art (MoMA) and the Cooper Hewitt, Smithsonian Design Museum in New York; the MAK in Vienna; the Design Museum in Helsinki and Vitra Design Museum in Weil am Rhein.

The past two decades have witnessed an increasing number of design museums opening globally, inspired by the development of design museums across Europe. In 2007, 21_21 Design Sight opened in Tokyo. In the following year, the Design Museum of Barcelona was established, and in 2009 the Gallery of Australian Design opened in Canberra. Inspired by these models, China has established its first design museums in Shanghai and Shenzhen, and recruited its first design curators.[7] In April 2018 the China Design Museum opened in Hangzhou in east China's Zhejiang Province. The museum is located on the campus of the China Academy of Art (CAA). The building, designed by

---

[5]Cooper Hewitt, Smithsonian Design Museum: Press Release, 'Cooper Hewitt Reopens after Three-Year Renovation', 9 December 2014. Available at: https://www.si.edu/newsdesk/releases/coo per-hewitt-reopens-dec-12-after-three-year-renovation (accessed 3 October 2019); Holland Cotter, 'Newly Playful, by Design: Cooper Hewitt, Smithsonian Design Museum Reopens', *New York Times*, 11 December 2014. Available at: https://www.nytimes.com/2014/12/12/arts/design/cooper-hewitt-smithsonian-design-museum-reopens.html. (accessed 3 October 2019).
[6]Liz Farrelly, 'Media in the Museum: Fashioning the Design Museum Curator at the Boilerhouse Gallery, Victoria and Albert Museum, London', in Leah Armstrong and Felice McDowell (eds), *Fashioning Identities: Identity and Representation at Work in the Creative Industries*, London: Bloomsbury, 2018: 29.
[7]Brendan Cormier, 'Introducing "Values of Design" and China's First Design Museum', *V&A Blog*, 1 June 2007. Available at: https://www.vam.ac.uk/blog/international-initiatives/introducing-values-of-design-and-chinas-first-design-museum (accessed 20 October 2019).

Portuguese architect Alvaro Siza, covers a total floor area of 16,800 square metres with design studios, a children's workshop and a roof garden. In a series of interviews shortly after the museum's opening, Youmin Yuan, deputy curator, commented that it was the country's first specialist design museum and one of a few professional design museums on such a large scale around the world.[8] In November 2021 M+, Asia's first global museum of contemporary culture, opened in the West Kowloon Cultural District of Hong Kong. Designed by world-renowned architecture practice Herzog & de Meuron, the 65,000-square-metre building brings design together with visual art, architecture and moving image across thirty-three galleries and other display spaces in the museum. Doryun Chong, deputy director and chief curator, explained that M+ was founded with an ambitious mission 'to create a new kind of multidisciplinary cultural institution dedicated to visual culture … grounded in Asia like no other in the world'.[9]

Design exhibitions are popular and attract large audiences. Over the last four decades, design-focused temporary exhibitions and permanent displays have taken place not only in design museums and galleries but also in other public spaces across the world. Increasingly museums and venues that have traditionally presented exhibitions focusing on fine art or the decorative arts have started to realize the potential of the design exhibition to reach a wider audience. Since the early 2000s, London venues such as the V&A, Barbican and Somerset House have staged contemporary design exhibitions that have attracted substantial audiences and media coverage. As an example, in 2015 the V&A presented *Alexander McQueen: Savage Beauty* (14 March–2 August 2015). The exhibition was first staged at the Metropolitan Museum of Art in New York in 2011. Curated by former V&A curator, Andrew Bolton, the exhibition attracted over 650,000 visitors in three months, a record for a fashion exhibition at the museum. In 2015 *Savage Beauty* opened at the V&A, London. The exhibition, curated by Claire Wilcox, was the first retrospective of McQueen's work in Europe and the largest showcase of his work.[10]

In the same year the Barbican hosted *The World of Charles and Ray Eames* (21 October 2015–14 February 2016), an exhibition that explored the work of two of the most influential designers of the twentieth century

---

[8]Xinhua/Weng Xinyang, 'China Design Museum Launches First Exhibitions in Hangzhou', *SINA*, 9 April 2018. Available at: http://www.china.org.cn/photos/2018-04/09/content_50847922.htm (accessed 20 October 2019).

[9]'M+ – Asia's First Global Museum of Contemporary Visual Culture – to Open This November in Hong Kong', M+: Press Release, 8 September 2021. Available at: https://www.westkowloon.hk/en/press-release/m-asia-first-global-museum-contemporary-visual-culture-open-november-hong-kong (accessed 20 October 2019).

[10]Will Coldwell, 'London Visitor Numbers Hit Record Levels', *The Guardian*, 20 May 2016. Available at: https://www.theguardian.com/travel/2016/may/20/london-record-visitor-numbers-2015-31-5-mill ion (accessed 3 October 2018).

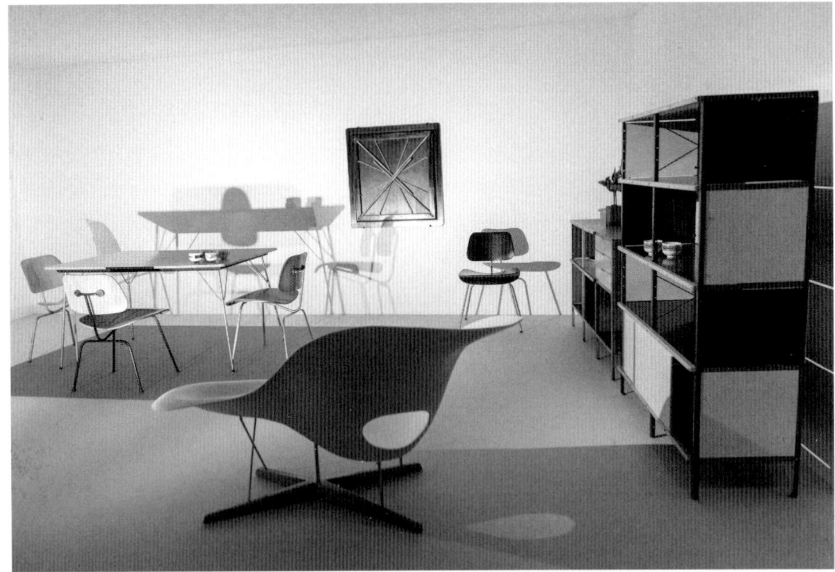

FIGURE 0.3 The World of Charles and Ray Eames, *Barbican Art Gallery, London, 21 October 2015–14 February 2016.* © *Tristan Fewings / Getty Images.*

(Figure 0.3). Featuring photography, film, architecture, exhibition-making, furniture and product design, the exhibition provided an insight into the lives of the designers, the Eames Office and the breadth of their groundbreaking work across many fields.[11] The exhibition was curated by Catherine Ince who is now chief curator at V&A East, a significant new museum project that will celebrate global creativity opening in 2025 at Queen Elizabeth Olympic Park, London.

At the end of 2015, Somerset House presented *Big Bang Data* (3 December 2015–20 March 2016), an exhibition exploring the way in which data is transforming the world through the work of artists, designers, journalists and visionaries. As the data explosion accelerated, the exhibition aimed to foster a greater understanding of the meaning and implications of data for the future.[12] The exhibition was curated by Olga Subirós and José Luis de Vicente whose curatorial work sits between the intersection of culture, technology and design. All of the exhibitions explored subjects across a range of design disciplines. They generated extensive media coverage and drew substantial audiences,

---

[11] 'The World of Charles and Ray Eames', Barbican: Press Release, 21 October 2015–14 February 2016. Available at: https://www.barbican.org.uk/the-world-of-charles-and-ray-eames (accessed 15 June 2019).

[12] Somerset House: Press Release. Available at: http://bigbangdata.somersethouse.org.uk (accessed 15 June 2019).

which further expanded when the exhibitions toured to international museum venues.

In 2018 the Institute of Contemporary Arts (ICA) presented the first UK exhibition of the work of the research-led design and architecture practice, Forensic Architecture (*Counter-Investigations: Forensic Architecture*: 7 March–6 May 2018), who were shortlisted for the Turner Prize in the same year. The ICA hosted a solo show by the Dutch design practice, Metahaven (*Metahaven: Version History*: 3 October 2018–13 January 2019). In 2020 the Serpentine Galleries presented an exhibition by the research-based design studio, Formafantasma (*Cambio*: 29 September–15 November 2020). The multidisciplinary exhibition highlighted the role that design can play in the environment and its responsibility to look beyond the edges of its borders as a discipline. This shift in art institutions bringing design into their exhibition programmes reflects an acknowledgement of design as a critical subject and investigative tool. Design is seen as intrinsic to contemporary art practice and implies an acceptance of the design exhibition within the wider framework of art and design. It also suggests that there is a public appetite for such exhibitions, which help to open up design to larger and more diverse audiences. Design curation has now emerged as a specific site of practice on an international stage. The results of this practice can be seen not only in museums and galleries but also at biennials, design festivals and trade fairs. But what does design curating entail and how do design curators curate? It is these questions that form the central focus of this book.

It seems a particularly important moment to be asking such questions. Curating design is an evolving and dynamic practice, but it remains an underexplored area of contemporary curatorial practice. In her essay, *Who Cares? Understanding the Role of the Curator*, international art curator Kate Fowle focuses attention on the nature of curating in a contemporary context. Fowle argues that the role of the curator has come a long way from its traditional definition as a 'guardian', 'overseer' or 'carer' of collections.[13] She reflects on how curating has expanded beyond its traditional parameters to become a diverse practice, located within the institution and outside of it:

---

[13]Harald Szeemann, 'Does Art Need Directors?', in Carin Kuoni (ed.), *Words of Wisdom: A Curator's Vade Mecum on Contemporary* Art, New York: Independent Curator's International, 2001: 167. Szeemann explores the root of the word *curare*, meaning 'to take care of'. While the word stems from the Latin, in English it evolved to mean 'guardian' or 'overseer'. From 1362, 'curator' was used to signify people who cared for (or were in charge of) minors or lunatics, and in 1661 it began to denote 'one in charge of a museum, library, zoo or other place of exhibit'. In each case, a curator is someone who presides *over* something, suggesting an inherent relationship between care and control.

> The curator is having an identity crisis. Curating is now an industry, constructing its own histories as it evolves. At the same time, it is an increasingly multifaceted practice that gives rise to much speculation as to how it functions and what it entails.[14]

She urges that such a rapid development has brought about a need to understand the field, and this call to action has influenced the rationale for this book.

As new design museums are built, and existing museums redefined, there has been a simultaneous boom in museum studies and curator-led publications. During the 1990s and 2000s one of the main developments driving change in the sector was the emergence of publications that examined the development of curatorship more broadly as an evolving practice.[15] Jens Hoffmann, in explaining his rationale for creating a journal of curatorial studies *The Exhibitionist*, commented that 'one measure of the vitality of a discipline is the intensity of the debate surrounding it'.[16] Hoffmann considers that the discussion around curatorial practice has intensified over the last decade, including the founding of numerous academic programmes, the creation of conferences and the publication of an increasing number of specialized books. He also notes that the discipline has not, up until now, had a consistent platform of more frequent and interconnected conversations that bring together the many fragments of the current dialogue.

In spite of the fact that design curating has been a rapidly expanding field of practice, the area remains largely undocumented, seeming to occupy 'a blind spot' in histories of curating with few critical histories of the practice. Design historian and a former curator at the V&A, Gareth Williams has noted that design in the museum context has historically occupied a peripheral position within exhibition-making:

> Museums have had a chequered relationship with design, at various times seeing it as the poor relation of architecture, as commercialised fine art, as evidence of social or technological history, or as the antithesis of craft skills. Design practice, as opposed to other disciplines implied in this list,

---

[14]Kate Fowle, 'Who Cares? Understanding the Role of the Curator Today', in *Cautionary Tales: Critical Curating*, New York: apexart 2007: 26.

[15]Publications include Reesa Greenberg, Bruce W. Ferguson and Sandy Nairne, *Thinking about Exhibitions*, London: Routledge, 1996.

[16]Jens Hoffmann (ed.), *The Exhibitionist: Journal on Exhibition Making – The First Six Years 2010–2016*, New York: Artbook/D. A. P., 2017: 29.

seems to find it hard to be considered as an autonomous subject ... design has been in the blind spot of museums.[17]

Liz Farrelly and Joanna Weddell note in their introduction to *Design Objects and the Museum* that design museums have received far less critical attention than art museums. The authors observe that 'the museology of the art museum has been extensively discussed, published and taught while that of the design museum has received less attention'.[18] They suggest that this imbalance reflects the status and position of the functional objects housed by museums of design compared with fine art together with a lack of historical depth of scholarship. They argue that the specific concerns of design museums continue to be neglected and that this seems to confirm broader uncertainties about the status and value of design museums' collections and displays.

The views of Williams, Farrelly and Weddell connect to a broader discussion about a lack of understanding around what curators do, and how this is overlooked in both academic and more public-facing literature. In newspaper reviews and design journals, the final exhibition is publicly critiqued but curators rarely reveal or publish the thinking, inspiration and processes behind an exhibition. While art curating has an evolved historiography with self-reflective practitioners interested in charting the history and practice of its output through books, conferences and contributions to online forums, the history of curating contemporary design is marginally covered. This becomes particularly apparent when reviewing the multiple texts that explore the development of curatorial practice over the last two decades.[19] The studies are either anthologies that comprise the collected writings and interviews of a single curator or which bring together the perspectives of a group of curators. The publications are generally intended to undertake a mapping of the terrain of curating from a critical perspective and by drawing on the insights of leading practitioners, but specifically with reference to the field of art.

---

[17]Gareth Williams, 'On the Problematic Relationship between Institutions and Critical Design Thinking', in Frida Jeppsson (ed.), *In Case of Design – Inject Critical Thinking*, Stockholm: Frida Jeppsson, 2010: 27.

[18]Liz Farrelly and Joanna Weddell (eds), *Design Objects and the Museum*, London: Bloomsbury, 2012: xx.

[19]Publications include Hans Ulrich Obrist, *A Brief History of Curating*, Zurich: JRP/Ringier, 2008; Carolee Thea, *On Curating: Interviews with Ten International Curators*, New York: Distributed Art, 2009; Hans Ulrich Obrist, *Everything You Always Wanted to Know about Curating*, Berlin: Sternberg Press, 2011; Paula Marincola (ed.), *What Makes a Great Exhibition?*, Philadelphia: Philadelphia Exhibitions Press, 2006; Terry Smith, *Thinking Contemporary Curating*, New York: Independent Curators International, 2012; Jean-Paul Martinon (ed.), *The Curatorial: A Philosophy of Curating*, London: Bloomsbury, 2013; Jens Hoffmann, (ed.), *Ten Fundamental Questions of Curating*, Milan: Mousse, 2013.

Curating is a practice under scrutiny with the term now used to describe activities in many different contexts. Today everything is 'curated', from menus and interiors to playlists and phone apps. Google invites users to curate their profiles across a range of digital platforms. Restaurants and bars provide menus curated by a food expert. The windows and displays inside department stores and fashion boutiques are often described as being curated, and include artwork and props in their carefully designed interiors. In the commercial world, the term 'curator' has come to designate someone who pulls together, sifts through and selects to create some sort of sense. This type of curating is not situated in museums and galleries but in restaurants, department stores, boutiques and online.

In a digital age, the rise of social media has enabled anyone to share their opinions, to select and present or curate a scenario through a plethora of digital platforms such as Facebook, Instagram, Pinterest and Twitter. With a flood of content being published on the internet every day, the process of curation has become an important part of how users find and personalize content. The term 'content curation' is now a recognized term to describe the process of sorting through the vast amounts of content on the web and presenting it in a meaningful and organized way around a particular theme. A content curator is continually and consistently staying on top of a topic area and is a trusted resource for their audience. They are required to be discerning, discriminating and selective in only sharing the most relevant content. They specialize in a single specific topic and over time have the opportunity to become an authority, and perhaps even a thought leader on that subject.

These new contexts enable everyone to 'curate', with the result that the traditional role of curating within the museum is increasingly less understood. These changing contexts for curating have generated a significant debate on the role of the curator. David Balzer has defined the shift as 'curationism', which he describes as the acceleration of the curatorial impulse to become a dominant way of thinking and being.[20] He suggests that since the 1990s, society has been living in the 'curationist moment' in which institutions and businesses rely on others, often variously credentialed experts, 'to cultivate and organise things in an expression-cum-assurance of value and an attempt to make affiliations with, and to court, various audiences and consumers'. He argues that, as these audiences and consumers, we are also 'cultivating and organizing our identities'.[21]

Many have argued that the appropriation of the term represents a cynical exploitation of its traditional meaning. Curator and documentary filmmaker

---

[20]David Balzar, *Curationism: How Curating Took Over the Art World and Everything Else*, London: Pluto Press, 2015: 2–3.
[21]Ibid.: 2–3.

Steven Rosenbaum has identified this development as part of a 'curation nation' with brands, publishers and content entrepreneurs embracing the concept of curation to grow an existing business or launch a new one. Rosenbaum suggests that, as the sheer volume of digital information in the world increases, the demand for quality and context becomes more urgent and that curation is the only way to be competitive in the future.

Rosenbaum accepts that museum curators are forced to compete with media curation but he also makes two important distinctions. First, that curation is about adding value from individuals who add their qualitative judgement to whatever is being gathered or organized, implying that the use of the term 'curator' in any context lends an authority and status to the activity. Second, that there is amateur and professional curation, and the emergence of amateur and 'prosumer' curators is not in any way a threat to professionals.[22] Similarly, Jean-Paul Martinon has suggested that the very fact that the curatorial seeps and bleeds into many different fields and practices, which some complain is a problem, is precisely what gives it its power and potential. It is also 'what makes it quintessentially of our time and, inevitably, a difficult thing to define'.[23]

As curatorial and exhibition-making activity is increasingly performed by professionals who are not aligned to a particular institution or responsible for a collection, debate over the definition and use of the term continues, and alternative meanings are sought to accurately describe the activity of devising and producing exhibitions. Sociologists Nathalie Heinich and Michael Pollack describe the role of an exhibition 'auteur', who devises the exhibition concept and also determines content and design. They reference the field of film studies where the term has been used to describe the role of a film director who applies a highly centralized and subjective control to many aspects of a collaborative creative work.[24]

The artist and critic Robert Storr proposes the term 'exhibition-maker' in relation to the activity of exhibition production as an alternative to curator because 'it acknowledges the existence of a specific and highly complex discipline and separates the care or preservation of art – a curator's primary concern – from its variable display'.[25] Storr's definition implies a compression of activities traditionally seen as being the remit of distinct individuals, the curator and the exhibition designer.

---

[22]Steven Rosenbaum, *Curation Nation: How to Win in a World Where Consumers Are Curators*, New York: McGraw Hill, 2010: 3.
[23]Martinon (ed.), *The Curatorial*: 3.
[24]Nathalie Heinich and Michael Pollak, 'From Museum Curator to Exhibition Auteur', in Greenberg, Ferguson and Nairne (eds), *Thinking about Exhibitions*: 231–50.
[25]Robert Storr, 'Show and Tell', in Paula Marincola (ed.), *What Makes a Great Exhibition?*: 14.

In response to a practice under scrutiny and a growing discourse on the subject, Sarah Pierce asks, 'How did we get to a place where the curatorial means so much? Does it matter? How? To when? Is the curatorial a condition? A device? Is it a field or subject?'[26] There is clearly a need to understand what constitutes this multifaceted practice, specifically in relation to curating design. It is into this body of work, and a perceived gap in literature on the practice of curating contemporary design, that this book is positioned. *Curating Design* seeks to understand and represent the practice of curating design. It responds to developments in the field over the last four decades: the development of design-focused museums globally, an expanding design industry, the growing popularity of design exhibitions and new postgraduate programmes to train curators. In addition, a number of key shifts such as rising museum attendances, the popularity of the 'blockbuster' exhibition, increased media coverage and the proliferation of new curatorial platforms such as the international biennial have translated into a growing interest in the role of the curator and curating practice.[27] These broader shifts have inevitably impacted on the practice of curating design.

The book draws extensively on my own experience of curating design exhibitions over a period of twenty-five years within the context of a design museum. The book is also informed by my experience of teaching curating practice as part of a design-focused masters programme and research undertaken for a practice-based PhD. The research presented in this book is by no means exhaustive, but rather presents some of the developments and wider shifts that have shaped the practice. The book aims to contribute to the ongoing debate around design curating practice, examined through the practitioner's lens. *Curating Design* is organized into three sections.

Part One, 'Displaying Designed Objects in Museum and Exhibition Contexts, 1800s–2000', contextualizes the investigation by mapping the history of displaying designed objects in museum and exhibition contexts, as a means of identifying the key moments that are pertinent to the development of the design museum and the design exhibition. The emergence of public museums and the development of their organizational structures influenced the role of the professional curator in the early twentieth century. The historical, theoretical and cultural discussions that have informed the development of the design museum and curating practice are discussed with reference to relevant literature and case studies.

Part Two, 'The Curatorial Turn, 1980–2020', identifies and analyses the culture around curating since the 1980s. It examines the main discursive

---

[26]Sarah Pierce, 'The Simple Operator', in Jean-Paul Martinon (ed.), *The Curatorial*: 97.
[27]Paul O'Neill provides an analysis of the rise of biennial culture in *The Culture of Curating and the Curating of Culture(s)*, Cambridge, MA: MIT, 2012: 51–85.

trends and broader shifts that have emerged within contemporary curating practice, with particular reference to the UK. These developments have been interpreted as part of a broader cultural shift or 'curatorial turn'.[28] It is a period marked by moments when the boundaries constituting the role of the curator and the field in which they operated significantly expanded. The research contributes to an understanding of when and why certain issues emerged in relation to broader political, economic, social and technological changes and how they impacted museums and the visitor experience. It examines how such shifts had an implication for curating in the wider sector, and how they influenced the way in which design exhibitions, displays and programmes were conceived and presented.

Part Three, 'Interviews with Eight International Design Curators', presents a series of interviews with design curators working in the UK and internationally. Drawing on the research methodology of the 'reflective practitioner', eight curators were invited to reflect on their practice and the contexts in which they are working. The curators have acquired their knowledge and expertise through directly engaging with the new institutions and curatorial models that have emerged in the last two decades. The interviews connect to the research presented in Parts One and Two and provide eight different perspectives on the more recent developments in design curating as practice and discourse. The interviews are designed to reveal what has been largely concealed; how design is curated and the distinctiveness of the design curator's role.

The book concludes with a reflection on the way in which the design curator's role is understood in the present moment and how it may evolve in the future. In so doing, the book aims to contribute meaningfully to a growing historiography of design curation and to an understanding of the necessary and ever-expanding role of the design curator.

---

[28]The term was first proposed by critic Paul O'Neill in an essay, 'The Curatorial Turn: From Practice to Discourse', in Judith Rugg and Michèle Sedgwick (eds), *Issues in Curating Contemporary Art and Performance*, Bristol: Intellect Books, 2007: 13–28.

PART ONE

Displaying Designed Objects in Museum and Exhibition Contexts, 1800s–2000

The idea of accumulating everything, of establishing a sort of general archive, the will to enclose in one place at all times, all epochs, all forms, all tastes, the idea of constituting a place of all times that is itself outside of time and inaccessible to its ravages, the project of organising in this a sort of perpetual and indefinite accumulation of time in an immobile place, this whole idea belongs to our modernity.

– MICHEL FOUCAULT (1986)[1]

[1] Michel Foucault, 'Of Other Spaces', *Diacritics*, Vol. 16 (Spring 1986): 22–7.

1.1

Cabinets of Curiosities and the Formation of the Public Museum

The practice of curating design is connected to a longer history of collecting and displaying objects that can be traced back to the fifteenth century. It is also connected to a more recent development; the formation of the public museum and various trade initiatives during the nineteenth century which placed a special focus on the manufactured and mass produced object.

In the essay, 'Of Other Spaces', philosopher Michel Foucault considers that the impulse to accumulate and archive is a modern phenomenon from which he derives his theory of the 'heterotopia'. He defines heterotopias as a range of cultural, institutional and discursive spaces that are somehow different, disturbing, intense, incompatible, contradictory or transforming. Heterotopias are worlds within worlds, mirroring and yet upsetting what is outside. Foucault provides many examples of these spaces. They include ships, cemeteries, brothels, prisons, gardens of antiquity, fairs, Turkish baths and also the library and the museum.

Referencing Foucault's theory of the heterotopia some ten years later, museologist Tony Bennett argues that the museum is characteristic of nineteenth-century Western culture, representing a new space of modernity fashioned to achieve order and rationality from the chaotic disorder that had characterized the museum's precursors.[1]

Much has been written about the formation of the public museum and its early development in the late-eighteenth and early-nineteenth centuries.[2] In

---

[1] Tony Bennett, *The Birth of the Museum: History, Theory, Politics*, London: Routledge, 1995: 2.
[2] Publications include Oliver Impey and Arthur MacGregor, *The Origins of the Museum: The Cabinet of Curiosities in Sixteenth and Seventeenth Century Europe*, Oxfordshire: Oxford University Press, 1985; Bennett, *The Birth of the Museum* and Kartsen Schubert, *The Curator's Egg: The Evolution of the Museum Concept from the French Revolution to the Present Day*, London: One-Off Press, 2000.

The Curator's Egg, published in 2000, Karsten Schubert explores the evolution of the museum concept from the French Revolution to the present day and, in so doing, demonstrates that from the outset the museum has been the subject of close scrutiny, perpetual critique and revision. As he notes in the introductory essay,

> the museum concept's own history has greatly contributed to the complexity of the picture: much of what constitutes today's museum is based on past record and institutional precedent. Without a look at history, today's museum would be virtually indecipherable.[3]

Schubert's observation supports the value of looking back in order to understand the present, particularly when dealing with a relatively recent phenomenon, the design museum. In order to be able to successfully interrogate and understand contemporary curating practice, it is necessary to identify the significant events that enabled the museum to become a site for collecting, conserving and studying the industrial object and manufacturing process. At a certain point, the design museum emerged from the general public museum to become a distinct cultural and operating institution, giving rise to a new type of curatorial practice.

An interrogation of literature in the broad territory of museum studies, design history and material culture reveals specific developments which have had an implication for the design museum. A number of historical, political, legislative, social and cultural factors informed the development of the public museum. They promoted shifts that were to set the scene for the development of the design museum, the design exhibition and its concomitant practice. Key to an understanding of the emergence of the design museum is the way in which objects, originally housed in cabinets and previously concealed from public view, were brought into new, open and public contexts. In addition, the types of objects collected that included the products of an industrial society went on to form the early collections of the modern public museum.

The first curators seem to have appeared under the name of *curatores rei publicae* around the year 100 AD. These 'curators of public affairs' were representatives of the imperial Roman government whose main task was to maintain public order and look after the finances of the city they were deputed to govern.[4] As Dr Stefan Nowotny has identified, these first curators had a well-defined responsibility which was oriented towards the good of the public and the common wealth. Modern curators, whose activities came to

---

[3]Schubert, *The Curator's Egg*: 10.
[4]Stefan Nowotny, 'The Curator Crosses the River: A Fabulation', in Jean-Paul Martinon (ed.), *The Curatorial: A Philosophy of Curating*, London: Bloomsbury, 2013: 61.

be related to museums, were for a long time confined to the more limited concerns of taking care of artefacts and objects that were considered to have some kind of extraordinary value or significance to human knowledge or that testified to an exceptional capacity of creation. These procedures were closely linked to the emergence of new fields of knowledge, from anthropology to aesthetics, and of new practices of appropriation and display.[5]

The foundation of Europe's great publicly funded institutions such as the British Museum and the Louvre go back more than two hundred years to the latter part of the eighteenth century. But, as Schubert has noted, there is an even longer history when the museum was first and foremost a study collection with a library attached – a repository for objects and a place of learning for scholars, philosophers and historians.[6] Such collections developed as a result of the collecting practices of individuals, typically monarchs, aristocrats and wealthy merchants. The collections inspired the 'cabinet of curiosities', a phenomenon which became fashionable throughout Europe in the sixteenth and seventeenth centuries. In July 1983 an international symposium, *The Cabinet of Curiosities*, was organized by Dr Oliver Impey and Arthur MacGregor of the Ashmolean museum in Oxford to explore the somewhat neglected subject of the nature and development of early collections and their relationship to the early history of museums. The papers delivered at the symposium were published in 1985 as *The Origins of the Museum: The Cabinet of Curiosities in Sixteenth and Seventeenth Century Europe*. Impey and MacGregor argue that the cabinet of curiosities were the main Western precursors to museums. The first signs of the modern design museum also unfold directly from these beginnings.[7] Three areas of this development have implications for the later development of design museums and the practice of displaying designed objects: the purpose of the collection; the content of the collection and its arrangement; and a gradual move towards cataloguing content and enabling public access.

As Impey and MacGregor's research identifies, the passion for collecting emerged in Renaissance Europe and derived from the secular collecting practices of European princes and monarchs who amassed art and artefacts of every conceivable kind. The earliest collections comprised the products of antiquity with statues and architectural fragments uncovered through the excavations of Roman ruins conducted from 1450 to 1550. From this classical starting point, collections soon proliferated in bewildering diversity. The discovery of the New World and the opening up of contacts with Africa, Southeast Asia and the Far East enabled collectors to establish collections of

---

[5]Ibid.: 62.
[6]Schubert, *The Curator's Egg*: 17.
[7]Impey and MacGregor, *The Origins of the Museum*: 1.

animal specimens, clothing, weapons, tools and utensils, which promoted a growing awareness of these objects as representative of the societies that produced them. As art historian, Oleg Neverov, has commented,

> the desire arose to amass tangible evidence of all the exciting, new, and hitherto unsuspected discoveries being made all over the world in that dynamic age. Exotic animals and plants, strange clothes and tools, ritual objects from distant tribes or from neighbours closer to home – all became objects of fascination and interest to collectors.[8]

The collections of Italian princes were characterized by an absence of specialization and by the juxtaposition of natural and artificial objects. One of the largest and most important princely collections was the studiolo of Francesco I de' Medici in Florence, Italy (Figure 1.1). Created between 1569 and 1570 by Giorgio Vasari and scholars, Vincenzo Borghini and Giovanni Batista Adriani, the studiolo was a small, windowless room in the Palazzo Vecchio. The function of the room was as a simple repository for the collection. Resembling the interior of a precious cabinet, the doors of the cupboards were closed and the objects within were concealed from public view.

Most of the collections were housed in cabinets that made their first appearance in the sixteenth century. The names given to such collections, the Italian *Studiolo*, the French *Cabinet des Curiosités* and the German *Wunderkammer*, indicate something of the aura of mystery that enveloped the cabinets and their contents. They were typically housed in a small, windowless room, the location of which in the palace was often secret. The walls of the room were lined with cupboards and the objects they contained were arranged around a central point of inspection where occupancy was reserved solely for the prince.

The cabinets of curiosities of princes and statesmen were not only places of study but also served to communicate important political messages. Julian Raby has suggested that the cabinets can be interpreted as spaces that represented the world in microcosm where the prince could symbolically claim dominion over the entire natural and artificial world.[9] Eilean Hooper-Greenhill has also referenced how the function of princely collections during the Renaissance was 'to recreate the world in miniature around the central figure of the prince who thus claimed dominion over the world symbolically as he did in reality'.[10] As Peter Vergo explains, 'the very act of collecting has a political

---

[8]Oleg Neverov, 'His Majesty's Cabinet and Peter I's Kunstkammer', in Impey and MacGregor, *The Origins of the Museum*: 54.

[9]Julian Raby, 'Exotica from Islam', in Impey and MacGregor, *The Origins of the Museum*: 253.

[10]Eilean Hooper-Greenhill, *Museums and the Shaping of Knowledge*, London: Routledge, 2015: 64.

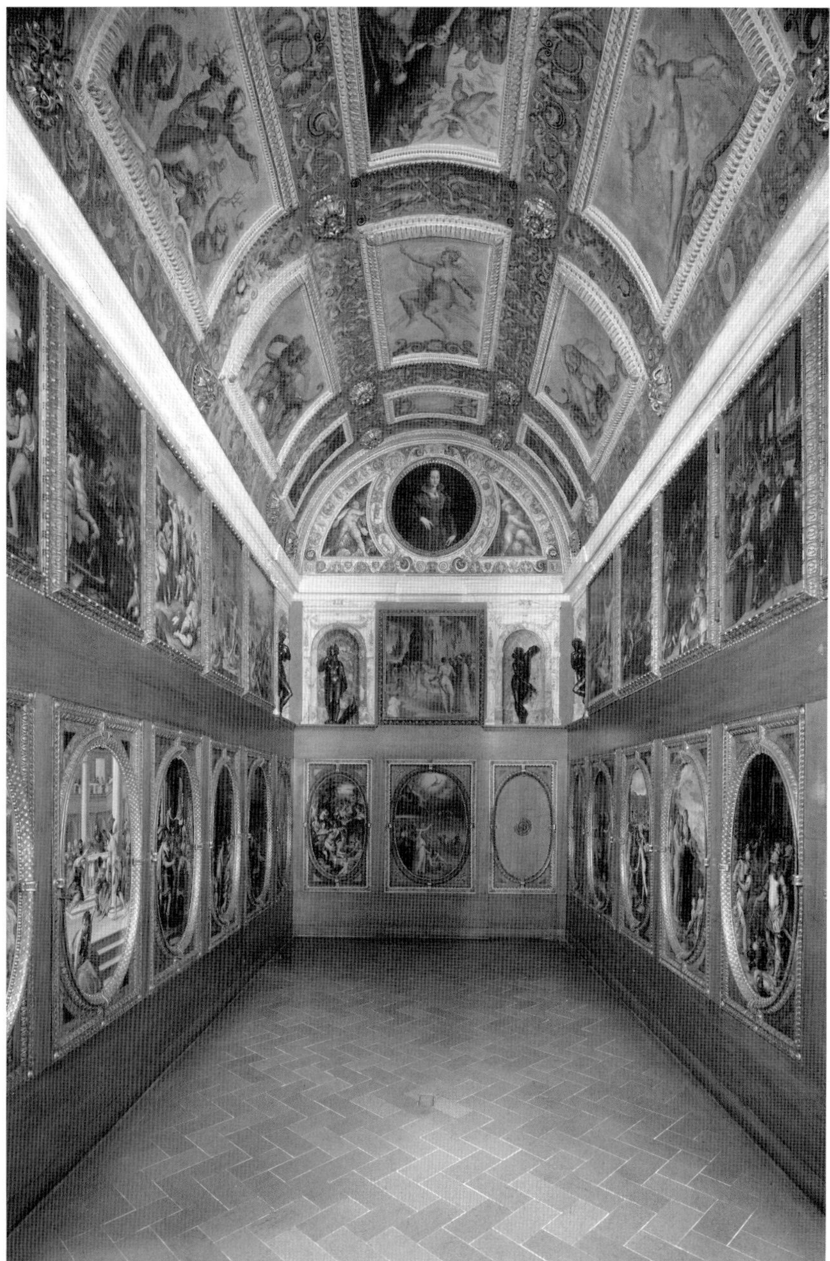

FIGURE 1.1 *Giorgio Vasari (1511–1574): Studiolo of Francesco 1, Palazzo Vecchio, Florence, Italy. © 2021. Photo Scala, Florence.*

or ideological or aesthetic dimension which cannot be overlooked'.[11] Most importantly, many of the objects brought back to Europe were incorporated into private collections where they were studied, catalogued and placed on display. The collections were an important precursor to the collections of the early public museums and their evolving systems of classification.

A second important aspect of the cabinet of curiosities was the method of displaying the objects. The cabinets as physical containers sometimes took the form of spacious closets or took over entire rooms. They were often constructed from fine woods, inlaid with lapis lazuli or decorated with jewels. The interiors were sectioned into shelves, drawers, partitions, niches and other receptacles.[12] Some enthusiasts concentrated on coins and medals, others on books and manuscripts and others on zoological and botanical specimens. One collection which had an enormous influence across Europe was that of Olaus Worm (1588–1654), which was particularly strong in archaeological objects and contained a large number of fossils (Figure 1.2).

By the early years of the seventeenth century, illustrated catalogues of the collections were published and fashionable trips abroad were arranged for the sole purpose of journeying from one collection to another. Collections soon proliferated in incredible diversity ranging from antiquities, books, coins, manuscripts, medals, sea shells, minerals, fossils, zoological and botanical specimens, human and animal remains to mathematical and scientific instruments, watches and automata.[13] The Kunstkammer of Friedrich Wilhelm of Brandenburg (1640–88) in Berlin contained more than 4,900 items listing coins, gems, bronze figures and vessels, ceramics, glass and porcelain.[14] The extensive list of material collected by the Milanese physician Lodovico Settle passed, after his death, into the keeping of his son in the early 1630s. The collections were arranged in four rooms in the family house in Milan, which eventually became the Settala Museum.[15]

The collections are notable not only due to the quantity, variety and rarity of their contents but also because objects represented the areas of technology, science, art and craft. An increasing number of collectors across Europe began to cultivate cabinets devoted predominantly, or even exclusively, to one type of material. Collections focused on plants, minerals, fossils, shells and

---

[11]Peter Vergo (ed.), *The New Museology*, London: Reaktion Books, 1989: 2.

[12]As Impey and MacGregor point out, tremendous advances were made in the design of the lathe during the sixteenth century, which allowed for the manufacture of specialized items in wood.

[13]Foucault, 'Of Other Spaces': 22–7.

[14]Christian Theuerkauf, 'The Brandenburg Kunstkammer in Berlin', in Impey and MacGregor, *The Origins of the Museum*: 110.

[15]Antonio Aimi, Vincenzo de Michele and Alessandro Morandotti, 'Towards a History of Collecting in Milan in the Late Renaissance and Baroque Periods', in Impey and MacGregor, *The Origins of the Museum*: 25.

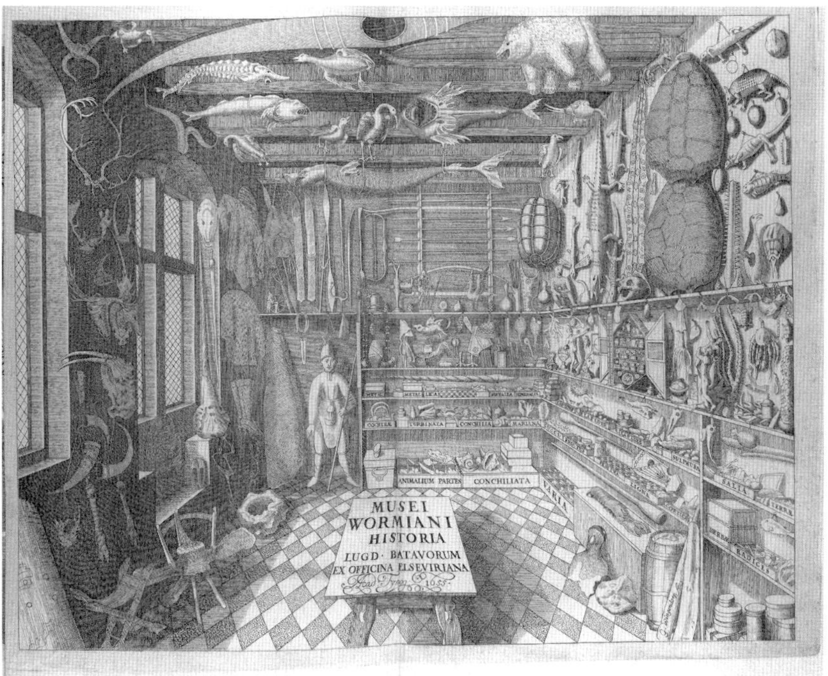

FIGURE 1.2 *Ole Worm (1588–1654): The Museum Wormianum of Ole Worm, engraved plate from the book 'Museum Wormianum', published in Amsterdam, 1655. © 2021. The British Library Board/ Scala, Florence.*

zoological specimens gave rise to a new type of museum, the natural history museum. Many collections were the forerunner of the scientific and technical museums, archaeology and ethnography museums, art museums, history museums and the decorative arts museum.

Most modern public museums contain a nucleus of objects from the earlier cabinets of curiosities. In 1584 the collection of Francesco I de' Medici was transferred into the new and more public context of the newly opened Uffizi Gallery in Florence. In Britain the collection of John Tradescent the elder (d. 1638) at Lambeth was the precursor of the Ashmolean Museum in Oxford. There were over a hundred thousand specimens in the collection of Sir Hans Sloane (1660–1753), president of the Royal Society and Royal College of Physicians, which came to form the foundation of the British Museum established in 1753.[16] Rare and precious objects once destined for the private contemplation of the prince alone were now on view to all. The dispersal of these collections and their reconstitution in public museums placed objects

---

[16]Schubert, *The Curator's Egg*: 17.

in less enclosed spaces and enabled wider access. From being museums of everything and for the limited few, museums were becoming accessible to a larger section of the public.

In recent decades, the early collecting practices of princes and scholars have provoked controversy in the cultural sector. The debate has brought about a growing demand for the restitution of artefacts taken from indigenous communities by European colonists during the nineteenth century. Tristram Hunt, director of the V&A, has noted how the V&A's collections expanded in line with the growth of the British Empire across southern Asia. The museum showcased Indian textiles, Burmese lacquerware, Chinese porcelain and Persian carpets, alongside British industrial designs and European Renaissance treasures. As Hunt explains, 'the V&A as a museum born of the imperial moment, the question of provenance and ownership in a post-colonial age is particularly germane'.[17] He asks how an institution like the V&A can respond to this new cultural climate, and honour its responsibilities as a global museum. He suggests that museum directors and curators need to be open and transparent about their colonial past, and consider carefully how to address its legacy.

---

[17]Tristram Hunt, 'Should Museums Return Their Colonial Artefacts?' *The Guardian*, 29 June 2019. Available at: https://www.theguardian.com/culture/2019/jun/29/should-museums-return-their-colonial-artefacts (accessed 17 September 2019).

1.2

International Exhibitions

The design museum also derived its impetus from a series of exhibitions of culture and industry that became popular in the nineteenth century. The public display of objects deemed to be examples of 'good taste' has its origins in nineteenth-century commercial trade fairs. Between 1880 and 1920 expositions became a regular feature of the European and American cultural landscape. Like museums, they professed an explicitly educational function. Exhibits followed a similar hierarchy of classification, their buildings reflected the neoclassical styles of museum architecture and the objects they displayed represented the best in quality. Unlike museums, the expositions made no effort to mask their entertainment function; the sheer novelty and technical wizardry of their exhibits boldly mixed pleasure with serious instruction, and visitors flocked to see them.

A series of international exhibitions, or world's fairs, were devoted largely to the display of industrial objects, machinery and processes. Each country celebrated its industrial strength by displaying, alongside other industrial nations, products and scientific and technological achievements that were seen to be material signifiers of progress. The exhibitions also demonstrated an ability to attract and entertain a mass urban public on a large scale.

On 1 May 1851 the 'Great Exhibition of the Works of Industry of All Nations' was opened by Queen Victoria. Housed in a temporary glass-and-steel structure constructed for the occasion in Hyde Park, the exhibition ran until 15 October 1851 and attracted over six million visitors (Figure 1.3). Contemporary accounts reveal that the event was considered to be a historic national achievement, not least for the sheer scale of the enterprise. The exhibition claimed to include every type and process of manufacture then known. It was considered to successfully appeal to all classes of the population, stimulate trade and have an educational benefit to the country. The exhibition's organizer, Henry Cole, later wrote:

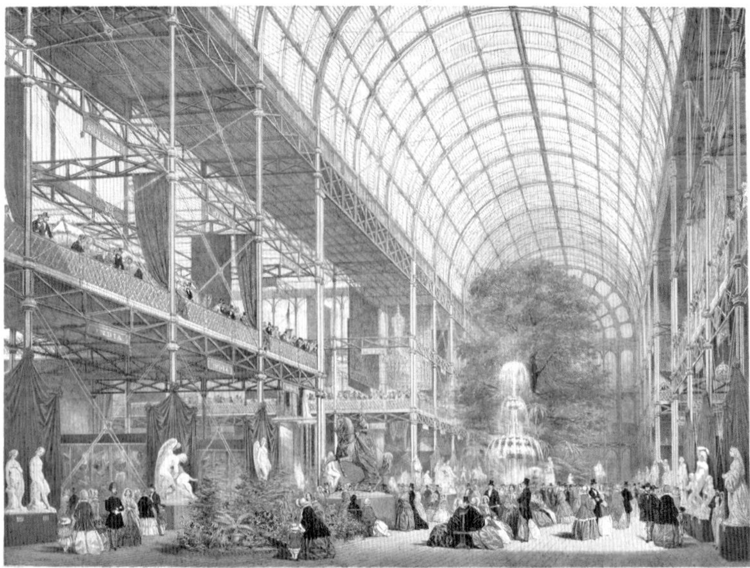

FIGURE 1.3 *Joseph Nash (1809–1878):* Great Exhibition, *Crystal Palace, Hyde Park, London, 1851, London Metropolitan Archives (City of London).* © *2021. Photo Scala, Florence / Heritage Images.*

The history of the world I venture to say records no event comparable in its promotion of human industry, with that of the Great Exhibition of the Works of Industry of all Nations in 1851. A great people invited all civilised nations to a festival to bring into comparison the works of human skill.[1]

A principal characteristic of the Great Exhibition, and one which has resonance for the development of the design museum, consisted of its arrangement of displays of manufacturing processes and products which were intended to raise the profile of new inventions and patents. It was an attempt to display the fruits of Britain's industrial revolution, its empire and its wealth, while also showcasing the manufactured goods produced by the rest of the world. The eastern half of the Crystal Palace was allocated to foreign countries and the western half to Britain and the Empire. The space was divided into national subdivisions, and exhibits within them were divided according to the classifications of Raw Materials: 'Machinery'; Manufactures: 'Textiles',

---

[1] Henry Cole as quoted in Victoria & Albert Museum, *The Great Exhibition of 1851: A Commemorative Album*, London: His Majesty's Stationery Office, 1950: 5.

'Fabrics'; Manufactures: 'Metallic', 'Vitreous' and 'Ceramic'; Miscellaneous and Fine Arts.

The Great Exhibition of 1851 brought together a range of disciplines and techniques of display that had been developed within earlier exhibiting platforms. In a study of the development of the Mechanics' Institute Movement in Britain, Martyn Walker explains that the Great Exhibition of 1851 had its antecedents in the modest provincial exhibitions organized by the Mechanics' Institutes some twenty years earlier.[2] The first large exhibition was held at the Lancashire and Cheshire Union Manchester Mechanics' Institute in 1837. The exhibitions were devoted largely to the display of industrial objects and processes and were intended to educate the public about new technical developments. The regional exhibitions attracted tens of thousands of visitors, and in 1849 the Birmingham Mechanics' Institute opened its exhibition to foreign products.

Following the success of the Great Exhibition in 1851, Britain used its exhibition tradition to explore new ways to develop its economy. This is most visibly demonstrated when in 1887 the organizers of the new Earls Court complex took the decision to stage a series of international exhibitions focused on promoting the products of specific countries. The Indian and Colonial (1886), American (1887), Italian (1888), French (1890) and German (1891) exhibitions were unique in this regard. Each had the same categories including agriculture, mining and metallurgy, machinery, education and science, and fine arts. They also had extensive committee structures, juries, prizes, thousands of private and public exhibitors, and attracted audiences of up to two million people.[3]

The exhibitions shared a number of commonalities. Temporary facilities were built on a sprawling site with products organized into national courts or display areas, which later developed into separate pavilions for each participating country. There was a wide range of categories of product, with at least a third of the space given up to foreign products. There was also a very vocal government participation, all designed to promote a rhetoric of progress.

The European and American exhibition tradition unfolded alongside the British in the second half of the nineteenth century. The Exposition or 'Expo'[4] and the World's Fair were concerned with not only national identity but

---

[2]Martyn Walker, *The Development of the Mechanics' Institute Movement in Britain and Beyond: Supporting Further Education for the Adult Working Classes*, London: Routledge, 2017.

[3]Paul Greenhalgh, 'Education, Entertainment and Politics: Lessons from the Great International Exhibitions', in Peter Vergo (ed.), *The New Museology*, London: Reaktion Books, 1989: 77.

[4]In 1931 the Bureau International des Expositions (BIE) was set up to provide a common organizational framework for the many Expos that had emerged as early as 1867. The BIE defines an Expo as a global event that aims at educating the public, sharing innovation, promoting progress and fostering

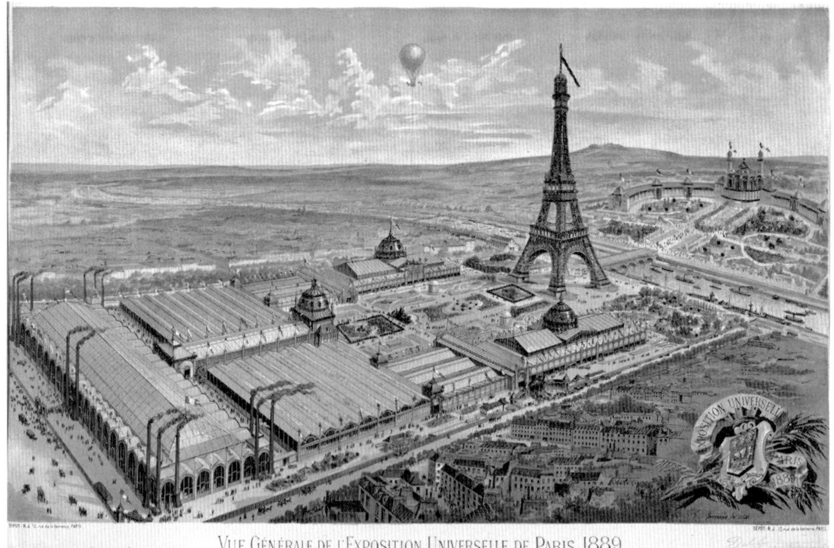

FIGURE 1.4 *Vue generale de l'Exposition universelle de Paris en 1889: Tour Eiffel, Trocadero, montgolfiere, 19th century, Musee Carnavalet, Paris.* © 2021. *Photo Josse / Scala, Florence.*

also with mass entertainment and spectacle. They comprised impressive buildings, machine halls, restaurants and cafes, and exhibited examples of technological inventions, fine and decorative art. The success of these events can be expressed in the numbers of visitors, which were substantial. The Paris Exposition Universelle of 1889 was even larger than the Great Exhibition of 1851, attracting more than thirty-two million visitors (Figure 1.4). It was the fourth of eight expositions held in the city between 1855 and 1937. The most popular attraction was the Eiffel Tower, a structure created for the exposition and which represented an astonishing achievement of modern design and engineering.

Over twenty-seven million people attended the World's Columbian Exposition, Chicago, in 1893. Chicago's Century of Progress Exposition in 1933 attracted almost forty-nine million people. In Britain, over twenty-seven million people attended the Empire Exhibition in Wembley in 1924 and twelve million people visited the Glasgow Empire Exhibition of 1938.[5]

---

cooperation. It is organized by a host country that invites other countries, companies, international organizations, the private sector, the civil society and the general public to participate. They are characterized by a diversity of participants, from top decision makers to children, and provide the setting for exhibitions, diplomatic and business meetings, public debates and live shows. Available at: https://www.bie-paris.org/site/en/about-the-bie/our-history (accessed 2 June 2019).

[5]John MacKenzie, *Propaganda and Empire – The Manipulation of British Public Opinion, 1880– 1960*, Manchester: Manchester University Press, 1984: 101.

Scholarship on international exhibitions and world's fairs comprises a rich and varied field of research which has focused on their social and cultural significance.[6] The exhibitions stimulated the development of public museums, often supplying them with their buildings and initial collections. The Great Exhibition of 1851 provided the impetus for the development of London's South Kensington Museum complex and set an example that was repeated elsewhere. Chicago's great public museums emerged from the World's Columbian Exposition in 1893. The exhibitions encouraged new ways of looking at the world and also created new forms of consumption. In this respect, the design museum connects to these new spaces of modernity that developed during the nineteenth century, which also included shopping arcades, railway stations, conservatories, market halls and department stores. As Tim Barringer has noted,

> the museum was redolent of the modernity of international exhibitions, the department store, liberal economics, technical design education and utilitarian reform ideology [as well as] the more traditional curatorial and aesthetic motivations.[7]

A number of characteristics set the international exhibition and modern fair apart as a distinctive grouping. Paul Greenhalgh, director of the Sainsbury Centre for Visual Arts, has described them as part of a 'serial exhibition phenomenon' which was to have an impact on the future structure and policies of museums, including the design museum. The exclusive emphasis on commercial and industrial subjects marked a decisive step away from the notion of the exhibition as a mass entertainment event, and towards that of specialist educator and informant. They established an educational pattern: objects were displayed, people explained and worked them and large numbers of people thronged to listen.[8] Greenhalgh has shown how the activities of the contemporary museum can be compared to policies formulated by the creators of the international exhibitions who needed to win sponsorship and fill their sites with people. They did this through policies such as introducing different days for different classes of visitors regulated by varying prices of admission.[9] Each of the international exhibitions was involved

---

[6]Scholarship includes David Raizman and Ethan Robey (eds), *Expanding Nationalisms at World's Fairs: Identity, Diversity, and Exchange, 1851–1915*, London: Routledge, 2017; Robert W. Rydell, *World of Fairs: The Century-of-Progress Expositions*, Chicago: University of Chicago Press, 1993; Robert W. Rydell, *All the World's a Fair: Visions of Empire at American International Expositions, 1876–1916*, Chicago: University of Chicago Press, 1987.

[7]Tim Barringer, 'Victorian Culture and the Museum: Before and after the White Cube', *Journal of Victorian Culture*, Vol. 11, Issue 1 (2006): 133–45.

[8]Paul Greenhalgh, 'Education, Entertainment and Politics: Lessons from the Great International Exhibitions', in Vergo (ed.), *The New Museology*: 76.

[9]Ibid.: 86.

in the practice of exhibiting industrial processes and goods to the public, and in promoting the themes of modernity and progress.

The earlier exhibitions from 1851 through to the middle of the twentieth century were strongly influenced by the Industrial Revolution and the colonial ambitions of the time. At the Great Exhibition of 1851 the value of an object, whether as raw material, instrument of production or finished product from Britain, India, France or America, was displayed as representative of a stage within an evolutionary process. Pavilions were constructed in which countries could showcase their material progress and trade pre-eminence based on technological innovation. The exhibitions were seen to represent progress and provided an opportunity for cultural and commercial exchange. Philosopher and cultural critic Walter Benjamin has described world exhibitions as 'places of pilgrimage to the commodity fetish'.[10] In his view, a defining characteristic was a glorification of the exchange value of the commodity. They constructed a universe of a new and exclusive category of goods which he describes as the 'spécialité'. The exhibitions directly pointed towards the future, unlike the contents of the eighteenth-century cabinet of curiosities which were very firmly rooted in the past.

The policies behind the first design museums can be seen to share similarities with the key characteristics of the international exhibition. The aim of the international exhibition was to educate the public, share innovation, promote progress and enable dialogue and shared experience. They were a unique way to reach out to a broad audience and a place where influencers, experts, politicians and the general public came together. For the organizers, the international exhibition was an important promotional tool for nation branding with its ability to attract world leaders and decision makers as well as millions of visitors. Participants were given an exhibition space or the opportunity to build a pavilion. In these designed spaces they were able to showcase their achievements, experience, products, innovations and ideas in relation to a specific theme and present to an international audience. For the visiting public, the exhibition was an experience that combined education and entertainment, and offered a wide variety of exhibitions showcasing innovative products and groundbreaking technologies, activities and shows.

The exhibitions were also popular for their exuberance and their entertainment value. Greenhalgh has observed how the international exhibition 'did show that it was possible to have high and popular culture in

---

[10] Walter Benjamin, *The Arcades Project*, translated by Howard Eiland and Kevin McLaughlin, Cambridge, MA: Belknap Press of Harvard University Press, 1999: 17. The full text of Benjamin's unfinished work, written between 1927 and 1940, was first published by Harvard University Press in 1999.

close proximity, and even that the one was capable of becoming the other'.[11] The exhibitions fused elements of high cultural standing such as the fine and decorative arts, displays of science and technology, anthropology and geography with trade fair stands and an amusement park. The exhibitions introduced entertainment zones. Rides such as the 'Wiggle-woggle', 'Flip-flap' and 'Witching-waves' were apparently popular amusement attractions.[12] The exhibition hall quickly became an essential part of the modern city. As Deyan Sudjic, a former director of the Design Museum, London, has noted, 'the expo itself evolved into a curious mixture of nationalism, utopian futures and fairground entertainment'.[13]

In later years the format of the international exhibition did much to open up the discussion of design to an expanded international audience. It helped to map, label and define the unfamiliar territories of design, style and taste during a period of intense interest in such topics. In 1923 the first *International Exhibition of Decorative Arts* was held in Monza, Italy. It moved to Milan in 1933 and became the Triennale di Milano, an exhibition held every three years to promote an international dialogue about design. Staged at the Palazzo dell'Arte, it hosted exhibitions and events showcasing the very latest examples of contemporary design. The first three editions were primarily dedicated to graphic arts, ceramics and decorative arts, while the fourth edition, the *International Exhibition of Modern Decorative and Industrial Arts*, focused on architecture.[14] In his autobiography Terence Conran, founder of London's Design Museum, cites the Triennale exhibitions in Milan during the 1950s as a crucially important platform where he was able to see first-hand the best of contemporary Italian and international design, at a time when Italian designers were dominant.[15] In 1961, also in Milan, the Salone del Mobile was established as a platform for designers to launch new collections to a captive design audience. It presented exhibitions with the aim of charting new directions in design and inspiring critical discourse around the designed object. The Salone del Mobile is now the largest trade fair of its kind in the world, attracting a substantial international audience each year.

---

[11] Paul Greenhalgh, 'Education, Entertainment and Politics: Lessons from the Great International Exhibitions', in Peter Vergo (ed.), *The New Museology*, London: Reaktion Books, 1989: 98.
[12] Ibid.: 85.
[13] Deyan Sudjic, *B Is for Bauhaus*, London: Penguin Books, 2014: 173.
[14] La Triennale de Milano website. Available at: https://triennale.org/en/about/history-and-mission (accessed 5 June 2019).
[15] Terence Conran, *My Life in Design*, London: Conran Octopus, 2016.

1.3

The Decorative Arts Museum and the Modern Art Museum

In the twentieth century, important precursors to the design museum were the decorative arts museum and the modern art museum. Alice Rawsthorn, a design critic and former director of London's Design Museum, has noted how historically objects found their way into design museums through two distinct museological avenues. The first approach involved decorative arts museums that focused on furniture, ceramics and fashion, such as the Victoria and Albert Museum (V&A). It inspired the first iteration of what is now the Museum of Applied Arts (MAK) in Vienna, which opened in 1864. A second approach saw museums of modern and contemporary art start to take a keen interest in industrial design. In this respect, the pioneering institution was the Museum of Modern Art (MoMA) in New York, where the world's first curatorial department devoted to architecture and design was established in 1932.[1]

The establishment of the V&A in London marked a significant turning point in the development of British museum policy. The V&A emerged from the profits generated by the Great Exhibition of 1851. Initially known as the Museum of Manufactures, it opened in May 1852 at Marlborough House with a nucleus of objects, covering applied arts and science purchased from the Great Exhibition. In September 1852 the collection transferred to Somerset House. By February 1854 discussions were underway to transfer the museum to its current site, and, in 1857, it opened as the South Kensington Museum.[2] The institution clearly enunciated the principles of the modern museum. It was conceived as an instrument of public education, from which both taste and technique could be learnt. Henry Cole, the first director of the museum

---

[1] Alice Rawsthorn, *Hello World: Where Design Meets Life*, London: Hamish Hamilton, 2013: 36–7.
[2] Anthony Burton, *Vision & Accident: The Story of the Victoria and Albert Museum*, London: V&A, 1999.

and an ardent advocate of the role museums should play in the formation of a rational public culture, wrote:

> The Museum is intended to be used, and to the utmost extent consistent with the preservation of the articles; and not only used physically, but to be taken about and lectured upon. For my own part, I venture to think that unless museums and galleries are made subservient to purposes of education, they dwindle into very sleepy and useless institutions.[3]

Administered eventually under the auspices of the Board of Education, the museum was officially dedicated to the service of an extended and undifferentiated public with opening hours and an admissions policy designed to maximize its accessibility to the working classes.[4] It proved remarkably successful, attracting over fifteen million visits between 1857 and 1883.

The establishment of the V&A has relevance to the subsequent development of the design museum, as it served to reinforce the idea that objects can, and should be, divorced from their original context of ownership and redisplayed in a different context of meaning. In addition, the museum provided a safe and neutral environment in which to display and mediate objects. The V&A was intended as an instructive demonstration to students and manufacturers of what design could achieve. The developing role of the design curator is most visibly seen in the history of the V&A. Here the curator's function was understood to be in the service of a collection. The curator brought to the public a recognized skill set around specialist subject expertise such as furniture, glass or ceramics. The curator cared for, researched and acquired historical and contemporary objects and there was an element of the job that was steadily growing in importance: the production of exhibitions.

In the early twentieth century, a number of influential museum directors and curators pioneered new methods of displaying objects. Writing in 1910, John Cotton Dana, the founder and first director of the Newark Museum in New Jersey, observed:

> Ancient conventions have museums firmly in hand; … most museums tend to become storehouses, used more to please and educate curators than to entertain and instruct the public; that they are quite averse to change; and that few among them exercise an influence on their respective communities at all commensurate with the cost of founding and maintenance.[5]

---

[3] Henry Cole, 'Report to the Department of Practical Art, 1854', in Vergo (ed.), *The New Museology*: 8.
[4] Burton, *Vision & Accident*.
[5] John Cotton Dana, *The New Museum: Selected Writings by John Cotton Dana*, edited by W. A. Peniston, Washington, DC: The Newark Museum Association, New Jersey, 1999: 157.

Dana advocated the museum as an alive and active institution offering entertainment, enlightenment and education. In a series of short pamphlets published between 1917 and 1920, he conceptualized the new museum, promoting it as an instrument for popular education and recreation: 'a good museum attracts, entertains, arouses curiosity, leads to questions – and thus promotes learning.'[6]

Dana hesitated calling the Newark a 'museum', preferring instead to describe the ideal museum environment as being 'an open workshop of delight and learning' and an 'institute of visual instruction'.[7] His many special exhibitions stretched the boundaries of conventional display by featuring applied and industrial arts, textile and clay products manufactured by local businesses, immigrant's handicrafts and inexpensive articles of good design. Dana hoped that these exhibits would draw new visitors to the museum, such as housewives and working people, who might have a natural interest in the objects on display. More important to Dana than what was displayed was how objects were used. He established new practices such as loaning objects to school classrooms, shops and hospitals. He created a teacher-training course at local colleges, opened a junior museum specifically for children and established branch museums in local libraries.[8]

New and radical curatorial practices were introduced by Alfred H. Barr at MoMA in New York during his tenure as director from 1929 to 1943. Curator Philip Johnson's 1934 exhibition, *Machine Art*, elevated design to the level of art by investing the object with an almost auratic status (Figure 1.5). In the exhibition, everyday machine-made objects such as airplane propeller blades, ball bearings, coils, springs and laboratory flasks were placed on cedar and walnut pedestals like pieces of sculpture, or under glass cases, and displayed in front of walls covered in oil cloth, stainless steel, aluminium and natural linen. A humble Tupperware container was elevated to the status of a modernist icon by putting it on a pedestal and emphasizing the simplicity of its form. A single ball bearing was appreciated for its sculptural quality. This display technique ensured that the objects were highlighted as works of art and communicated as exemplars of modern design to be admired as much for their formal beauty as for their functionality.[9] The display strategy deliberately divorced the object from its everyday, utilitarian context and social function and enabled the object to be seen and understood from a new angle.[10]

---

[6]Ibid.: 65.

[7]Ibid.: 65.

[8]Lisa C. Roberts, *From Knowledge to Narrative: Educators and the Changing Museum*, Washington, DC: Smithsonian Institution Press, 1997: 61.

[9]Zoë Ryan (ed.), *As Seen: Exhibitions That Made Architecture and Design History*, London and New Haven: Yale University Press, 2017: 18.

[10]Ibid.: 18.

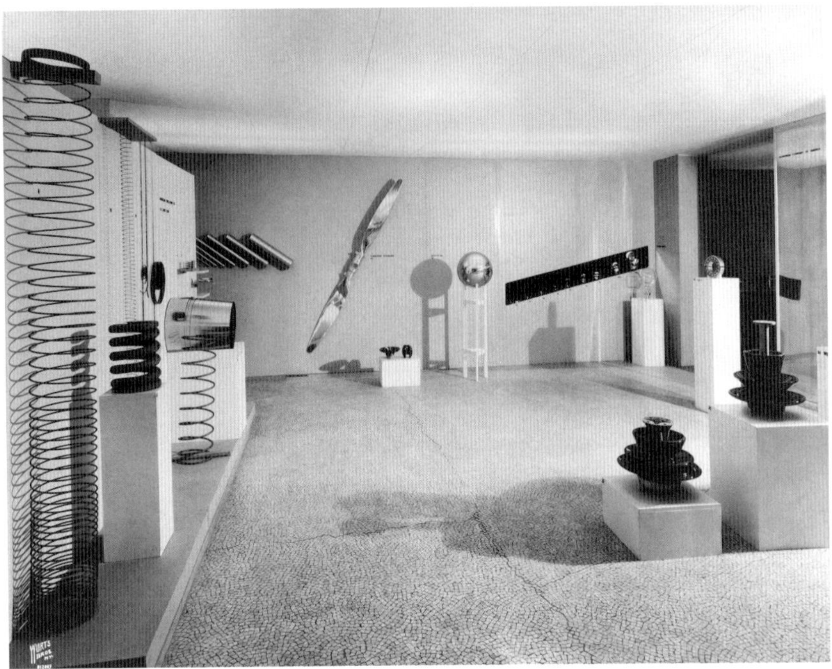

FIGURE 1.5 *Installation view of the exhibition* Machine Art *Museum of Modern Art (MoMA, 1934), New York. Photo by Wurts Brothers; IN34.2. © 2021. Digital image. The Museum of Modern Art, New York / Scala, Florence.*

Visitors to the exhibition were invited to vote for their favourite exhibits. The exhibition catalogue included a price list and manufacturer's contact information, encouraging visitors to purchase the objects for display in their own homes. A selection of the objects from the exhibition would later form the foundation of the design collection at MoMA. The innovative display strategy adopted by the curators of the exhibition would also influence the way in which objects were presented in the newly established design museums across Europe.

1.4

The Emergence of the Design Museum

Since their formation in the nineteenth century, museums have changed in response to broader political, economic, social and technological changes. The development of the design museum can be interpreted as a response to wider shifts and to an increasing focus by museums on contemporary concerns.

When the Design Museum opened in London in 1989, it was the first in the UK of a new type of specialist museum focusing on the collection, study and exhibition of modern and contemporary design. At the time of its opening, it was one of a small number of high-profile design and applied arts museums internationally that included the Museum of Modern Art (MoMA), New York and the Cooper Hewitt, Smithsonian Design Museum in New York; the MAK in Vienna; the Design Museum in Helsinki and Vitra Design Museum in Weil am Rhein.

Stephen Bayley, writing a few months before the official opening of the Design Museum in London, positioned the new museum within a broader development of museums. He identified it as a unique platform for reflecting and communicating contemporary concerns:

The creation of any museum is unusual; the creation of a Design Museum even more so. Since they betray contemporary preoccupations, a history of the national temperament could be written in terms of the museum. You have classical archaeology in the age of the 'grand tour', ethnography as explorers pushed into darker continents, science in the century of mechanised war and now, approaching a millennium … design.[1]

---

[1] Stephen Bayley, *Commerce and Culture: From Pre-Industrial Art to Post-Industrial Value*, London: Design Museum, 1989: 5.

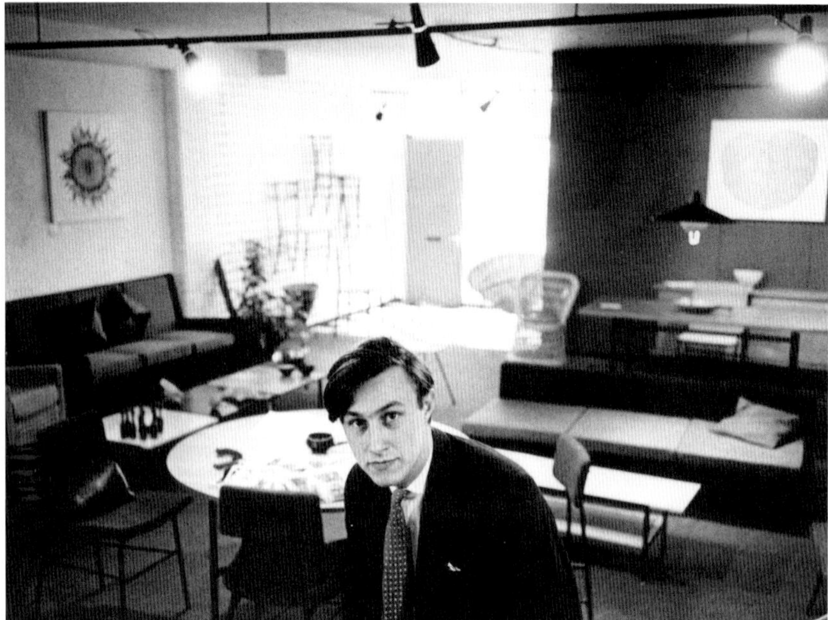

FIGURE 1.6 *Terence Conran photographed inside the first Habitat store, Fulham Road, London. c.1964. © Popperfoto / Getty Images.*

London's first design museum provides an interesting case study, particularly in view of the fact that its origins connect closely to a decorative arts museum, the V&A. Within this context, the museum developed as an institution that focused attention on the cultural value of design and began to develop an audience for the subject.

The Design Museum was founded by designer, retailer and business entrepreneur, Terence Conran, in the belief that design had a vital part to play in shaping and understanding the world. In his autobiography published in 2016, Conran reflects on how since the 1950s he had been involved in selling design to the public and to industry. In 1951 he decided to abandon his studies in textiles at the Central School of Art and Design to work on the Festival of Britain.[2] The following year he established Conran & Company, making furniture in a modern style.

His first shop, Habitat, opened on London's Fulham Road in 1964 (Figure 1.6). For a generation growing up in the austerity of post-war Britain and who did not necessarily share their parents' tastes, Habitat offered a different kind of home store. The store combined European and American modernism juxtaposing

---

[2]Conran, *My Life in Design*: 14–15.

leather lounge chairs and tubular steel furniture alongside Japanese paper lanterns, French earthenware, German consumer electronics by Braun and new continental imports like the duvet, which became a bestseller. Customers identified with a lifestyle which Habitat promoted through thoughtfully designed store displays and catalogues of beautifully photographed interiors. In its first catalogue, Habitat offered 'instant good taste … for well-switched-on people'.[3] Stephen Bayley later reflected that Conran's great achievement was in elevating design to a commodity:

> A scrubbed wooden table from a French monastery, a coarse glass jug holding a single daffodil stem, a Bauhaus chair, a French white porcelain *batterie de cuisine* and modern jazz from a Dieter Rams SK4 record player … It was about fine things enjoyed by civilised folk. He has always been reluctant to acknowledge the role of taste in his own judgements.[4]

Habitat grew into an international chain and was regularly featured in the Sunday colour supplements during the 1970s and 1980s. In 1977 Habitat catalogues began to be sold on UK news-stands and in branches of high-street newsagents highlighting the far-reaching popularity of the concept. For Conran, coming out of the dreary and austere post-war years, there was the opportunity to reshape the world in a new, more enjoyable image and add a little colour to life. As he later reflected, 'we had looked at the Bauhaus in Germany and what they had achieved and hoped that we could extend those ideals to Britain'.[5]

Habitat's founding principles reflect this new attitude. Writing in 2011, Ben Highmore, professor of cultural studies at the University of Sussex, suggests that Habitat's success owed much to the fact that it offered a new type of shopping experience, which was the antithesis of the department store, 'a world of glass cabinets, with a mausoleum-hush, gives way to a world of informality, where the haughty advice of shop assistants (assistants who might be more snobbish than their clientele) is replaced by the authority of knowledge gained from touching and feeling'.[6] Habitat promoted a lifestyle and supplied the material support for it in the form of interior decoration and furnishings. Some of this was achieved through the pedagogic strategies of the shop and the catalogues. As Highmore points out, the selecting and

---

[3]Tom Wilson, *The Story of the Design Museum*, London: Phaidon Press , 2016: 17.

[4]Stephen Bayley, 'How the Design Museum Lost Its Way', *The Spectator*, 13 August 2016. Available at: https://www.spectator.co.uk/2016/08/how-the-design-museum-lost-its-way-by-co-founder-step hen-bayley/ (accessed 23 May 2018).

[5]Conran, *My Life in Design*: 16.

[6]Ben Highmore, 'Feeling It: Habitat, Taste and the New Middle Class in 1970s Britain', *New Formations*, Vol. 88 (Spring 2016): 105–22.

connecting of items was the point of Habitat. As the store's first press release quoted:

> We hope we have taken the foot slogging out of shopping by assembling a wise selection of unusual and top-quality goods under one roof. It has taken us a year to complete this pre-digested shopping programme.[7]

This process of selecting and displaying goods sourced from around the world can be connected to an earlier role of museums as connoisseurs and subject specialists. It also connects to the future development of the design museum. Habitat was bringing modern design within everyone's reach and, in so doing, invoking its founder, Terence Conran, as a designer, retailer, tastemaker and prototype curator. In the late 1970s, and after Habitat became a public company, Conran began discussions with Paul Reilly, formerly director of the Design Council, to realize an ambition to create a museum of industrial design in Britain featuring products from across the world.[8] Reilly introduced Conran to Stephen Bayley, a lecturer in art history at the University of Kent, who had produced research on the design sector for the Design Council. Conran and his team embarked on the search for a location to create a purpose-built structure which would combine the functions of exhibition space, permanent collection, archive, library, study and design facilities. In 1978 Conran asked Bayley to undertake a feasibility report into the creation of a new museum of industrial design and funded a research trip around Europe and the United States. Bayley discovered that while New York's MoMA and the Pompidou Centre in Paris had collections of industrial design, these tended to be subsumed within wider art collections. The outcome of his research confirmed that there was no major institution internationally focused on industrial design.

The final substantial report, completed in May 1979, proved key to Bayley's future role.[9] The document laid out the team's aim of opening a 'Museum of Industrial Design in Britain', in Milton Keynes, with the help of Fred Roche, who had been part of the planning team for the new town, and was partner to Conran in the architectural and planning consultancy, Conran Roche. This document represents one of the first steps in the process of creating the Design Museum, positioning the museum within a developing discourse of design, and flags up the importance of its name, in this case the 'Museum of Industrial Design'.[10]

---

[7]Habitat: Press Release, 11 May 1964 cited in Highmore, 'Feeling It': 105–22.
[8]Tom Wilson provides a summary of the search for a suitable site for a new museum of design and the development of the Boilerhouse Project in *The Story of the Design Museum*: 21–9.
[9]The Conran Foundation, Feasibility Report, Undated, the Design Museum Archives, London.
[10]Paul Reilly Files, Boilerhouse Papers, V&A Archives, London.

After discussions to open a museum in Milton Keynes fell through, Sir Roy Strong, the director of the V&A, offered Conran a temporary exhibition space at the museum. Two sites were identified, one called Clinch's Hole in the middle of the museum, the other the old Boilerhouse yard on the museum's western boundary, opposite the entrance to the Science Museum. The Boilerhouse location was chosen and in 1982, following an ambitious refurbishment of the Boilerhouse yard, it was ready for use.

The exhibition space was essentially a concealed white cube, its walls and floor were covered with bright, white tiles and lit by Erco spotlights. It corresponded to the ideological construction of the white cube, a foundational concept of modern Western art museums since the early twentieth century. It also specifically referenced the display strategies of modern art, which connect back to the exhibition, *Machine Art* at MoMA in 1934. The white cube's unique features were later described by Brian O' Doherty:

> The outside world must not come in, so windows are usually sealed off. Walls are painted white. The ceiling becomes the source of light … The art is free … to take on its own life.[11]

The Boilerhouse exhibition space was often described as clinical by contemporary commentators. The art critic Brian Sewell described it as 'a subterranean installation so aesthetically hygienic that it seemed to have been sanitised for our protection',[12] while cultural commentator Peter York referred to it as 'Emergency Ward 10'.[13]

Conran's vision for the Boilerhouse Project had a strong educational purpose and was born of a passionate conviction:

> It was the feeling that we could use intelligent design to change and improve Britain, so acting as a catalyst for social and economic change … I kept coming back to the realisation that design education was not being well understood by the government and that it could be vitally important to the future of our country.[14]

As a model, Conran had looked to the Triennale exhibitions in Milan where he had seen first-hand the best of contemporary Italian and international design. Conran's aim was to not only establish a permanent collection of mass-produced consumer products, for consumers, but also to provide strong

---

[11] Brian O'Doherty, *Inside the White Cube: The Ideology of the Gallery Space*, California: University of California Press, 1976: 15.
[12] Brian Sewell cited in Peter York, 'Chic Graphique', in *Modern Times*: 26.
[13] Peter York, 'Chic Graphique', in *Modern Times*: 26.
[14] Sir Terence Conran, Foreword in Wilson, *The Story of the Design Museum*: 7.

exemplars for business and industry. The intention behind the Boilerhouse Project was to 'stage an exemplary and challenging series of exhibitions about the history, theory, process and practice of design that explored the relationships between design, industry and commerce'.[15]

Bayley wanted the Boilerhouse Project to be a vital and living institution and to concentrate on a contemporary exhibitions programme that freed it from the burdens of archiving, conservation and cataloguing, and which allowed it to be light on its feet and quick to react to developing events. The higher ambition was to contribute towards reversing the prejudice against mass production, as opposed to limited-edition art or craft pieces, and to foster an appreciation of the process and practice of design. In the five years it was open, the Boilerhouse Project held many lively, original and acclaimed exhibitions. They included shows on the Italian avant-garde group Memphis, Issey Miyake, Dieter Rams and a case study of the development of the Ford Sierra.

An early promotional brochure for the Boilerhouse quotes the American designer and writer George Nelson. In comparing modern living with life in the Middle Ages, Nelson claimed that, as far as artists and designers are concerned, 'you've either got the Church or you've got IBM', in other words, a belief in either religion or technology.[16] The brochure carried images of contemporary mass-produced design of the twentieth century; a drawing by the Porsche design office for a Volkswagen prototype (early 1930s), an Olivetti poster designed by Xanti Schawinksy (1935), a circuit board (1982) and a fan blade from a Rolls Royce turbine engine (1987). As Bayley later reflected,

> No one had put a car on display in the V&A before because with the Victorian taxonomy no one could decide if a car came under 'metalwork' or 'sculpture'. We did. It was a Saab.[17]

Bayley's explicit reference to a car as an example of twentieth-century industrial design was in direct opposition to the way in which contemporary design was viewed by museums of decorative arts where commerce and culture have often sat uncomfortably together. As Joanna Weddell's research has shown, Sir John Pope-Hennessy, director of the V&A in the 1970s, had been dismissive about the museum's relationship between culture and

---

[15]The Conran Foundation, Promotional brochure for a new Design Museum, 1988, the Design Museum Archives, London.

[16]Promotional Brochure for The Boilerhouse, Undated, the Design Museum Archives, London.

[17]Stephen Bayley, 'Behind the Scenes at the Museum', *The Independent*, 17 September 2006. Available at: https://www.independent.co.uk/news/uk/this-britain/behind-the-scenes-at-the-mus eum-415998.html (accessed 27 October 2018).

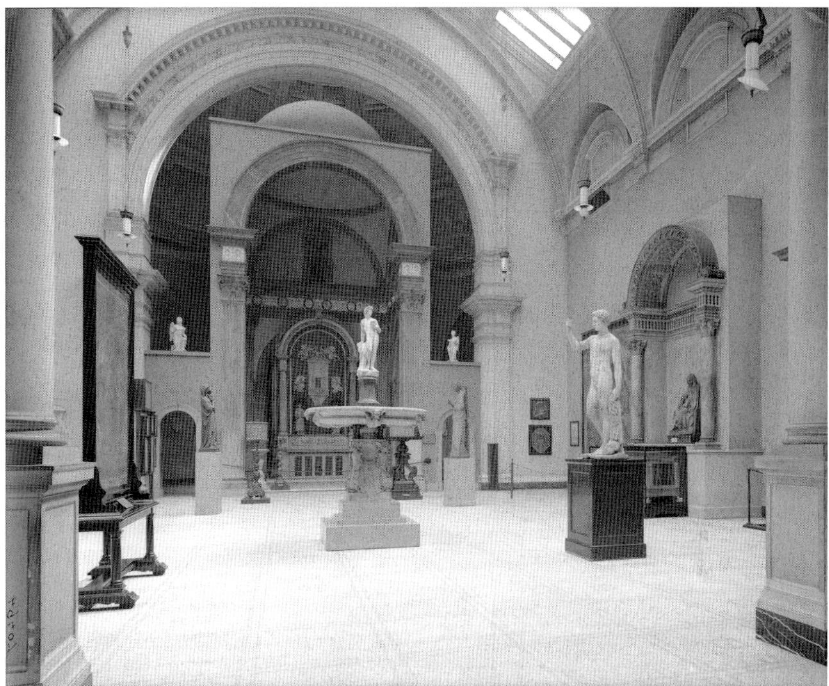

FIGURE 1.7 *The East End of the East Hall, Gallery 50, looking east, Victoria and Albert Museum, London, December 1920. © Victoria and Albert Museum, London.*

commerce.[18] As an Italian Renaissance scholar he had little interest in the products of twentieth-century industrial design. Such things were only allowed into the V&A under the guise of the increasingly marginalized 'circulating collections'. Set up in 1948, the Circulation Department, known as 'Circ', sent small- and large-scale touring exhibitions to museums and art schools around the UK. Circ was specifically engaged with the contemporary, and was the only V&A department to seriously pursue the acquisition and display of new design objects during the period. From her analysis of the published writings of Peter Floud, Circ's keeper during the 1950s and 1960s, Weddell notes the tensions and oppositions between art and industry, with 'industrial design' being a particularly contested item. Contemporary design took second place to what was regarded as the more elevated study of artefacts which were untainted by the concerns of modern consumerism, such as classical sculpture or ceramics (Figure 1.7).[19]

---

[18]Joanna Weddell, 'The Ethos of the Victoria and Albert Museum Circulation Department 1947–1960', in Liz Farrelly and Joanna Weddell (eds), *Design Objects and the Museum*, London: Bloomsbury, 2012: 15.
[19]Ibid.: 15.

However, this marginalization was not necessarily a problem. Maurice Davies, a cultural consultant and former deputy director of the Museums Association, has suggested that the tentative place of the Boilerhouse 'squatting at the V&A, perhaps both symbiotic and parasitic', gave it the confidence to be not just highly creative but also rather mischievous:

> My favourite show there was about national characteristics in design. It managed to be simultaneously insightful and hilarious in identifying national stereotypes. I still miss the Boilerhouse's brave combination of intelligence and parody.[20]

The first year of the Boilerhouse Project saw five exhibitions; the first, *Art and Industry: A Century of Design in the Products We Use*, opened on 14 January 1982. The exhibition was the first of a series of exhibitions about the history, theory and practice of design. It celebrated the work of influential designers and their relationship with manufacturers through a series of case studies. Objects were placed on white display stands and included Raymond Loewy's duplicator for Gestetner, Ettore Sottsass's typewriter for Olivetti, Walter Dorwin Teague's work for Boeing and a petrol pump designed by Eliot Noyes for Mobil, which remains part of the Design Museum's permanent collection.

The second exhibition presented a complete contrast, a history of *Sony*, the Japanese manufacturer of consumer electronics, with a detailed survey of production. The product packaging was used as the display structure in the exhibition with products displayed on piles of empty boxes.

This exhibition was followed by a monographic exhibition on the German designer *Dieter Rams* and an exhibition titled *52 Months to Job One: How They Designed the Ford Sierra*. The year ended with an exhibition, *Memphis Milano in London*, a presentation of furniture, glass, ceramics and fabrics produced by the Italian avant-garde design group. Later exhibitions included subjects as diverse as design from Denmark, advertising and art direction, a history of taste, robotics and the ergonomics of hand tools.

When interviewed in 1989, Bayley reflected on his achievements at the Boilerhouse and his approach to exhibition-making, which he considered to be more akin to theatre:

> I'm convinced that to make exhibitions effective, you have to regard them as a form of theatre, which is why I like to use as many sophisticated devices as possible. I want to educate and interest people, and so I'll

---

[20]Maurice Davies, Blog Post, 23 November 2016. Available at: https://charlessaumarezsmith.com/2016/11/22/boilerhouse-project/ (accessed 27 October 2018).

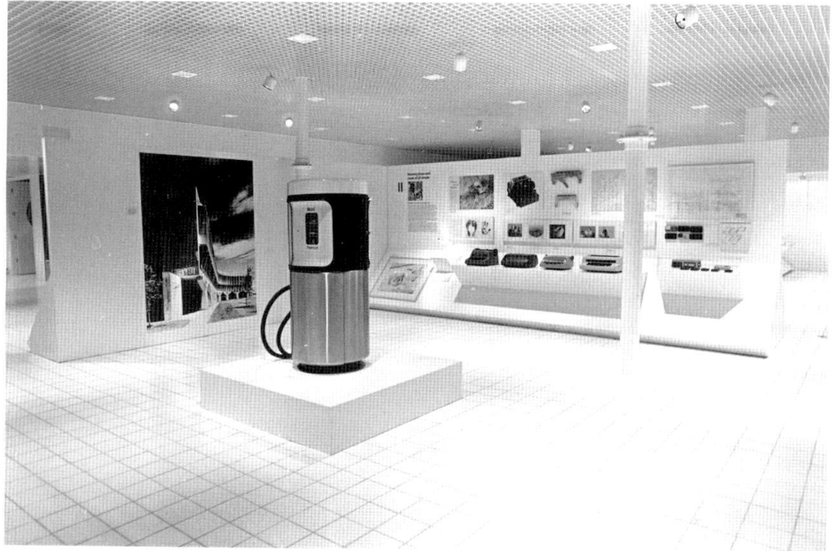

FIGURE 1.8 *Petrol pump designed by Elliot Noyes for Mobil in the Boilerhouse exhibition*, Art and Industry, *1982. © Design Museum, London.*

consider anything. Part of my job is to create debate, if people get angry, at least they start thinking and talking.[21]

In order to create a sense of theatricality, Bayley used attention-grabbing display approaches that moved away from the conventional method of objects housed in glass cases. In 1993 he chose a dustbin as display device in an exhibition on the subject of taste. *Taste: An Exhibition about Values in Design* presented objects displayed on upturned galvanized steel dustbins or on white plinths, according to Bayley's judgement of their taste value. For the exhibition on Japanese fashion designer Issey Miyake, the immaculate, white-tiled gallery was pumped full of black foam rubber from which bald, glossy black mannequins protruded and floated above the foam. In 1984 Bayley employed John Pawson's extreme minimalistic design for the exhibition, *Hand Tools* which used long, low black wedges to display the objects forcing the visitor to bend down to view the exhibits.

The Boilerhouse Project positioned itself firmly at the forefront of new and contemporary design, but it was met with both praise and criticism. The exhibitions often evoked a strong response, for example, one visitor was shocked at seeing a petrol pump in a museum of applied arts (Figure 1.8). The *Observer* described the Boilerhouse as a strange nether region declaring

---

[21]Stephen Bayley Press Cuttings Files, the Design Museum Archives, London.

that 'the work of the industrial designer would be sinister were it not mildly ridiculous'. The *Guardian* felt that the exhibitions had been 'calculated to distance the public'. The strength of the critical responses attests to the novelty of showing industrial design in a museum context. But the project also had its supporters. Radio 3's *Critics Forum* described the inaugural exhibition, *Art and Industry*, as 'very intelligent … a model exhibition'.[22]

In spite of a mixed critical response, the enormous popularity of the Boilerhouse Project with the public and its success in bringing attention to the importance of the industrial designer was clear to see. The Boilerhouse was a small gallery within a national institution but in terms of visitor numbers of 1.5 million, the twenty-three exhibitions it presented over five years proved to be some of the more successful ones in London.

Writing in 2016, Charles Saumarez Smith, formerly chief executive of the Royal Academy of Arts (RA), London, recalls the Boilerhouse Project 'which was no more than a creative cell in the basement of the V&A where Stephen Bayley held court in a glass office surrounded by piles of magazines' and remembers the exhibitions as being 'lively and very inventive'.[23] For Bayley, 'they tapped and thereby demonstrated the existence of a massive latent interest in design', supporting Conran's rationale for a permanent museum devoted to the study of industrial design.[24]

In 1981, Terence Conran led a consortium to win the bid for a mixed-use development at Butler's Wharf, a 13-acre site on the south bank of the River Thames. The search for possible locations for the new Design Museum began as early as 1984. In 1986 Conran moved the Boilerhouse Project to the area. The site chosen for the new museum was a derelict 1950s banana-ripening warehouse on the riverfront in a location overlooking Tower Bridge and across from the city of London. The building was converted by Richard Doone of Conran Roche, who created space for two floors of exhibition galleries, education and events spaces, as well as a cafe and a restaurant overlooking the river.

Doone devised a scheme that stripped back the brickwork and used the steel structure to create a simple, white-walled building with generous balconies that was deliberately reminiscent of the International Style of the 1930s exemplified by the Bauhaus and which stood in direct contrast to the

---

[22]Stephen Bayley Press Cuttings Files, the Design Museum Archives, London.

[23]Liz Farrelly presents an account of Stephen Bayley's trajectory from 'enfant terrible' and journalist to curator and director of the Boilerhouse Gallery in 'Media in the Museum: Fashioning the Design Curator at the Boilerhouse Gallery, Victoria and Albert Museum, London', in Leah Armstrong and Felice McDowell (eds), *Fashioning Identities: Identity and Representation at Work in the Creative Industries*, London: Bloomsbury, 2018: 29.

[24]Tom Wilson (ed.), *Designs of Our Times: 10 Years of Designs of the Year*, London: Design Museum, 2017: 29.

Victorian warehouses along the riverfront. Stephen Bayley later recalled that people would often refer to the museum as 'Bauhaus on Thames'. Barbara Usherwood's detailed description of the Design Museum in 1991 describes the renovated warehouse in Shad Thames as a skin-deep simulacrum of modernism with ocean-liner decks, a faux corporate reception desk and pristine marble-and-white interiors (Figures 1.9a and 1.9b).[25]

An early promotional brochure produced by the Design Museum set out a bold ambition for the new museum:

> In a building of outstanding architectural character and quality on a remarkable site close to London's financial centre, the Design Museum will offer a range of resources which designers, industry and business may draw on to create better products, while providing a stimulating environment in which to view, experience and evaluate design. When the Design Museum opens in Spring 1989 it will take the concept of the museum out of the nineteenth century and into the twenty-first century.[26]

The brochure states that the museum would house a permanent study collection of noteworthy design from the Industrial Revolution to the age of electronics with products supported by information about marketing, materials and performance, which enables an object to be understood in context. In 1989, in his regular editorial column in *Blueprint*, Deyan Sudjic praised Bayley's approach, pointing out that many institutions show objects as art whereas Stephen Bayley wanted to put objects into context.[27]

Drawing on the experience of the Foundation's successful Boilerhouse Project in the V&A, the new Design Museum would provide a unique range of resources for students, professional designers, industry and commerce. Through its permanent collection, temporary exhibitions, continuously changing reviews, lecture programmes and study facilities, the Design Museum recognized that 'industry is our culture'.[28] It was acknowledged that design was not one subject but many: furniture, packaging, office equipment, transport and leisure. Design encompassed materials science, ergonomics, mechanical engineering and styling.

From the beginning, the museum was deliberately international in its outlook. In 1988 Conran and Bayley set up an International Advisory Council.

---

[25]Barbara Usherwood, 'The Design Museum: Form Follows Funding', *Design Issues*, Vol. 7, No. 2 (1991): 76–87.

[26]The Conran Foundation, The Design Museum at Butler's Wharf Promotional Brochure, Undated, the Design Museum Archives, London.

[27]Deyan Sudjic, Editorial, *Blueprint*, July/August 1989.

[28]Stephen Bayley, Design Museum Hymn Sheet, 24 June 1987, the Design Museum Archives, London.

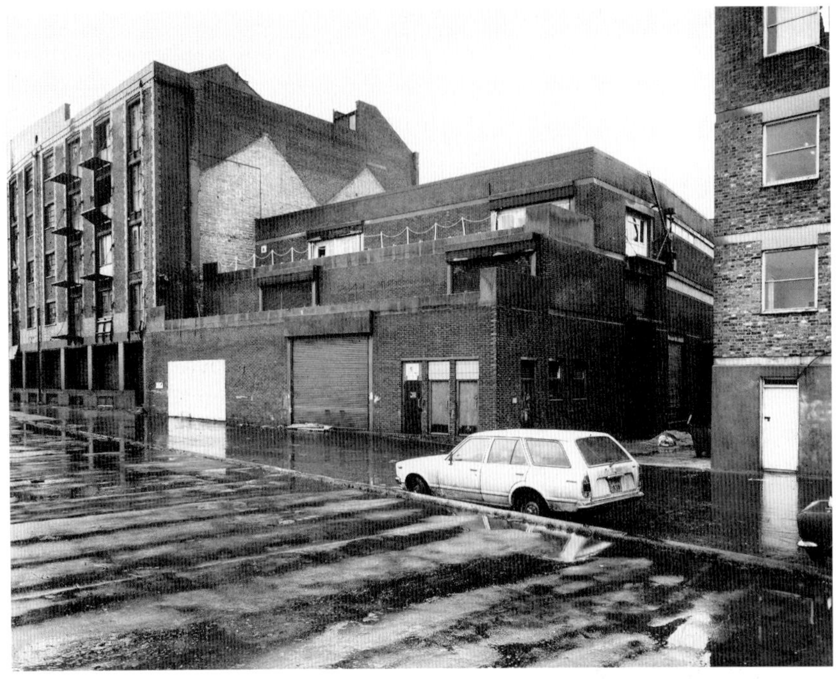

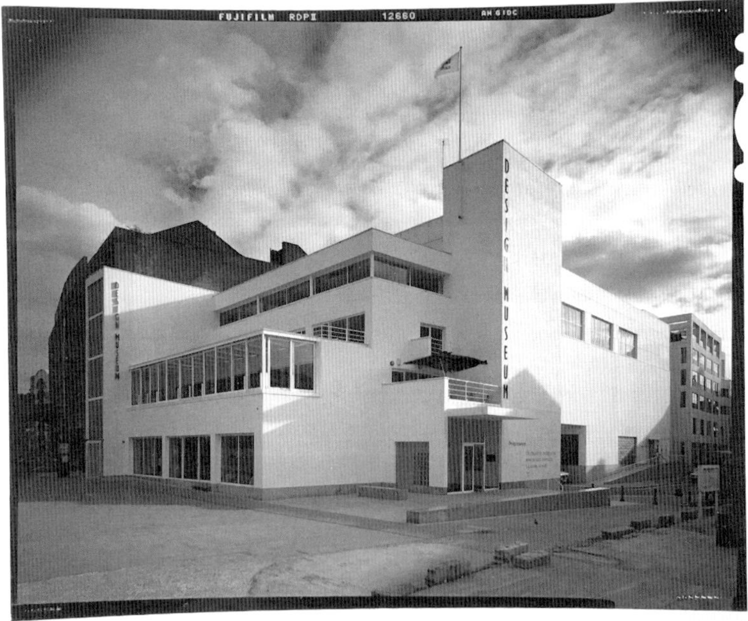

FIGURE 1.9 *The Design Museum prior to conversion in 1987 (Figure 1.9a) and just before its official opening in 1989 (Figure 1.9b). © Design Museum, London.*

The participants included directors of design institutions such as the Design Arts Programme at the National Endowment for the Arts in Washington, the Palazzo Grassi in Venice, the Deutsches Architekturmuseum in Frankfurt, the Taideteollisuusmuseo in Helsinki and the Cooper Hewitt, Smithsonian Design Museum in New York.[29] By so doing, it was hoped that the new Design Museum would be able to benefit from best practices in Europe and the United States. The role of the council was to advise on themes, issues and developments in design that might influence the exhibition and education programmes at the new museum. The Design Museum was also vocal about its position as an independent institution whose purpose was 'to increase public understanding of industrial society through the study of the artefacts it produces'.[30] It was also clear that it would not endorse a notion of good design or taste, in an attempt to distance itself from the position communicated at the Boilerhouse and to establish the museum as an independent institution.[31] The Design Museum was opened by the UK prime minister Margaret Thatcher on 5 July 1989 (Figure 1.10).

The first exhibition, *Commerce and Culture: From Pre-Industrial Art to Post-Industrial Value*, set the agenda for the new Design Museum. In a foreword to the accompanying exhibition catalogue, Design Museum director Stephen Bayley asserted that commerce and culture were not separate entities but were all one, stating:

> Our modern muses are commerce, industry and technology, and we're trying to make a home for them ... Commerce and culture are all part of the same thing. The only difference between a museum and a department store is that in one of them, the goods are for sale.[32]

The exhibition included full-scale reconstructions of the entrance to an American shopping mall, a Corinthian-style column from the Earls Court Sainsbury's Homebase store together with Brucciani's gallery of casts from the V&A. Now that they were free from the institutional shackles of the V&A, the exhibitions at the new Design Museum were able to depart from what was presented at the earlier Boilerhouse and could more explicitly embrace commerce.

The earlier Boilerhouse Project at the V&A and, later, the Design Museum at Butler's Wharf, offered independent spaces in which to think seriously

---

[29]Design Museum International Advisory Council, First Meeting: Agenda and Briefing Notes, 12 April 1988, the Design Museum Archives, London.
[30]Positioning Paper, the Design Museum, February 1989, the Design Museum Archives, London.
[31]Bayley, 'Behind the Scenes at the Museum'. Available at: https://www.independent.co.uk/news/uk/this-britain/behind-the-scenes-at-the-museum/ (accessed 20 October 2018).
[32]Positioning Paper, the Design Museum, February 1989, the Design Museum Archives, London.

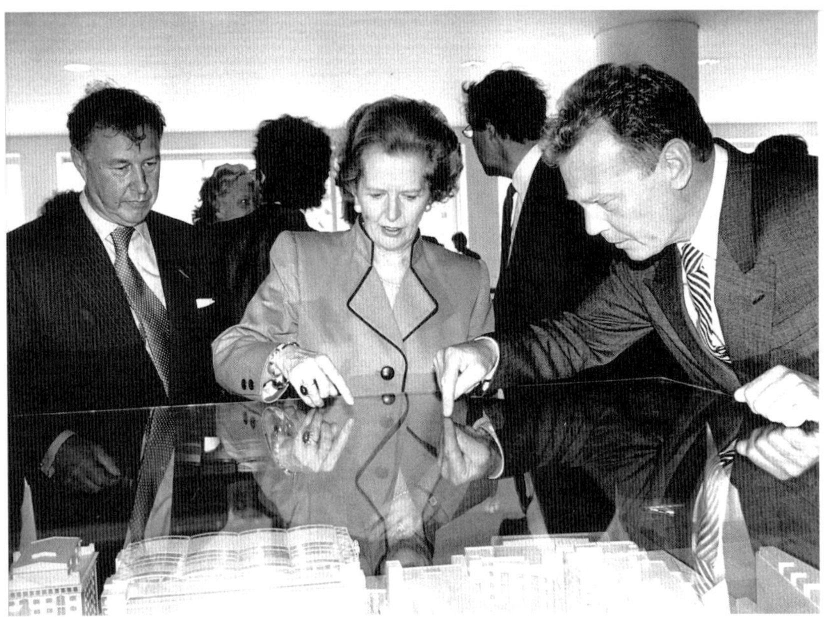

FIGURE 1.10 *Terence Conran and Prime Minister Margaret Thatcher at the opening of the Design Museum, 5 July 1989. © Design Museum, London.*

about design and, through a temporary exhibitions programme, permanent collection and learning programme, communicate its value in the broadest cultural sense. This continuing debate has, over time, informed the mission of the institution and underpinned curatorial approaches. Official documents produced by the Design Museum between 1989 and 2017, including press releases, monthly bulletins, annual reports and corporate plans, reflect these changing mission statements and programming policies.

Writing in 1988 at a time when many more museums were being launched or were reinventing themselves, Neil Kotler and Philip Kotler's research identified that museums were starting to develop mission statements to more clearly define their functions, roles and purpose.[33] Over time, they can also be interpreted as markers in the development of the design museum, reflecting gradual shifts in thinking and strategic direction. From the late 1980s, in response to a series of rapid political, social and cultural changes, museums became more aware of their audiences and attempted to make their venues more attractive, their exhibitions more didactic and their names

[33]Neil Kotler and Philip Kotler, *Museum Strategy and Marketing*, San Francisco, CA: Jossey-Bass, 1998: 28.

more appealing.[34] During the 1990s, there is a noticeable shift in focus as design museums attempt to redefine themselves by changing their names and shifting the focus of their acquisition policies. Research by Javier Gimeno-Martinez and Jasmijn Verlinden has documented the impact of this shift.[35]

In 1995 the Museum voor Sierkunst (Museum of Decorative Arts) in Ghent changed its name to Museum voor Sierkunst en Vormgeving (Museum of Decorative Arts and Design). In 2001 the institution's name underwent a further change and became the Design Museum Gent. For trustees at the museum, design reflected a wider concept of which decorative arts formed only a part. The term decorative arts was seen to be archaic and did not accurately reflect the museum's acquisition and exhibition policies. In 2002 the Taideteollisuudmuseo (Museum of Applied Arts) in Helsinki, Finland, changed its name to Designmuseo (Design Museum). In the same year, New York's American Craft Museum changed its name to the Museum of Arts and Design.

Gimeno-Martinez and Verlinden argue that the name changes addressed two key concerns. First, that museum directors wanted to raise the institution's profile, and second, that they wanted to gain international status and, because of a rising public interest in design, felt that the word 'design' helped them to achieve both of these aims.[36] Veteran institutions with decorative art collections, like the V&A in London and the Cooper-Hewitt, Smithsonian Design Museum in New York, began to call themselves national museums of art and design. The V&A name change became effective in January 2002. The association with the field of design clearly had connotations as something modern, global and progressive.

Alongside a new focus on contemporary design within these institutions, the role of the curator was undergoing key changes. Curators continued to research and care for the collection, and acquire historical and contemporary objects, but there was an element of the job that was steadily growing in importance and that was the production of exhibitions. It was the expansion of this role that was to have a direct impact on curatorial practice in the design museum.

---

[34]Eilean Hooper-Greenhill has charted this shift in museums in a series of studies including *Museums and Their Visitors*, London: Routledge, 1994 and *The Educational Role of the Museum*, London: Routledge, 1999.

[35]Javier Gimeno-Martinez and Jasmijn Verlinden, 'From Museum of Decorative Arts to Design Museum: The Case of the Design Museum Gent', *Design and Culture*, Vol. 2, No. 3 (2010): 259–83.

[36]Ibid.: 272.

1.5

A Rising Public Interest in Design

From the 1960s, the antiques trade, auctions and retail influenced a growing consumer demand for design. In London, and across Europe, retailers and gallerists established spaces in which to promote the work of contemporary designers. This development influenced the establishment of private collections that focused on contemporary design. Since the mid-twentieth century, furniture companies such as Vitra and Herman Miller had produced and sold reproductions of design pieces. Working with designers such as George Nelson and Charles and Ray Eames, Herman Miller produced pieces that would become popular examples of industrial design and which later entered the collections of design museums. In 1989 Vitra opened a museum on its campus in Weil am Rhein to collect and exhibit the work of twentieth-century architects and designers. The collection had been established by Rolf Fehlbaum who transferred it to the Vitra Design Museum when it opened. Originally a private collection, it became part of the institutional framework of the new museum.[1] The collection has gradually been expanded by the museum's directors, Alexander von Vegesack (1989–2010), Mateo Kries and Marc Zehntner (since 2011), and it now numbers among the largest of its kind worldwide. The collection comprises seven thousand pieces of furniture, more than a thousand lighting objects and numerous archives, including the estates of designers Charles and Ray Eames, Verner Panton and Alexander Girard.

A further factor in a rising consumer demand for design was a developing antiques trade. During the 1960s in London, a group of gallerists initiated research on obscure or long-forgotten designers, invested in emerging ones and produced the kind of scholarship and monographs that had traditionally been the exclusive domain of art galleries. In 1966 John Jesse set up a stall

---

[1] Interview with Susanne Graner, Head of Collections, Vitra Design Museum, 19 May 2016. Available at: https://www.vitra.com/en-us/magazine/details/susanne-graner (accessed 12 November 2018).

in Portobello Market specializing in Art Nouveau and Art Deco. Two years later, he opened a gallery on Kensington Church Street and established himself as a leading dealer of twentieth century decorative arts, sourcing works for collectors and museums worldwide. During this time London was producing some of the earliest champions of contemporary design, among them Themes & Variations which opened in Notting Hill in 1984 and David Gill who launched his art and design gallery on Fulham Road three years later. These were bold moves at a time when furniture and decorative antiques were very much the prevailing taste.[2]

Gill initially focused his collection on early modern masters such as Jean-Michel Frank, Émile-Jacques Ruhlmann and Eileen Gray. From the early 1990s he started to represent artists and designers who represented the vanguard, such as Donald Judd, Grayson Perry and Garouste & Bonetti, explaining that he 'wanted to take people on a journey between historical pieces and contemporary design'.[3] Connoisseurs and collectors such as the banker Jacob Rothschild and the interior designer David Mlinaric became regular buyers. Later Gill shifted the gallery's focus to contemporary designers such as Zaha Hadid, the Campana Brothers and Fredrikson Stallard.

The early 2000s saw the opening of a number of independently curated spaces for design that exhibited the work of contemporary designers in their early careers. The Aram Gallery was established in 2002 by Aram Store founder, Zeev Aram, and curator, Daniel Charny. Located on the third floor of the Aram Store in Covent Garden, the opening exhibition, *Small Step* (25 October–18 December 2002), presented the experimental works of ten design graduates across a range of disciplines. The gallery was interested to show how designers' explorations, ideas and uses of new materials translated into new typologies. The Aram Gallery built up a strong profile, presenting the work of established and emerging designers who were selected because of their experimental design thinking. As a non-commercial space, the gallery staged five new shows every year addressing relevant topics within contemporary design. The diverse programme of exhibitions included solo and group shows, with a thematic-, material- or process-led focus.[4]

The gallery's location above the Aram Store selling contemporary design connected its cultural and commercial activities. This model resonates with the furniture company Vitra that established a design museum in Weil am

---

[2]'Kensington Church Street Bids Farewell to John Jesse', *Antiques Trade Gazette*, 12 July 2005. Available at: https://www.antiquestradegazette.com/news/2005/kensington-church-street-bids-farewell-to-john-jesse/ (accessed 2 June 2019).

[3]Marisa Bartolucci, 'The Ultimate Guide to Collecting Contemporary Design', *Introspective Magazine*, 15 February 2016. Available at: https://www.1stdibs.com/introspective-magazine/collecting-contemporary/ (accessed 3 June 2019).

[4]Aram Gallery website. Available at: https://www.thearamgallery.org (accessed 5 September 2019).

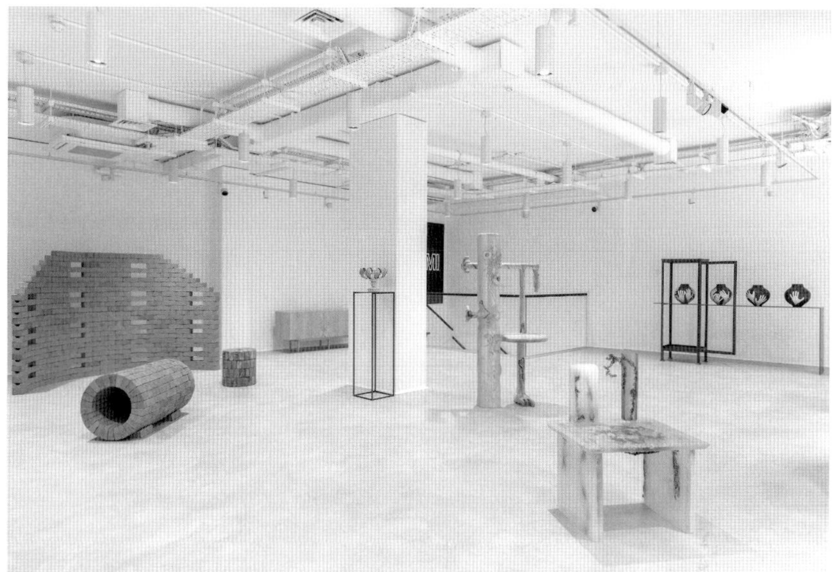

FIGURE 1.11 Together/The Power of Collaboration/Group Show, *Gallery FUMI, London, 16 September–12 November 2021.* © *Tom Joseph Wright / Penguins Egg.*

Rhein in 1989 and the Design Museum, London, established by the retailer and founder of Habitat, Terence Conran, also in 1989. The close link between commerce and culture is something which directly influenced the origin of design museums and which also connects to an earlier history of the display of designed objects at international exhibitions.

The opening of commercial galleries in London, promoting the work of contemporary designers, influenced the establishment of private collections of contemporary design. In 2006 Julien Lombrail and Loic Le Gaillard opened a space in Chelsea in a former carpenter's workshop. The Carpenters Workshop Gallery was set up to represent international artists and designers who work 'outside their traditional territories of expression'. The gallery is actively involved in the research and production of limited-edition pieces. In 2008 the gallery opened a second gallery space in Mayfair and in 2015 a workshop space in Roissy, France. The gallery became the first to integrate a production facility dedicated to research and the development of collectable design.[5]

Gallery FUMI was established in Mayfair by Sam Pratt and Valerio Capo in 2008 (Figure 1.11). Both came from non-design backgrounds and their aim was the promotion, commission and sale of high-level craft, with an emphasis on

---

[5]Carpenters Workshop Gallery website. Available at: http://carpentersworkshopgallery.com (accessed 5 September 2019).

the conceptual and practical.[6] The gallery has established a series of long-term relationships with a core group of designers. Objects are usually handmade by the designer in a small workshop context, or in small-batch production by specialist crafts practitioners. Many use traditional techniques such as carving, glass-blowing, cabinetry and lacquering while others apply digital technologies in their making. The gallery has built creative relationships with institutions, interior designers and collectors. It runs an ambitious programme of exhibitions alongside a presence at international design fairs. In 2018 the gallery celebrated its tenth anniversary with an exhibition, *Now and Then*. Curated by Libby Sellers, the exhibition charted the trajectory of the gallery's programme since its opening in 2008.

Over time, the growing client bases of commercial design galleries attracted the interest of auction houses, which began to establish twentieth-century and contemporary design departments. Alexander Payne had previously headed a small design department at Bonhams in London. In 1999 he joined Phillips with the aim of building a new international design department. He began by developing their design market initially in America and then in the UK and internationally. In an interview Payne revealed:

There's a broader approach to collecting design, and no specific area has been ghettoed, as such. But I think that's what's really exciting – the fact that there's not a narrow approach to collecting, and now there's a renaissance in understanding where design and decorative arts have come from. What's happening is collectors, perhaps from the modernist era of the 1920s and 1930s, are seeing how they can potentially connect the likes of Newson, Laarman and Hadid to their collections, their homes, or other areas of their lives.[7]

The field of collectable design has existed under different names and in different guises, as art furniture, functional art, design art, experimental design and fine design. Edwin Heathcote has written about this changing landscape for commercial design. He points out that twenty years previously design was called the 'applied arts'. The auction houses periodically held sales of classic and contemporary design pieces but they were few and far between. Pieces by celebrated designers such as Frank Lloyd Wright and Eileen Gray sold for just a few thousand pounds, as Heathcote comments:

---

[6] Presentation by FUMI Director Sam Pratt to MA Curating Contemporary Design students, the Design Museum, 4 October 2017.

[7] Alex Easthope, 'An Introduction to Collecting Design with Phillip's Alexander Payne', *Classic Driver*, 14 April 2017. Available at: https://www.classicdriver.com/en/article/design-furniture/introduction-collecting-design-phillips-alexander-payne/ (accessed 17 May 2019).

Then, in the noughties, something happened. Designers, seeing the vast sums to be made in the contemporary art sales, decided they would become artists. Rather than designing to commission or for manufacture, as they had traditionally done, they began to create one-off pieces, to launch 'editions', borrowing the tropes and language of the art market.[8]

In June 2005, Christie's sold a 1948 Carlo Mollino trestle desk, owned by contemporary art collector Dakis Joannou, for an unprecedented $3.9 million, much more than the estimate of $200,000. The sale represented a significant shift when compared with the previous auction record for twentieth-century design of $1.9 million reached in 2000 for a 1929 chromed-metal and lacquer desk by Émile-Jacques Ruhlmann. The Mollino desk was purchased by Cristina Grajales, one of New York's leading gallerists in modern and contemporary design, for a client who was keen on creating a mid-century design collection. Design was seen to be a marketable and a commercial asset. The hybrid came to be known as 'design art' and resulted in works reaching stratospheric art-world prices. This shift famously culminated in Marc Newson's Lockheed Lounge which sold at Phillips de Pury for £1.1 million in 2009.[9] In the same year a Dragon armchair by Eileen Gray from the collection of Yves Saint Laurent sold for €21.9 million at a sale at Christie's in Paris. As a result, designers were feted across the world in magazines, festivals, fairs and galleries. It seemed that design now had a market with auction prices comparable to the art market.

The art market has been extensively studied with artists' values widely published and discussed.[10] But there has been a distinct lack of data about the design market and understanding conventional markers for the value of design pieces. In 2005 Rabih Hage, a gallerist, designer and founder of online design think tank DeTnk, commissioned and published a report which set out to quantify the sales of contemporary design by designers.[11] DeTnk described itself as a think tank and marketplace for modern contemporary design, architecture and interiors. It was also an online curated space, showcasing the

---

[8]Edwin Heathcote, 'Collecting Special: Designs on the Market', *Financial Times*, 27 May 2011. Available at: https://www.ft.com/content/1ca5efac-87f6-11e0-a6de-00144feabdc0 (accessed 17 October 2019).

[9]Marcus Fairs, 'Newson Chair Sells for Design-Art Record 1.1 Million Record', *Dezeen*, 30 April 2009. Available at: https://www.dezeen.com/2009/04/30/newson-chair-sells-for-design-art-record-11-million-pounds/ (last accessed 17 October 2019).

[10]Academic literature includes Natasha Degen, *The Market (Documents of Contemporary Art)*, London: Whitechapel Gallery, 2013; Peter Watson, *From Manet to Manhattan: The Rise of the Modern Art Market*, London: Random House, 1992. *The Art Newspaper*, an online and print publication, was founded in 1990 by Umberto Allemandi and Anna Somers Cocks and publishes reviews and in-depth commentary on the international art market.

[11]'DeTnk: A New Way of Collecting Design and Architecture'. Available at: https://www.detnk.com (accessed 20 October 2019).

work of emerging and established designers and a platform for providing the latest and most interesting news, articles and discussions on contemporary design. The platform, aimed at design enthusiasts and collectors, was intended to bring a fresh perspective to the contemporary conversation on design while expanding the margins of design discourse and debate into a public forum. *The DeTnk Market Report, the Rise of the Collectible Design Market 2005–11* set out to analyse design sales and provide a holistic analysis of the emerging collectible design market. In an interview, Hage explained why he had initiated the report:

> We were all talking about the rise in the design market, but wondering, was there really a rise? Was there really a design market? We started looking at the market … collecting data and observing the sales and changes and over the years the market has proved not only to exist but to be solid. It seems it is here to stay.[12]

The 2016 report focused on sales from five of the largest auction houses including Christie's (New York, Paris, London); Sotheby's (New York, Paris, London) and Phillips (New York, London). It confirmed that the global collectable design market had steadily grown with 25.3 per cent more lots offered for sale and a 36.35 per cent increase in total value of sales in 2016. The research undertaken by DeTnk also showed that design was still a relatively fledgling market. Jean Prouvé sold for less than £2 million at auction, a small sum compared with some of the well-known names in art and a single Picasso selling for as much as £65.5 million.[13] Nevertheless, the research indicated that design was being taken as seriously as art. It also revealed that contemporary design promoted by the commercial gallery and the auction house played an important part in driving and sustaining a commercial market for design.

In Britain during the 1990s, a government focus on the creative industries, enabled by funding from new sources such as the National Lottery, resulted in a proliferation of exhibitions, trade shows and travelling showcases of contemporary design. Government-funded organizations such as the Department for Trade and Industry (DTI), the Design Council and the British Council initiated a number of projects to promote British design across the UK and overseas, much like the international exhibitions during the nineteenth century. The DTI was particularly active during the 1990s, arranging a series of trade-promotion initiatives and exhibitions to promote British design.

---

[12]Heathcote, 'Collecting Special: Designs on the Market'. Available at:https://www.ft.com/content/1ca5efac-87f6-11e0-a6de-00144feabdc0 (accessed 17 October 2019).

[13]'2017 DeTnk Collectible Design Market Report: An Analysis of Design Sales during 2016'. Available from: https://www.detnk.com/node/142519 (accessed 20 October 2019).

Design was also promoted regionally across the UK, notably through city-specific design festivals such as the Glasgow UK City of Architecture and Design in 1999. The festival was directed by Deyan Sudjic, then editor of the design magazine, *Blueprint*. Design was also a key focus in the controversial *Millennium Experience*, which opened to the public at Greenwich in 2000.

In 1996 Emily Campbell was appointed the first head of Design and Architecture at the British Council, the UK's international organization for cultural relations. In an interview, she described her role as a design ambassador with the aim of promoting British design around the world and raising awareness of design issues. During Campbell's tenure, the British Council were commissioners and curators of exhibitions and design showcases at a range of venues, including the Venice Biennale.[14] They also introduced initiatives such as the International Young Design Entrepreneur Award. The exhibitions and publications produced by the British Council provide well-documented surveys of the culture and industry of design during the 1990s and 2000s. From 2011 to 2014, a series of papers were published by the Architecture, Design, Fashion Department (ADF). The ADF papers invited critics and curators to explore new directions in British architecture, design and fashion through specific themes or a series of case studies. Subjects included design collectives, fashion as installation, sustainability in design, 3D printing and social design. The ADF papers did much to bring attention to current and emerging debates in contemporary design at that time.[15] Campbell went on to become head of design at the Royal Society for the encouragement of Arts, Manufactures and Commerce (RSA), where she continued to focus her attention on the promotion and debate of design and its emergent issues.

---

[14]Kristina Gill, 'Interview with Head of Design of British Council Emily Campbell', *Three Layer Cake*, 10 December 2007. Available at: http://www.yankodesign.com/2007/10/12/interview-with-head-of-design-of-british-council-emily-campbell/ (accessed 16 March 2018).
[15]ADF Papers, published by the British Council's Architecture, Design, Fashion Department, were launched on 28 July 2011. Available at: https://design.britishcouncil.org/blog/2011/jul/28/launch-adf-papers/ (accessed 16 March 2018).

1.6

The Growing Popularity of Design Exhibitions

From the 1990s, exhibitions were seen by museums as a major way to build an institutional brand, attract larger visitor numbers and generate income. The growing demand for contemporary exhibition programming started to offer new opportunities to curators that were independent of collection responsibilities. It was the expansion of this role that was to lead to wide-ranging changes in contemporary curatorial practice. It also suggested new roles for the design curator, in terms of curating exhibitions and displays that communicated contemporary culture and that brought fresh thinking to a museum's collection.

The years leading up to the millennium saw the creation of a number of large-scale design exhibitions that presented intriguing and innovative concepts in engaging ways. Curators started to experiment with new formats and approaches. Significantly, the exhibitions were curated by individuals or agencies operating outside the institutional context of the museum and who were described by *Design Week* in 2001 as 'a new breed of curators'.[1] Restructure was established in 1999 by Libby Sellers and Helen Evenden, graduates of the MA Design History programme at the Royal College of Art (RCA), run jointly with the V&A. The curatorial agency provided design-related and architecture-related content for a variety of clients and institutions including RIBA, Habitat, L'Oreal, Wordsearch and the Design Council. As part of a month-long design festival, UKinNY, Restructure was commissioned by the Design Council to curate a major touring exhibition, *Great Expectations: New British Design Stories*, to be installed in New York's Grand Central Terminal, Vanderbilt Hall.

---

[1] 'Structure This', *Design Week*, 2 August 2001. Available at: https://www.designweek.co.uk/issues/2-august-2001/structure-this/ (accessed 5 October 2019).

worked as an independent curator throughout the 1990s and was responsible for a number of high-profile design exhibitions including *Powerhouse: UK: British Creativity Now* in Horse Guards Parade (1998); *Stealing Beauty: British Design Now* at the Institute of Contemporary Art (1999) and *Food: Design and Culture* for Glasgow 1999. In 2000 she co-founded Scarlet Projects with Sarah Gaventa, also a graduate of the RCA Design History programme. The agency established a reputation for innovative work that brought design and architecture to a wider public. They also pioneered a new approach to commissioning, offering a strategy which placed exhibitions, installations and events in public spaces, commercial and business settings, as well as in museums and galleries. Clients were wide-ranging and included the British Council, the V&A, Science Museum, Wellcome Trust, Selfridges and Bloomberg.

In 2012 Catterall was appointed director of exhibitions at Somerset House. She implemented a distinctive programme of design exhibitions, including *SHOWstudio: Fashion Revolution* (17 September–23 December 2009); *Maison Martin Margiela 20 the Exhibition* (3 June–5 September 2010); *Tim Walker Storyteller* (18 October 2012–27 January 2013); *Valentino: Master of Couture* (29 November 2012–3 March 2013); *Isabella Blow: Fashion Galore!* (20 November 2013–2 March 2014); *Big Bang Data* (3 December 2015–20 March 2016) and *Hair by Sam McKnight* (2 November 2016–12 March 2017). Catterall also devised and curated the venue's acclaimed annual contemporary graphic art fair, *Pick Me Up*.[3] Somerset House continues to present exhibitions and installations but as part of a wider remit. The programme now also supports young creatives and businesses by providing workspaces for those working at the intersection of design and technology.

During the 2000s, design exhibitions explored a range of subjects to appeal to broad audiences. Many were notable in the way that they highlighted the design and manufacturing process. The exhibitions were intended to bring visitors closer to design practice and the world of the design studio. *In the Making* (22 January–4 May 2014) at the Design Museum, London, showcased the work of Ed Barber and Jay Osgerby, the award-winning designers of the London 2012 Olympic torch. The designers had a long-held technical curiosity and fascination for the making process, and the exhibition explored unfinished products with industrial objects interrupted at various stages in their manufacturing processes. The objects were wide-ranging and included a tennis ball, a bank note and a diamond. The exhibition gave visitors a rare insight into how objects are made and the prototypes that are created before the final design is delivered.

---

[3]Somerset House website. Available at: https://www.somersethouse.org.uk (accessed 15 May 2018).

In 2013, the Design Museum explored new territory by giving a platform to the emerging discipline of critical or speculative design. *United Micro Kingdoms: A Design Fiction* (30 January 2012–28 April 2013) showcased the work of designers and educators Anthony Dunne and Fiona Raby and examined a series of speculative futures. Dunne and Raby, who had established the Design Interactions course at the RCA, weave speculative narratives around objects and designs that extrapolate current trends and offer witty critical commentaries on contemporary culture. The Design Museum exhibition, curated by Dunne and Raby, explored the future interface between science, technology and design. It imagined an alternative version of England governed by four extreme lifestyle tribes. The designers devolved the country into four new counties, each conceived as an experimental zone with its own form of governance, economy and lifestyle, and visitors were encouraged to decide which tribe they might want to align themselves with. These fantastical worlds were depicted through models and props, arranged on a central table in the exhibition space. As a review of the exhibition noted, 'by suspending reality for a moment and indulging in speculation, with a very English sense of humour, *United Micro Kingdoms* provides the very lens we need to make our contemporary social, political and environmental predicament all the more clear. It is beautiful, funny and clever and may just change the way you look at the world'.[4]

At this time, design curating practice was starting to expand outside of the museum and gallery. It was extending to new locations and became a key area of practice in the rapidly changing fields of contemporary science and health care. The Science Museum and the Wellcome Trust commissioned curators, artists and designers to communicate the complexities of modern science and technology to the widest audience.

Examples include the Wellcome Trust's groundbreaking exhibitions at Euston Road, whose subjects have included the human heart, hygiene and mental health. At the Science Museum, a series of curated events such as family sleepovers were introduced and art collectives used performance art to explain issues such as climate change. In 1996, the first Maggie's Centre opened offering groundbreaking support for cancer patients. From the beginning, the organization commissioned contemporary architects and designers to create a new environment for high-quality health care that was designed to feel very different from a hospital.[5]

---

[4]Oliver Wainwright, 'Are Nuclear Trains and Cars Made of Skin: The Future of Travel?', *The Guardian*, 30 April 2013. Available at: https://www.theguardian.com/artanddesign/architecture-design-blog/2013/apr/30/united-micro-kingdoms-design-museum/ (accessed 23 September 2019).
[5]Catherine McDermott, 'Curating Contemporary Design – 20 Years of Change', *Design Journal*, Vol. 20, No. 3 (2017): 307–12.

Perhaps the most visible expression of a rising public interest in design and an awareness of design's increasing economic value was the establishment of the London Design Festival (LDF) in 2003. LDF was conceived by Sir John Sorrell, formerly chair of the Design Council, and Ben Evans, a graduate of the MA History of Design at the RCA and formerly content editor for the exhibition spaces at the Millennium Dome in 2000. Their concept was to create an annual event that would promote the city's creativity, drawing in the country's greatest thinkers, practitioners, retailers and educators to deliver an unmissable celebration of design. LDF would celebrate and promote London as the design capital of the world. The launch of the first Festival took place at Bloomberg on 25 March 2003, with a huge show of support from design, education, government and business.[6]

A review of the early years of London Design Festival reveals a steady increase in scale and ambition. By 2004 LDF had doubled in size and in 2005 it had become part of London's cultural calendar with then prime minister, Gordon Brown, praising it for 'cradling the British genius'. In 2006 the Festival was opened by Sir Terence Conran and attended by over three hundred thousand people. In 2009 the V&A became the hub for LDF with a programme of commissions and exhibitions that took place at the museum during the Festival. Distinct 'design districts' began to emerge where leading international brands, independent retailers, neighbourhood restaurants and cultural institutions joined forces. The aim was to revitalize the heritage of each area as a place where people could come together to share, enjoy and learn about design in its broadest sense, whether design, culture, fashion or food.[7] There are now ten design districts with the Festival commissioning high-profile designers and architects, as well as emerging talents, to create installations in some of London's most prominent spaces, including the V&A and Trafalgar Square.

In 2007 LDF introduced the London Design Medal to recognize the contribution made by leading design figures to London and the design industry. The first recipient of the medal was the architect and designer, Zaha Hadid. In 2020 the medal was awarded to a design curator, Paola Antonelli, senior curator of the department of Architecture and Design at MoMA, New York. From the very beginning of her career at MoMA, Antonelli's exhibitions have engaged audiences with contemporary design practice and discourse. *Mutant Materials in Contemporary Design* (1995) was her first major exhibition and highlighted how designers were working with new materials to create products as wide-ranging as consumer electronics, sports equipment and medical devices. Her

---

[6]London Design Festival website. Available at: https://artdaily.cc/news/15042/London-Design-Festival-Launched-at-National-Gallery#.Yhy2AcbLd-U (accessed 15 May 2018).

[7]Ibid. Available at: https://www.londondesignfestival.com/design-districts/ (accessed 5 June 2019).

subsequent exhibitions, *Workspheres* (2001), *Safe: Design Takes on Risk* (2006), *Design and the Elastic Mind* (2008) and *Design and Violence* (2015), have all been issue-driven and aimed at expanding dialogues about design. The award was a clear acknowledgement of the important contribution of the curator in promoting a public understanding of design and its impact on the world.

LDF promoted the city as a centre for contemporary design to a global audience. It also provided a new platform for curatorial practice, generating new roles for the curator in developing programmes and events for the festival that took place outside the traditional context of the museum and gallery.

The more discursive approach of the design festival and the biennial has focused attention on, and helped to build confidence in the contemporary as a subject. They have become global stages for world-leading contemporary design and design-led innovation, creativity and research. The Venice Biennale Arte, established in 1895, is the oldest and most prodigious of its kind, with each iteration drawing half a million visitors to the city. It has two primary components; a central curatorial presentation and the national pavilions. Since 1999 each Biennale has been organized by a different curator nominated by the Biennale organization and reflects that curator's choice of exhibition, approaches and themes which range from painting and sculpture to film, performance and dance.

For design curators, journalists and writers, the design biennial has become an important platform for sharing new design knowledge and practice. The biennial has also created new roles and opportunities for the design curator. The themes, content and design approaches proposed by biennial and festival curators are actively shaping curatorial practice. Paola Antonelli, Jan Boelen, Joseph Grima, Marina Otera, Mariana Pestana and Yesomi Umolu are curating large-scale biennials that directly address urgent global issues and highlight how design can respond.

Established in 2012, the Istanbul Design Biennial organized by the Istanbul Foundation for Culture and Arts (IKSV) brings together a diverse cross section of design ideas once every two years. The 5th edition of the Istanbul Design Biennial in 2021 was curated by London-based, Portuguese architect Mariana Pestana. The Biennial was designed to be a slowly expanding format, partly physical and partly digital, due to the limitations imposed by the Covid-19 pandemic. In her curatorial statement, Pestana sets out the theme for the Biennial as *Empathy Revisited*:

Designs for more than one, which explores the feeling of empathy and its care in design and how the mode of empathy can, 'foreground practices of care, localism and new models of co-existence'.[8]

---

[8] 'Curator Mariana Pestana and Director Deniz Ova Highlight Details for Istanbul Design Biennial', *Turkey Architecture News*, 15 October 2020. Available at: https://worldarchitecture.org/article-links/

The projects on display encouraged visitors to rethink practices of care and civility at such a critical moment in time, and to collectively build new systems and structures for reconnecting.

The structures of the design exhibition, the design festival and the biennial have done much to open up the subject of contemporary design to an expanded audience. In the same way, the design journal also helped to map, label and define the new and unfamiliar territories of design, style and taste. Jeremy Myerson has described the 1980s as 'a schizophrenic decade when Britain presented a picture of design in all its schizophrenic glory'.[9] It was the decade of *The Face*, the Lloyds Building, Next and the Channel 4 logo and a time of innovation, ambition and restless entrepreneurialism. In the 1980s, new magazines were launched, with the intention of surveying and critically assessing developments in the design sector, and began to focus on the design exhibition as a subject for discussion.

Launched in 1983, *Blueprint* was the first magazine to address both architecture and design. It was established by architect Peter Murray and edited by design critic, Deyan Sudjic, with the financial backing of leading architects and designers including Terence Conran, Rodney Fitch, Norman Foster and Richard Rogers. The range of subject matter and the magazine's tabloid format, designed by art director Simon Esterson, was influenced by the content of the New York–based magazine, *Metropolis*, established in 1981.[10] In *B Is for Bauhaus*, Sudjic recalls the early ambitions for the magazine:

> *Blueprint* set out to be iconoclastic, disposable, and tried to root architecture, design, graphics, fashion and the visual world in the popular culture of the time.[11]

Blueprint positioned itself as London's leading magazine of architecture and design, and offered a fresh and unconventional approach aimed at keeping readers updated on the latest styles and trends in the design community. The magazine presented profiles of designers such as Rei Kawakubo, Katherine Hamnett, Paul Smith and Issey Miyake, together with articles on nightclubs, restaurants and boutique hotels. It offered an opportunity to examine a range of design disciplines from fashion to car design, and to explore new and

---

eghgn/curator-mariana-pestana-and-director-deniz-ova-highlight-details-for-istanbul-design-biennial/ (accessed 12 December 2020).

[9] Jeremy Myerson, 'A Schizophrenic Decade', in 'Best of British: 1960–1999 Four Decades of Design', *The Observer* in association with D&AD, 1999: 16.

[10] *Metropolis* website. Available at: https://www.metropolismag.com/about-metropolis/ (accessed 3 May 2019).

[11] Deyan Sudjic, *B Is for Bauhaus*, London: Penguin Books, 2014: 43.

influential centres of design such as Tokyo. The magazine was also unique in featuring portrait photographs of designers, rather than products or buildings, on its covers and, by so doing, conferring an almost celebrity status on their subjects.[12] This interest in the individual designer was reflected in the ongoing dominance of monographic design exhibitions at museums in London and internationally.

Other new publications dedicated to design, advertising and marketing were launched during this period and also helped to open up design to a wider audience. *Creative Review* launched in 1980, *Design Week* in 1996 and *Wallpaper* in 1996 by journalists Tyler Brûlé and Alexander Geringer. Alice Twemlow has noted the important role of these independent design publications describing them as 'public sites of debate and exchange'.[13]

Many youth culture-and-style magazines aimed at a more populist market were launched during the period such as *The Face*, *Sky*, *Blitz* and *Arena*. Alongside music and fashion, the magazines carried features on design. The May 1985 issue of *The Face* featured articles on contemporary architecture and included profiles of designers Nigel Coates, Ron Arad and the magazine's art director Neville Brody. The June 1985 issue carried a profile of design entrepreneur Terence Conran, who would later establish the Design Museum in 1989.[14]

New television programmes also helped to open up the subject of design to non-specialist audiences. In 1981 the BBC launched a series of Horizon programmes, *Little Boxes*, about design and scientific thinking written and presented by design critic Stephen Bayley and directed by producer Patrick Uden. It featured interviews with industrial designers such as Raymond Loewy and Dieter Rams. In 1986 the *BBC Design Awards*, presented by the broadcaster Janet Street-Porter, attempted to engage viewers by inviting them to vote for their favourite example of contemporary design. The BBC also began a *Design Classics* series in 1987. Commissioned by Alan Yentob, the thirty-minute episodes were fronted by design experts and discussed the design and impact of products such as the Volkswagen Beetle, Sony Walkman, Barcelona chair, Coca-Cola bottle and Levi's 501 jeans. In 1984 Channel 4's *Hey Good Looking* series devoted programmes to four subjects; style, architecture, design and advertising. They were written

---

[12]Past editors of *Blueprint* have included Rowan Moore, formerly director of the Architecture Foundation, Marcus Field, formerly arts editor of *The Independent on Sunday* and now founder and editor of *Dezeen* and Vicky Richardson, formerly director of the Architecture, Design, Fashion Department at the British Council, London.

[13]Alice Twemlow, *Sifting the Trash: A History of Design Criticism*, Cambridge, MA: MIT Press, 2017: 138.

[14]*The Face*, May 1985 and June 1985, the Design Museum Archives, London.

and presented by Peter York, Deyan Sudjic, Stephen Bayley and Janet Street-Porter.[15]

These new and very visible promotional vehicles for design were not intended solely for those working in the sector but helped to open up design to a wider public audience. What is also significant is that many of the individuals involved in the launch of these platforms, namely Terence Conran, Stephen Bayley and Deyan Sudjic, went on to play a significant role in the development of a permanent platform for contemporary design in London, the Design Museum.

---

[15]Alice Twemlow, *Sifting the Trash: A History of Design Criticism*, Cambridge, MA: MIT Press, 2017: 140.

1.7

New Programmes to Train Curators

The increasing number and popularity of design exhibitions required curators who could make sense of a rapidly changing landscape for design. These wider developments had the effect of not only creating new areas of practice for the curator but they also called for a specialist skill set. Notable in the exhibitions discussed in the previous section are the number of curators who were graduates of the MA Design History programme at the RCA, run jointly with the V&A.

During the 1990s, a proliferation of curating courses began to emerge aimed at training students across all fields of curating. In 1982 the RCA had been one of the first higher educational institutions to establish a masters programme in the History of Design in partnership with a major museum, the V&A. The programme was significant in that it recognized a need to teach both theory and practice, taking curatorial research outside of the university and into the museum. The course put a strong focus on the study of the intellectual and theoretical discipline combined with vocational training in curatorial practice.

A significant development for the study of curating design was an MA in Curating Contemporary Design, which was validated at Kingston University in 2001.[1] The masters programme was devised in close partnership with the Design Museum, London, to deliver a training programme that responded to an important sector-demand for creative people who could interpret and explain design culture within the museum, cultural and creative industries. In 2017, founding course director Catherine McDermott reflected that, twenty years previously, 'design curation was a practice discipline that simply did

---

[1] 'Curating Contemporary Design: Definitive Field Document', Faculty of Design, Kingston University, June 2000, MA CCD course files, the Design Museum Archives, London.

not exist … it was evident that there was a skills gap around the curation of contemporary design'.[2] McDermott noted that there were no emerging curators trained to work with end of twentieth-century creative practice.[3]

The MA in Curating Contemporary Design was devised by Design Museum director Paul Thompson and design historians Catherine McDermott and Penny Sparke, who had joined Kingston University from the RCA in 1999.[4] In September 2000 an advertisement for the course appeared in *Museums Journal*, which stated the following:

> The Design Museum and Kingston University will launch an MA in Curating Contemporary Design in Autumn 2000. This will be the first postgraduate course to prepare students for a career in the museums sector, event management or trade venue specialising in contemporary design.[5]

The advertisement explained that students would receive a strong grounding in the specialized nature of curating contemporary design and knowledge of the interpretative, educational, marketing and financial aspects of the discipline. They would be involved in all aspects of planning and organizing live exhibitions. Leading practitioners and visiting tutors would be invited to hold lectures and seminars that identified the key areas of curating contemporary design.

The promotion for the new course communicates two key shifts. The partnership with the Design Museum alludes to the specificity of design with a strong focus on the curating of design, rather than art. It also suggests the ambition for an expanded field of practice in preparing students not just for a career in museums, but also for areas outside the traditional museum or gallery, such as retail, events management or trade fairs.

The masters in Curating Contemporary Design, offered by Kingston University in partnership with the Design Museum, was quickly followed by other postgraduate curatorial programmes. Together they formed an extensive international portfolio of training opportunities in this new field of practice. Individually, they offered a specialist focus in different areas of curatorial practice such as MA Fashion Curation established at London College of Fashion and MA Narrative Environments at Central Saint Martins.

The postgraduate training programmes have contributed to an increased critical focus on the practice of curating in the UK and internationally. They

---

[2] McDermott, 'Curating Contemporary Design – 20 Years of Change': 307–12.

[3] Ibid.: 307–12.

[4] 'Curating Contemporary Design: Definitive Field Document', Faculty of Design, Kingston University, June 2000, MA CCD course files, the Design Museum Archives, London.

[5] 'MA Curating Contemporary Design, a Unique Course Starting Autumn 2000', Training and Conferences, *Museums Journal*, September 2000: 49, the Design Museum Archives, London.

have also produced curators who are now promoting contemporary design in a range of different global contexts and cultural locations. Interviewed for an article exploring the rise of postgraduate programmes in curating in 2006, Professor Catherine McDermott, then course director for MA Curating Contemporary Design, commented on this expanding field:

> We don't see curating as a museum activity. We're interested in developing a group who can respond to whatever the creative industries require, be that in design practice, retail, government policy or public space. Our graduates could end up curating for anyone from the Science Museum to Selfridges.[6]

The development of masters programmes has contributed to a growing pedagogy around design curating and its concomitant practice in the UK. Sarah Pierce has suggested that the new programmes in design curating have signalled 'a turning tide', not just in the field of curating but in the way that curators, artists and designers were beginning to understand the relationships between research and exhibition-making which fell outside the specialist knowledge areas of art history or fine art.[7]

The academic programmes can be interpreted as the first stage in the emergence of a new curatorial discourse which was being led by, and for, a new generation of curators. The new courses were training curators and equipping them with skills that addressed traditional forms of research, writing and exhibition-making alongside training in new online platforms, broadcasting and more experimental media and display formats. More importantly, these new training programmes indicate that design curating was developing as a new academic discourse and professional opportunity.

---

[6]Tim Walker, 'Exhibiting an Eye for the Contemporary', *The Independent*, 18 May 2006. Available at: https://www.independent.co.uk/student/postgraduate/exhibiting-an-eye-for-the-contemporary-478702.html (accessed 3 March 2019).
[7]Sarah Pierce, 'The Simple Operator', in Martinon (ed.), *The Curatorial*: 97.

PART TWO

The Curatorial Turn, 1980–2020

Museums must change or die. They must compete in the modern world for their audiences and their resources against other leisure activities and – in a time when there are too many museums and other heritage attractions with new ones still opening and the audience at best static – against each other.

– GRAHAM BLACK (2005)[1]

---

[1] Graham Black, *The Engaging Museum: Developing Museums for Visitor Involvement*, London: Routledge, 2005: 267.

2.1

A Changing Political Landscape for Museums

In 2005 museums and heritage specialist Graham Black delivered a call to action. In *The Engaging Museum*, he argues that museums must transform themselves if they are to remain relevant to twenty-first-century audiences. For most of the nineteenth and twentieth centuries, the primary role of museums had been to collect, classify, document and conserve objects and put them on display. Black was recognizing that, since the 1980s, society had changed bringing with it new demands on the cultural sector. Modern museums needed to justify their existence, generate far more of their own income, broaden their audience bases, reflect their communities and enhance their role as learning institutions.

Black was also indicating that audiences had changed and, with more demands on their leisure time, were far less willing to accept a passive role as cultural consumers. This would increasingly mean that museums would need to expand their offer to meet the varying needs of different audience segments and individuals, and to reflect the fact that most visitors will demand a multiple range of experiences during their visit. Black proposed a clear vision for a museum of the future that 'engages, stimulates and inspires the publics it serves'.[1]

Black's position was connecting to a debate that had dominated the museum sector since the late 1990s. In 1998 academics and marketing consultants Neil Kotler and Philip Kotler had acknowledged a similar shift as museums faced the twenty-first century:

---

[1] Ibid.: 268.

> The most successful museums offer a range of experiences that appeal to different audience segments and reflect the varying needs of individual visitors … successful museums provide multiple experiences: aesthetic and emotional delight, celebration and learning, recreation and sociability.[2]

In the same year Caroline Reinhardt, writing in *The Spectator*, was one of a number of cultural commentators who detected a similar shift:

> There is something happening behind the scenes at the museum. A revolution has taken place in its philosophy, which would like to see the glass cases smashed. Today's museum aims to be genuinely populist. It welcomes – indeed seeks out – all sectors of the community, and eschews anything that smacks of elitism. Explanatory material, preferably using state-of-the-art technology, is pitched at the simplest possible level. And, above all, the new museum seeks to pull its head out of the historical sand to address issues in the contemporary world.[3]

These debates were in direct response to a rapidly changing landscape for culture, particularly in the UK. They were driven by a series of political and social changes that were to have a major impact on museums in the years leading up to the millennium. The shift was also due to new challenges facing the sector, most notably cuts in government funding for the arts, increasing competition from other sectors such as retail and leisure and declining visitor numbers. Museums were forced to look sideways in order to understand what was happening around them and to question the very nature of the visitor experience they offered in an attempt to engage and expand audiences.

An analysis of these key shifts is helpful as a way of defining the debates that were circulating in the museum and cultural sector during the late 1990s and early 2000s. The shifts influenced many different aspects of curatorial practice, from exhibition design, display techniques, interpretive tools and marketing strategies to the changing relationship between the areas of curatorial and education in the museum. These developments presented both opportunities and challenges for curators and marked a moment when the boundaries constituting the role of the curator and the field in which they operated significantly expanded. Such shifts in curatorial practice led to an expanding curator-led discourse but they were discussed largely in relation to curating fine art, neglecting the area of design curating altogether. The

---

[2] Neil G. Kotler and P. Kotler, *Museum Strategy and Marketing: Designing Missions, Building Audiences, Generating Revenue and Resources*, San Francisco, CA: Jossey-Bass, 2008: xx.
[3] Caroline Reinhardt, 'History with Attitude: Elitism Is Out, Populism Is In', *The Spectator*, 4 April 1998: 43–4.

'curatorial turn' is a term that was first used by curator and writer Paul O'Neill to describe such shifts in contemporary art curating practice. The term can also be applied to professional practice in contemporary design and the changing approaches of curators working in the field.[4]

The first noticeable shift was in response to changing government policies towards culture and their impact on the museum sector. In 1980s Britain, the role of the museum was scrutinized as never before and became the subject of heated debate within professional cultural heritage circles and at government level. Margaret Thatcher became prime minister in 1979. The policies of a new conservative government changed Britain significantly during the 1980s. With a post-war economy defined by competitive global trading, old industries declined and new service economies and digital manufacturing developed and boomed. One of the main tenets of the Thatcher government was a move away from a culture of dependency to one of enterprise and a new approach on self-reliance across all sectors.[5]

In the cultural sector cuts were swiftly implemented, which severely impacted cultural institutions. Previously 'high culture', a term which included museums, had not needed to justify its existence. Frances Spalding has described how up until 1989 the Tate Gallery employed a single accountant to file all the institution's accounts, and trustees were rarely issued with any breakdown of the annual accounts.[6] Karsten Schubert summarizes the prevailing situation when he states:

> In the past, the curator was considered primarily the guardian of the collection he was in charge of, and his duties could be summed up as sourcing new acquisitions, researching, conserving and displaying. The director was a benign scholarly figure at the helm, overseen by an equally amenable board of trustees, an air of eccentricity and amateurism hung over everything. The museum was the ivory tower par excellence where questions of accountability – ideological or financial – hardly ever came up, a place reassuringly insulated from the bustle of the outside world and the perceived ugliness of politics.[7]

---

[4]Paul O'Neill, 'The Curatorial Turn: From Practice to Discourse', in Judith Rugg and Michèle Sedgwick (eds), *Issues in Curating Contemporary Art and Performance* , Bristol: Intellect Books, 2007: 13–28.
[5]Roger Bootle, 'Margaret Thatcher: The Economic Achievements and Legacy of Thatcherism', *The Telegraph*, 8 April 2013. Available at: https://www.telegraph.co.uk/news/politics/margaret-thatcher/9979362/Margaret-Thatcher-the-economic-achievements-and-legacy-of-Thatcherism.html (accessed 5 June 2019). Michael Adrian Peters, 'Education, Enterprise Culture and the Entrepreneurial Self: A Foucauldian Perspective', *Journal of Educational Enquiry*, Vol. 2 (November 2001). Available at: https://www.researchgate.net/publication/251429444_Education_Enterprise_Culture_and_the_Entrepreneurial_Self_A_Foucauldian_Perspective/ (accessed 5 June 2019).
[6]Frances Spalding, *The Tate: A History*, London: Tate Gallery, 1998: 252–3.
[7]Kartsen Schubert, *The Curator's Egg: The Evolution of the Museum Concept from the French Revolution to the Present Day*, London: One-Off Press, 2000: 70–1.

By the mid-1980s, public sector museums were under enormous pressure to become more economically viable. Stephen Deuchar, formerly director of Tate Britain before moving to the Art Fund, recalls the time when public funding for the arts was cut while simultaneously demanding greater tangible outputs from those museums receiving funding. As Deuchar noted, 'partly in response there arose a more overtly populist and commercially driven approach to display and exhibition making'.[8]

Museums now had to prove themselves in the marketplace and were subjected to the same level of scrutiny applied to other state-funded areas, such as education and health. They were required to demonstrate that they provided a necessary service at a reasonable cost. As a result museums changed from state-funded institutions to revenue-generating enterprises, increasingly involved with marketing and fundraising. The audience and its needs were, for the first time, key to the success of the enterprise. Museums started to track their attendance figures and established separate fundraising, development and marketing departments. As Fiona Candlin's research has demonstrated, museum directors and curators began to adopt the languages of management, marketing and accountancy as fluently as that of museology and art history.[9]

In 1993 additional capital funding for museums was announced through the newly established state lottery, made possible by the National Lottery Bill. This allowed institutions to address the results of decades of neglect and to bring their buildings and facilities up to date. With the establishment of The National Lottery, responsibility for the UK-wide distribution of National Lottery proceeds was allocated to the Heritage Lottery Fund (HLF). The funds were directed at a range of heritage projects and many were aimed at encouraging more people to visit museums, either through developments such as exhibitions, restaurants, expanded shops and upgraded galleries or by building entire new museums.

The museum boom of the late 1980s and 1990s generated a debate about the role and character of museums, and the visitor became the focus of curatorial thinking. Museums considered new strategies to increase attendance figures, in order to justify public expenditure and attract sponsorship. In a journal paper reflecting on the British heritage debates of this period, Fiona Candlin explains how museums needed to generate income with many following the lead of larger and more commercially-minded independent organizations.[10]

---

[8]Stephen Deuchar, 'Whose Art History? Curators, Academics and the Museum Visitor in Britain in the 1980s and 1990s', in G. Kavanagh (ed.), *Making Histories in Museums*, London: Leicester University Press, 2002: 105–15.

[9]Fiona Candlin, 'Independent Museums, Heritage, and the Shape of Museum Studies', *Museum and Society*, Vol. 10, No. 1 (March 2012): 28–41.

[10]Ibid.: 28–41.

This resulted in a flurry of blockbuster exhibitions and the evolution of experience-centred initiatives such as theme and leisure parks. A number of new venues were established by private individuals, special interest groups or businesses and they largely operated independently of the public sector. They had relatively low budgets, small numbers of staff and concentrated on a diverse range of subjects that included pasta, whisky, wurlitzers, barbed wire and immigration. Museums went through something of a makeover and introduced merchandising and catering facilities and embraced other moneymaking enterprises. As Candlin comments, 'cafes, corporate hire and gift shops are no longer the signs of vulgarity but of survival'.[11] Museums started to position themselves as brands and commissioned new graphic identities, all of which prompted the cultural historian Frederique Huygen to comment that British museums had started to look like shops, and shops like museums.[12]

The results of this shift can be seen most visibly at the V&A, London. Director Elizabeth Esteve-Coll caused uproar by restructuring the senior staffing, changing the traditional duties of curators and sanctioning more popular culture exhibitions, which had the result of provoking the resignations of senior curators. Esteve-Coll was accused of taking the prestigious museum downmarket by her decision in 1998 to commission the advertising agency, Saatchi & Saatchi, to devise a marketing campaign of six posters describing the V&A as 'an ace caff, with quite a nice museum attached' (Figure 2.1). The campaign series, produced by Paul Arden and Jeff Stark for Saatchi & Saatchi, was part of the V&A's campaign to make the museum more appealing and accessible to the general public. The depiction of an eighteenth-century ivory sculpture in the V&A collections, *Venus and Cupid* (c.1718) by David Le Marchand, combined with the plain-spoken language in the poster's copy was intended to emphasize the easy, democratic nature of accessing the V&A collections. Alan Borg, who followed Esteve-Coll as director, faced similar opposition when he brought in compulsory admission charges. These moves resulted in a rapid decline in visitors and very public tensions with museum trustees.[13]

A change of government in 1997 introduced reforms that were in direct opposition to what were perceived as Tory cuts, indifference and neglect. When Labour came to power, they demanded that it was time to deliver opportunities for all. With education at the top of its agenda, government policy forged a national purpose for rapid and radical improvement in schools,

---

[11] Ibid.: 34.

[12] Frederique Huygen, *British Design: Image and Identity*, London: Thames & Hudson, 1989.

[13] David Lister, 'V&A Gains Three Graces and Loses a Director', *The Independent*, 13 December 1994. Available at: https://www.independent.co.uk/news/uk/v-a-gains-three-graces-and-loses-a-director/ (accessed 15 April 2018).

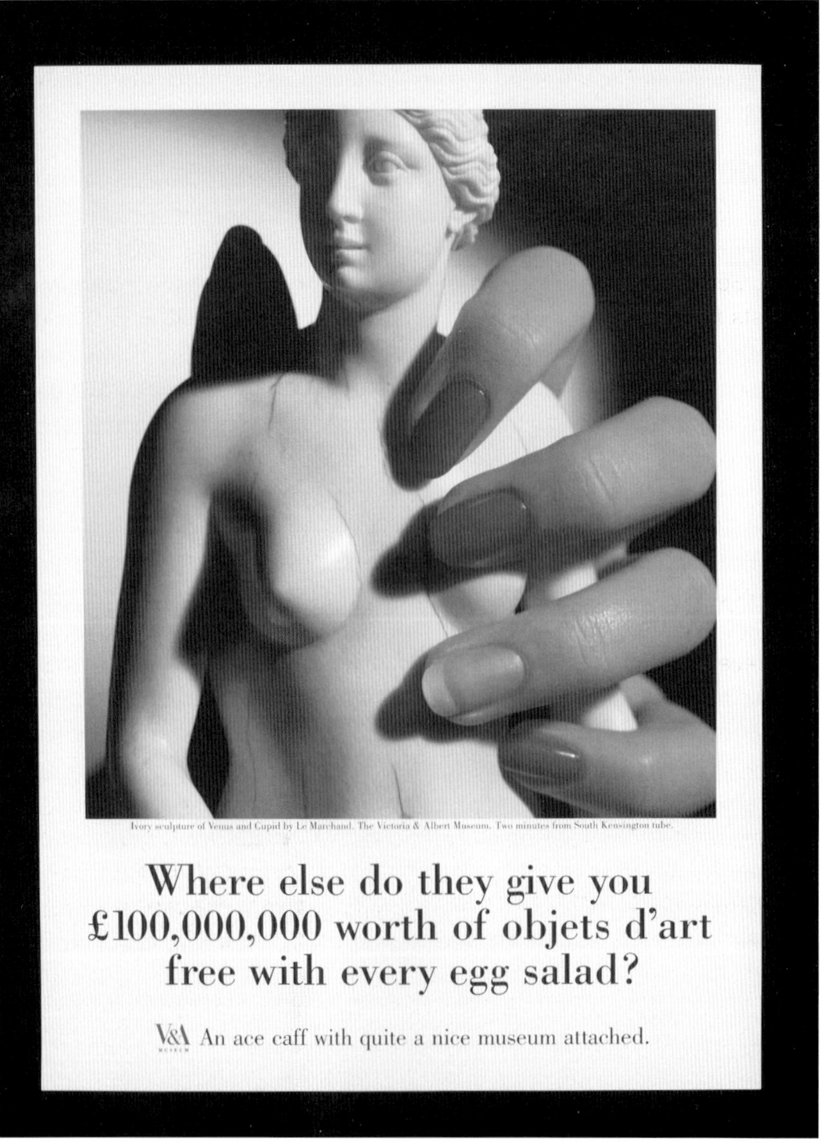

FIGURE 2.1 *'Where else do they give you £100,000,000 of objets d'art free with every egg salad?' Poster, produced by Paul Arden and Jeff Stark for Saatchi & Saatchi Advertising Ltd, London, UK, 1998. © Saatchi & Saatchi Advertising Ltd, London / Victoria and Albert Museum, London.*

colleges and universities. Labour's manifesto pledge became the rallying cry for a generation: 'Our top priority was, is and always will be education, education, education. To overcome decades of neglect and make Britain a learning society, developing the talents and raising the ambitions of all our young people.'[14]

Labour rejected the hard-nosed commercialism of the 1980s and increased funding for the cultural sector, enabling some museums to eliminate entrance fees. With museums receiving eighty-one million visits per year, Chris Smith, Secretary of State for Culture, Media and Sport, saw museums as catalysts for urban regeneration, and wanted more.[15] He claimed that more money was being spent on museums than on any other single sector in the culture industry. In a building boom unprecedented in its speed and intensity, museums received £524 million of HLF funding over a period of four years.[16]

Speaking at the European Museum Forum in 2000, Neil Cossons, director of the Science Museum in London, commented on the fact that museums had never been more numerous or more popular which, in turn, had generated a new and increasingly public debate about the nature of museums and their role in society:

> In recent months I have heard professional museum colleagues talk of paradigm shifts in the way in which museums relate to their audiences. They have observed a rate of change in museums that is apparently unparalleled.[17]

Cossons attributes this development to a combination of factors such as increases in people's disposable income, a progressive reduction in the cost of global travel and the advent of new digital communication technologies. In his view, society was becoming income-rich but time-poor. With growing competition for people's time compounded by improvements in mobility and access, he argues that such a seismic shift had caused a recalibration of cultural parameters. It was forcing museums to change in response to such debates from within the sector and a variety of drivers and pressures outside it.[18]

---

[14]A full text of Tony Blair's speech on education delivered at the Labour manifesto launch appeared in *The Guardian* on 23 May 2001.

[15]Chris Smith was appointed by Tony Blair as Secretary of State for Culture, Media and Sport in 1997, a post he held until 2001.

[16]Paul Teasdale, 'How to Measure the Value of Museums', *Frieze*, 14 March 2018. Available at: https://frieze.com/article/how-measure-value-museums/ (accessed 20 April 2018).

[17]Neil Cossons, *Industrial Museums in the New Millennium*, The 2000 European Museum Forum Lecture. Available at: http://www.europeanmuseumforum.info/elibrary/ (accessed 20 October 2018).

[18]Ibid. Available at: http://www.europeanmuseumforum.info/elibrary/ (accessed 20 October 2018).

At the same time, the Museums Association, the governing body for museums in the UK, was campaigning for change. It championed the role of museums in learning and stressed the importance of access for all. In 2001 Re:Source, the Council for Museums, Archives and Libraries, was commissioned by the Secretary of State for Culture, Media and Sport, Chris Smith to look into the current climate for museums and galleries in the English regions. The subsequent report, *Renaissance in the Regions: A New Vision for England's Museums*, advocated that museums, as one of the enduring legacies of the nineteenth century, were committed to education for all. They played a vital role in spreading knowledge and enjoyment, but were facing special challenges. The report stressed the need to shape and secure the future of museums and galleries, important national cultural assets that had been neglected for a generation or more.[19]

Funding agreements drawn up by the Department for Culture, Media and Sport (DCMS) to cover the period 2003 to 2006 show that the eighteen museums they directly funded were required to attract more visitors from ethnic minorities and increase the number of children who visited their exhibitions by a total of seven million.[20] In order to attract these new and diverse audiences, public museums needed to find more effective ways to engage with their audiences, and as a result new curatorial strategies were introduced.

Recognizing that audiences did not necessarily have prior knowledge of the museum's collections, explanatory wall texts and published guides were made more freely available. Expanded education programmes were devised with the intention of making collections more accessible to diverse audiences. Curators began to make provision for children and for visitors with special needs. Multimedia resources offered visitors the opportunity to pursue their own interests in greater depth. In the course of this transformation, museums also adopted some of the interpretation techniques pioneered by the independent museums such as live interpretation by costumed actors. The V&A introduced dressing-up boxes for children and the British Museum provided Roman soldier costumes for school groups.[21]

An analysis of the responses to these changes in the press and academic journals provides an indication of prevailing opinions in the sector at the time. The results of the National Lottery culture-building boom of the 1990s and 2000s had its many successes but, as curator Kieran Long later reflected, there were also plenty of institutions without a mission, with no clear sense of

---

[19]*Renaissance in the Regions: A New Vision for England's Museums* published by Re:Source, The Council for Museums, Archives and Libraries, September 2001.
[20]Candlin, 'Independent Museums, Heritage, and the Shape of Museum Studies': 34.
[21]Ibid.: 34.

public duty and with an offer pitched somewhere between didactic educational experience and theme park. He also noted that 'too many museums are obsessed with contemporary fine art, and not enough with the crossovers between artistic production and design, digital, architecture, technology, science, anthropology and history'.[22]

For some museum professionals, the frenzy of building new museums had led to the downgrading of staff and the dilution of expertise. Celina Fox, a founding curator at the Museum of London in the 1970s, commented: 'The danger is that marketing will consume the resources: you cannot run museums on style alone.'[23] Writing in 1999 Simon Tait, arts correspondent for the *Financial Times*, suggested that as museums compete with theme parks, multiplex cinemas and sports centres for attention, curators were being made redundant while the survivors were losing ground in the museum hierarchy to marketing managers and development directors. In Tait's view, curators were becoming an endangered species threatened by a new realism sweeping through museums: 'if they are to avoid extinction, curators need to break out of their glass cases and realise that they are part of the entertainment business.'[24]

For others, the shifts were interpreted as an inevitable part of progress. The newly appointed director of the Museum of London, Simon Thurley, declared: 'Curators don't really understand people, do they? We've got to give people reasons for coming here.'[25] Neil Cossons, director of the Science Museum, London, argued that visitors should get what they want from their trip: 'if curators can't supply it, then someone else will. To survive curators must become communicators.'[26]

Museums implemented a programme of exhibitions and displays to attract new visitors and established new criteria to grow their audiences. Growing visitor numbers equated with a more inspirational and imaginative offer and curators more attuned to the needs of their audiences. Tait concludes his article with the following comment:

> As we build ever more fabulous palaces of discovery, we will need more curators, not fewer. But they will need to understand that they are responsible for more than just the objects in their care, that they are part of

---

[22]Stella Duffy and Kieran Long, 'Are We Building Too Many Museums?', *RA Magazine*, 21 May 2015. Available at: https://www.royalacademy.org.uk/article/the-question-are-we-building-too/ (accessed 11 September 2018).

[23]Celina Fox cited in Simon Tait, 'Curatosaurus ex?', 'How to Spend It', *Financial Times*, Date/Month, 1999: 34.

[24]Ibid.

[25]Ibid.: 34.

[26]Ibid.

a multi-million pound entertainment industry for which they must learn the psychology and language of the consumer.[27]

When the V&A opened a £31 million refurbishment of its British Galleries 1500–1900 in 2001, it was the result of an ambitious, five-year project financed in part by the HLF. The galleries were extensive both in terms of floor space and the number of objects displayed. They also presented a new museological approach to the display of British decorative arts and were distinguished by their engagement with a broad range of historical themes, as well as by the use of a variety of interpretive methods aimed at providing for the needs of different museum visitors.[28]

In an article for the V&A's conservation journal, Nicholas Humphrey, a member of the project team for the galleries, explained the museum's approach to design and interpretation:

> What we know less about, and yet know to be crucial to the success of these galleries, is our audiences. They are certainly varied, from tourist visitors who may speak no English to school children and family groups, as well as specialists and students. Audience research into the ways museum visitors learn is being carried out, and the results fed back into the design process by educators working on three gallery teams. What is well established is that some people prefer to learn in museums from a practical 'hands-on' approach while others are more interested in starting from a theory and applying it.[29]

Humphrey explained that traditionally the V&A had presented displays for analytical learners, those who learn by thinking and watching and who look for facts and intellectual comprehension, but had offered less for those who like to try things out for themselves or who look for personal meanings in objects. The new galleries attempted to provide for all learning styles, creating spaces that were inspiring and welcoming but that also promoted enjoyment and learning.

The galleries included a number of new interpretive devices, placed next to the objects to which they related. In many cases, videos replaced conventional labels to communicate an object's story. These ranged from a video that showed how an object was made, a practical exercise reconstructing the

---

[27]Tait, 'Curatosaurus ex?', 'How to Spend It': 34.

[28]Christopher Wilk, *Creating the British Galleries at the V&A: A Study in Museology*, London: V&A, 2004.

[29]Nicholas Humphrey, 'The New British Galleries at the V&A', *V&A Conservation Journal*, Issue 27 (April 1998). Available at: http://www.vam.ac.uk/content/journals/conservation-journal/issue-27/the-new-british-galleries-at-the-v-and-a/ (accessed 4 April 2019).

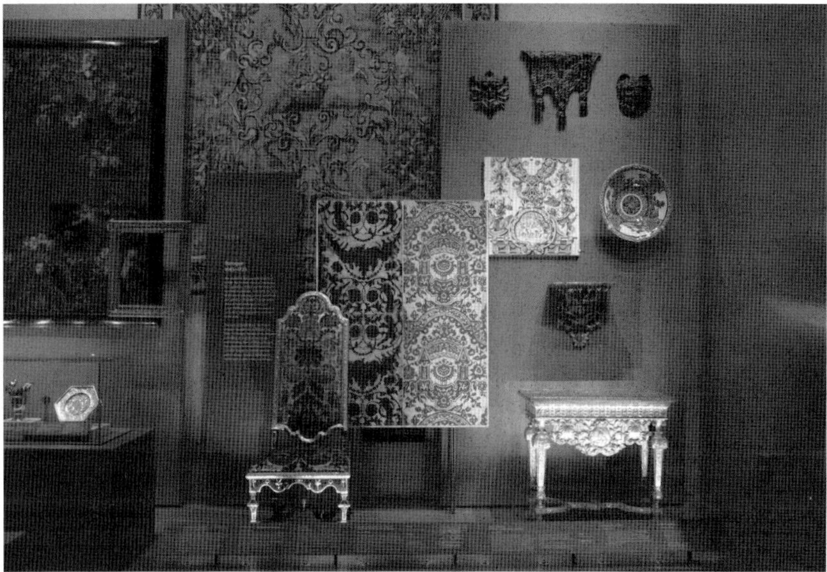

FIGURE 2.2 *Baroque Display, British Gallery, Victoria & Albert Museum, London, Autumn 2001. © Casson Mann, London / Victoria and Albert Museum, London.*

elements of a replica object, an activity asking visitors to spot the difference between objects and their imitations to an audio programme retelling the story depicted on an object. Reviewing the galleries for the *Telegraph*, Richard Dorment described it as 'combining entertainment and instruction, the V&A's new British Galleries are a triumph of curatorial ingenuity'.[30]

The galleries were designed by Casson Mann, an exhibition design company established in 1994 by Dinah Casson and Roger Mann (Figure 2.2). During the late 1990s, they were responsible for designing a number of high-profile museum galleries, displays and exhibitions. In 2000 they designed the Wellcome Wing at the Science Museum, London, which explored the impact of digital technology. In describing their intention behind the design of the British Galleries, the designers explained:

Our design intent was that visitors would *feel* and recognise the story rather than learn or read about it. We did away with too much text, too much dependency on eyes and we introduced touch and sound. We varied the pace, texture, acoustic, density, colour and interactivity. In this exhibition

---

[30]Richard Dorment, 'The Great British Variety Show', *The Telegraph*, 21 November 2001. Available at: https://www.telegraph.co.uk/authors/r/rf-rj/richard-dorment/ (accessed 25 September 2019).

> 3,000 objects are distributed over 3,000 square metres; but the story is irresistible.[31]

The new curatorial approaches also prompted accusations of dumbing down. Museums came under increasing criticism for their high-tech methods of display and interpretation and adoption of theme-park effects and 'disneyesque' techniques. At the opening of a £61 million redevelopment at the Ashmolean Museum, Oxford in 2009, journalist Kathy Brewis was highly critical of the loss of traditional showcases featuring a wide variety of objects and a move to themed galleries full of gimmicks, which she argued were actively discouraging the museum visitor from using their imagination:

> It's as though someone has taken all the worst facets of 21st century life – our reliance on gizmos and gadgets, our burden of political correctness and our constant need to be entertained – bottled them and piped them into the curator's brains while they were sleeping … what remains is educational in the narrowest sense: informational rather than thought-provoking.[32]

In spite of accusations of 'dumbing down', these new approaches to museum exhibitions and displays resulted in increased visitor numbers. Accusations of 'disneyfication' were also levelled at the National Trust by some of its members in response to a programme of decluttering properties to make way for the installation of interactive exhibitions and staff wearing period dress. In an interview for the *Sunday Times Magazine*, Hilary McGrady, director - general of the National Trust, suggests a reason why this approach has been so successful: 'Debate is good, it's what keeps us contemporary and relevant, and goes to the heart of the many paradoxes that exist in the trust.' The article concludes with the fact that the National Trust's membership was at the highest in its history.[33]

---

[31]'The British Galleries Project Overview'. Available at: https://www.cassonmann.com/projects/british-galleries (accessed 25 September 2019).
[32]Kathy Brewis, 'Who Are the Curators Kidding?, *The Times*, 27 October 2009: 10.
[33]Katie Glass, 'Has the Trust Lost the Plot?', *Sunday Times Magazine*, 25 March 2018: 24–7.

2.2

The Educational Turn: The Museum as an Ideal Learning Environment

From the 1980s, a growing professionalism in museums, along with a climate that focused on accountability, customer service and access for all, made education a serious and central function. An increasing number of educators joined exhibition development meetings and curators opened up to new areas of expertise. Educators brought visitor's perspectives to bear on the collections, offering insights into how they should be displayed and interpreted. The significance of these changes was considerable and marks a major shift. Lisa Roberts argues that educators have been at the forefront of what can only be described as a paradigm shift in museums:

> It would appear that these one time Towers of Babel comprise ... not a synopsis of wisdom but a multitude of voices. Theirs is an enterprise that is concerned less with knowledge than with narrative.[1]

The shift sparked a change in the way that the role of education was understood in the museum. The task of the education department was increasingly to make exhibitions and collections more accessible to visitors. It led to changing practices in the museum with the development of new learning programmes aimed at more diverse audiences. It also led to shifting responsibilities in museum programming teams, with more joined-up thinking between curators and educators.

---

[1] Lisa C. Roberts, *From Knowledge to Narrative: Educators and the Changing Museum*, Washington, DC: Smithsonian Institution Press, 1997: 3.

The theoretical underpinnings of this shift in perspective can be found in a number of new publications by specialists in the museum and heritage sector during the 1980s and 1990s. The studies became important disseminators of the key debates and proponents of new ideas. Studies by educational theorists advocated a new approach to museology by placing an emphasis on the visitor and their experience in the museum and argued for new thinking about accessibility, the social function of the museum, participation programmes and the increasingly important role of museum education.[2] The studies contested that a new visitor-centred approach would help museums to compete with other educational and leisure institutions in the contemporary world.

In a number of influential studies produced during the 1990s and 2000s, Eilean Hooper-Greenhill addressed the changing relationship of museums and galleries to their audiences. In *Museums and Their Visitors*, she asserted that museums were at a critical moment in their history. In order to ensure survival into the next century, museums and galleries had to demonstrate their social relevance and use. They needed to develop their public service functions through becoming more knowledgeable about the needs of their visitors and more adept at providing enjoyable and worthwhile experiences. She argues that this expansion in scope and ambition of programmes and activities would inevitably impact the role of the curator in contemporary museums:

> The thrust of the shift is clear – museums are changing from being static storehouses for artefacts into active learning environments for people. This change in function means radical reorganisation of the whole culture of the museum – staff structures, attitudes and work patterns must all mutate to accommodate new ideas and new approaches. In addition to looking inward to their collections, museums are now looking outwards to their audiences.[3]

Hooper-Greenhill was describing a radical shift which had implications for museums as their focus began to shift from collections to one that was increasingly visitor-engaged and public-facing. She argues that, for too long, museums had defended the values of scholarship, research and collection at the expense of the needs of their visitors. The challenge for museums was to not only preserve traditional museum concerns but also to combine them with the educational values that focus on how the objects cared for in museums can add to the quality of life for all. She urges that 'a new role has

---

[2]Publications include Peter Vergo (ed.), *The New Museology*, London: Reaktion Books, 1989 and Eilean Hooper-Greenhill, *Museums and Their Visitors*, London: Routledge, 1994.
[3]Hooper-Greenhill, *Museums and Their Visitors*: 1.

had to be found for museums'.[4] For Hooper-Greenhill, the museum presented itself as the ideal learning environment.

Informing this key development in museums were a range of learning theories, developed mainly by psychologists and researchers outside the museum sector, that had helped to build an understanding of how visitors learn in museums.[5] The main tenet underpinning the various theories is that visitors learn in different ways with each learning type exhibiting different characteristics. The museum artefact does not have a fixed meaning, rather it is subject to multiple interpretations shaped by the personal significance and meaning that the visitor brings to it. Museum educators and curators have drawn on this body of research in order to better understand how their visitors learn, and how learning can be encouraged in the museum environment.[6]

Prior to the 1980s, museums had traditionally been perceived as centres of research about their respective collections. As museum work began to be professionalized during the early twentieth century, it was marked by a period of increased specialization and a separation of fields of practice within the museum. In the first public museums, the areas of 'curation' and 'education' were presented as distinct areas of work, based on quite different sets of knowledge and experience. Traditionally, the relationship between them was hierarchical; first came the exhibition and then began the educational work of conveying its contents to as many people as possible. Priority was given to collections and research with education lagging far behind. Curators increasingly withdrew from a direct relationship with the visiting public, as their focus fell increasingly on curating exhibitions and maintaining the collection.

Most European museums remained enclaves for the scholar well into the nineteenth century. As Lisa Roberts's research has demonstrated, it was in the newly established museums of America that the doors were first fully opened to the general public, promoting equality for all through rational enlightenment.[7] In the early twentieth century, the experiences of museum directors such as John Cotton Dana did much to change this rigid structure. Writing in 1910, Dana, the pioneering founder and first director of the Newark Museum in New Jersey, observed:

> Ancient conventions have museums firmly in hand; ... most museums tend to become storehouses, used more to please and educate curators than to

---

4 Ibid.: 2.

5 A helpful summary of the key learning theories is presented by J. A. Palmer (ed.) in *Fifty Modern Thinkers on Education: From Piaget to the Present*, London: Routledge, 2001.

6 Helen Charman discusses the impact of these learning theories on her own practice in her PhD thesis 'The Productive Eye: Conceptualising Learning in the Design Museum', PhD thesis, Institute of Education, University of London, 2011.

7 Roberts, *From Knowledge to Narrative*: 4.

entertain and instruct the public; that they are quite averse to change; and that few among them exercise an influence on their respective communities at all commensurate with the cost of founding and maintenance.

He was highly critical of American museums, which he considered to be influenced by European-style art museums housed in buildings which were fashioned to look like remote Greek temples or Renaissance palaces. He suggested that a museum devoted entirely to the display of objects that had no connection to the lives of most of its potential visitors and was pointless. In his view, the true work of the museum was in enriching the quality of the lives of its visitors, and to entertain, interest and instruct.

Dana's observations have particular relevance to the development of the design museum. The modern museum bore many similarities to the area of commerce and the city department store; it was centrally located, easily reached, open to all at the hours when patrons wished to visit it, received all visitors courteously and issued information freely, its collections were classified according to the knowledge and needs of its patrons, it advertised itself widely and continuously, it changed its exhibits to meet daily changes in subjects of interest, changes in taste and the progress of invention and discovery, as he explained:

> We think the kind of museum best worth having in your community is the kind that is alive and active, is doing some rather definite work in the field of entertainment and of enlightenment and education.[8]

Since Dana, the concept of the museum as an active learning environment has been explored by a number of educational theorists.[9] Perhaps the most influential research has been the work of Howard Gardner whose theory of multiple intelligences, developed in 1983, promotes the notion that individuals think and learn in many different ways.[10] Gardner's theory proposes that there is not just one form of intelligence but several. He identifies seven human intelligences, or ways of thinking, that learners use to differing degrees to understand the world: linguistic, logical-mathematical, spatial, musical, bodily-kinaesthetic, interpersonal and intrapersonal. An individual's particular 'mix' of intelligences determines the way they learn and consequently learning experiences need to be created that attend to all intelligences. Like Dana before him, Gardner advocates the idea of the museum as a more open learning

---

[8]Ibid, x.
[9]A helpful summary of the key learning theories is presented by Palmer (ed.) in *Fifty Modern Thinkers on Education*.
[10]Howard Gardner, *Frames of Mind: The Theory of Multiple Intelligences*, New York: Basic Books, 1983.

environment than the controlled situation of the classroom. He recommends that museums should use a wide range of interpretive approaches that use all the senses, in order to cater for different ways of learning.[11]

This focus on the visitor experience in the context of the museum was key to John Falk and Lynn Dierking's research during the 1990s.[12] They developed a framework called a 'Contextual Model of Learning' which tracked thousands of people throughout their museum visits, observing them in specific exhibitions and conducting numerous interviews. This model suggests that three overlapping contexts, 'the personal, the sociocultural and the physical', influence the interactions and experiences that people have when engaging in free-choice learning activities such as visiting museums. The experience is influenced by the interactions between these three contexts. Falk devised five categories of 'identity lenses' that characterize personal museum-going motivations. Museum visitors may see themselves as 'explorers, facilitators, professionals/hobbyists, experience seekers, rechargers, respectful pilgrims or affinity seekers', and these various identities colour and characterize their museum experience.

A concept that expands on Falk and Dierking's research and which has particular relevance to the design exhibition is psychologist Mihaly Csikszentmihalyi's investigations into 'optimal experience'. His research reveals that what makes an experience genuinely satisfying is a state of consciousness called 'flow'. During flow, visitors typically experience deep enjoyment, creativity and a total involvement with life. The concept of 'flow' is a common experiential state described as 'a state of mind that is spontaneous, almost automatic, like the flow of a strong current'.[13] In this state, learning and satisfaction are optimized. In a museum environment, while interest and curiosity may first attract a visitor to an exhibit, the interaction with the exhibit needs to engage the visitor sufficiently for positive emotional or intellectual changes to occur. If a museum exhibit induces the 'flow' experience, the experience will be intrinsically rewarding and consequently will grow in sensory, intellectual and emotional complexity. Csiksgentmihalyi concludes with an appeal for more museums to become more active learning institutions and to take a more experimental approach to the interpretation of exhibits.

These educational theories have been particularly influential on the museum sector in helping curators and educators to understand visitor motivations and to tailor programmes accordingly. The impact can be seen in national initiatives established in the 1990s. The Campaign for Learning (CFL) was set

---

[11]Ibid.

[12]John H. Falk and Lynn D. Dierking (eds), *The Museum Experience Revisited*, London: Routledge, 2013.

[13]Mihaly Csikszentmihalyi, *Creativity: Flow and the Psychology of Discovery and Invention*, New York: Harper & Row, 1996: 110–13.

up in 1995 to conduct research and develop policies and campaigns to engage more people in learning. In 1999 David Anderson produced a report for the Department for Culture, Media and Sport in which he argued for the important role of education:

> Education is intrinsic to the nature of museums. Their educational mission drives every activity; it is an integral part of the work of all staff and an element informing the experience of every museum user. Unless museums make provision for education purposefully and with commitment, they are not truly museums.[14]

In 2004 the Museums, Archives and Libraries Association (MLA) defined learning in the museum as a process of transformation engendered by a museum visit:

> Learning is a process of active engagement with experience. It is what people do when they want to make sense of the world. It may involve the developing or deepening of skills, knowledge, understanding, awareness, values, ideas and feelings, or an increase in the capacity to reflect. Effective learning leads to change, development and the desire to learn more.[15]

Curators and educators were increasingly recognizing the importance of understanding their audiences and in developing exhibitions and learning programmes that catered to a wide variety of educational needs. The theories also inspired a whole range of visitor studies, and museums commissioned their own research in order to understand why people visit museums, what they do during their visit and what they take away from their experience. Museums initiated in-house evaluations of exhibitions and, in many cases, commissioned external agencies to undertake audience research.[16] The results of such research were used to not only strengthen the museum's offer but they also helped to identify underrepresented audiences such as disenfranchised racial, ethnic and socio-economic groups, individuals with special needs, young adults and older visitors. Museums were able to assess the effectiveness of their offer by monitoring visitor's responses to permanent displays, exhibitions and services, allowing them to more finely calibrate their activities, as Neil Kotler and Philip Kotler observed:

---

[14]David Anderson, *A Common Wealth, Museums in the Learning Age*, A report to the Department for Culture, Media and Sport, London, 1999: 8. Available at: https://gem.org.uk/wp-content/uploads/2021/01/DCMS-1999-A-COMMONWEALTH-MUSEUMS-IN-THE-LEARNING-AGE.-DCMS-LONDON.pdf (accessed 4 January 2019).

[15]MLA, *Inspiring Learning for All*, London: Resource, 2004: 1.

[16]A range of visitor research methods have been employed by museums to evaluate the impact of their programmes and to test out content and interpretation. These range from quantitative methods such as surveys, systematic tracking or observation to qualitative methods such as interviews, focus groups or open observation.

Today, museums are not only reaching out to larger audiences and building demand among new groups, they are designing proactively the arrangements, services and offerings which will generate satisfaction and positive outcomes for their visitors.[17]

The research also influenced the way in which design museums responded to their audiences. In 2009 the Design Museum, London, commissioned the research agency, Morris Hargreaves McIntyre (MHM), to undertake research to identify and explore attitudes to the Design Museum amongst 'general gallery goers' who had not yet visited the museum. The intention was to explore brand perceptions of the Design Museum and particularly to investigate why people did not visit. The research was also intended to test initial responses to the proposed move of the museum to a new location and to look at the potential impact on perceptions and visiting.

MHM is the largest cultural strategy and research agency in the UK which has, over many years, conducted research exploring the reasons why people visit museums. Their research has shown that visitor motivations can be broken down into four main reasons: 'educational, social, spiritual and emotional'. The dominant reason varies from visitor to visitor but all are almost there in one proportion or another. MHM's previous research suggested that, traditionally, museums had been willing to respond to the need to educate their visitors but had been less comfortable satisfying the other three motivations: social, spiritual and emotional.

MHM devised an online survey for the Design Museum which was emailed to over four thousand people, preselected by MHM, who had visited a London museum, gallery or cultural venue in the previous two years. The final report, *The View from Outside*, provides a range of fascinating data. Perhaps the most interesting outcome highlights the fact that visitors to museums were highly motivated and looking for a compelling proposition. The results of the research communicated that visitors were actively seeking out opportunities to visit museums and galleries in order to meet their needs for intellectual stimulation and emotional connection. Special exhibitions were a key driver in deciding to make a visit. The results suggested that, while the location of the building or ticket price is a factor in deciding whether to visit, the compelling reason to visit was the exhibition; 'a powerfully attractive exhibition will draw visitors over perceived barriers such as distance or cost if it is strong enough'.[18]

Exhibitions with a relatively broad appeal and interpretation suitable for non-specialists with hooks around wider popular culture, and an immersive

---

[17]Kotler and Kotler cited in Anderson, *A Common Wealth: Museums in the Learning Age*, London: DCMS, 1999: 167.
[18]From the MHM report, 'The View from the outside', the author's personal archive.

and fun visitor experience, were emphasized. The report also recommended that museums develop alternative approaches to marketing that focused less on the profile or significance of the designer or movement and more on the benefits that a visit will deliver to visitors and points of connection with their existing knowledge. There was a clear demand for more 'down-to-earth' exhibitions that provide an introductory route into fascinating subjects. The authors of the report were keen to emphasize that this was not a plea to 'dumb down' content, but rather 'to provide visitors with context and tools to help them appreciate the messages of the exhibition'.[19]

The results of the MHM research changed the way in which the museum responded to its audience and informed new programming and curatorial approaches. A comprehensive audience development strategy was developed that identified eight target audience segments, each characterized by their personal interests and motivations for visiting the museum. The information helped curators, educators and the communications team tailor their programmes to more precisely meet the needs of the different groups.[20]

As a result of this general shift in museums engaging more directly with their audiences, curators began to work more closely with education and marketing teams within institutions. Museum educators now actively contributed to exhibition development, organized events programmes, wrote education materials and provided outreach activities. In 2011 Helen Charman, a former director of Learning and Research at the Design Museum, London, examined the reasons for this new focus in her PhD thesis, *The Productive Eye: Conceptual Learning in the Design Museum*.[21] Charman noted a visible shift in the way museums viewed education, with the integration of curating and education beginning to change the nature of museum work. She observed how the traditional education model, which had perceived the visitor as an empty vessel to be filled with knowledge, had now shifted to a position that advocated a process of active engagement with experience. This had the effect of instigating a change in the visitor and a desire to learn more.

There was also a conscious shift in the language used by museums that moved away from 'education' to 'learning' and which emphasized the learner over the teacher. Education departments were renamed as Learning, Learning and Interpretation, and in some cases, Participation, as Nina Simon later commented:

---

[19]Morris Hargreaves McIntyre, *The View from Outside: How Visitors to Other London Museums and Galleries See the Design Museum*, October 2009: 28. London: Morris Hargreaves McIntyre.
[20]Presentation by Matteo Plachesi, Head of Marketing and Communications, the Design Museum, to MA CCD students at the Design Museum, 17 October 2018.
[21]Charman, 'The Productive Eye'.

> Museums now think of themselves as sites of knowledge exchange, places geared up for active engagements – the keyword is participation.[22]

Simon's observation derived from her study, *The Participatory Museum*, in which she offers fresh thinking as to how cultural institutions can become more dynamic, relevant and essential places. Her central argument advocates that curators should focus on creating participatory and audience-centred museum spaces. In Simon's view, the cultural sector had reached a critical point where many professionals believed in the 'why' of participation but needed good resources on the 'how'. Drawing on her background as a designer, she examines and shares a range of techniques for visitor participation available to the curator and the ways in which those techniques could impact the visitor experience and the outcome of a museum visit: 'what matters to me is that professionals pick design techniques that suit their mission statements … producing a high-quality museum experience for everyone.'[23]

This new emphasis on participatory learning in museums impacted the way in which the Design Museum, London, approached its learning remit. In 2009 the education department was renamed the learning team and expanded its programmes as well as the team required to deliver the programmes. Increasingly, educators worked more closely with curators to understand the aspects that constitute an effective learning experience. The results of this shift influenced new curatorial approaches in developing exhibitions that were able to respond to a range of learning styles. It also prompted new ways of working. Project teams were set up by the curator for each new exhibition, which opened up to other areas of expertise in the museum. The teams included a representative from Learning, Communications, Development, Front of House (later renamed Visitor Experience), Finance, Retail and Publishing to ensure that every aspect of the visitor experience was considered and maximized.

As Charman points out in her PhD thesis, this move reflected a broader museological shift towards a strategy that understands learning as bringing together both the intellectual (prescribed content knowledge within a formal curricula) and affective faculties (emotions and feelings) as modes of cognition. It also presented the museum less as a singular authority on its subject, and more as a catalyst or hub for discursive, critical engagement with design, both with the general public and the design community.[24] This increased focus by museums on the interests and motivations of their audiences had a further outcome. It led to the introduction of a new strand to the learning programme designed to engage with an adult audience: the public programme.

---

[22] Interview with Nina Simon, 'The Participatory Museum', *Museum Identity*, Edition 05, 2010: 36–40.
[23] Ibid.:36–40.
[24] Charman, 'The Productive Eye': 41.

2.3

Producing New Curatorial Formats: The Public Programme Curator

During the late 1990s and 2000s, a proliferation of curator-centred publications and international conferences sparked debates about an increasingly expanding field of practice. In 2007 Paul O'Neill first used the term 'curatorial turn' to describe these shifts. In his study, *The Curatorial Turn: From Practice to Discourse*, O'Neill undertakes a mapping of approaches to contemporary curating. He presents a short history of the practice by examining some of the issues that had emerged in curatorial discourse over the previous ten years, including the rise of biennial culture, the expansion of the artist as a meta-curator or 'creative-auteur' and the large-scale curated exhibition.[1] The issues identified by O'Neill are also relevant to the development of contemporary design and the developing role of the design curator.

O'Neill's argument focuses on a shift from the primacy of the artist to that of the curator, in line with what he identifies as a shift in the curator's role. No longer seen as the carers of institutional collections, curators would instead become the authors of a more critically engaged and experimental form of exhibition practice. As examples of this shifting practice, he cites the increasing number of global biennials and the rise of the nomadic curator disconnected to any specific institution. In 1997 curator and critic, Michael Brenson had identified this shift as the 'curator's moment' when certain individual curators started to achieve an unprecedented visibility.[2] In 2008

---

[1] O'Neill, 'The Curatorial Turn: From Practice to Discourse'.
[2] Michael Brenson, 'The Curator's Moment: Trends in the Field of International Contemporary Art Exhibitions', *Art Journal*, Vol. 57, No. 4 (Winter 1998): 16.

curator and theorist, Irit Rogoff described the new type of curator as 'jet-set flaneur'.[3]

As an outcome of this shift, O'Neill identifies an increasing proliferation in discursive practices such as discussions, lecture programmes, conferences, publications and events as a recurrent and integral part of exhibitions. Many of these practices took place outside the existing traditional educational and institutional structures.[4] Alongside exhibitions and learning activities, the public programme was now considered as an integral part of a museum's offering. Historically, these events had been peripheral to the exhibition, playing a supporting role. These discursive interventions were becoming central to contemporary practice, reflecting part of a wider educational turn in curating.

In an essay written in 2009, *Experiments in Integrated Programming*, Sally Tallant, director of the Liverpool Biennial, argues that today's institutions should place an equal emphasis on public programming as they do on exhibitions.[5] Tallant was head of programmes at the Serpentine Galleries between 2001 and 2011. In the essay, she comments on how education, learning and public programmes were often seen as secondary to, or as servicing, exhibitions. The programme had less importance than that of the exhibition; thus the public programme curator was viewed as less important than the exhibitions curator. She argues that the new institution should have equal emphasis on all programmes, such as talks and events as well as exhibitions. Public programming should be integrated into the exhibition-making process, as opposed to departmentalizing each area of work.[6]

In line with a shift in focus by museums on the interests and motivations of their audiences, public programming is now a curatorial practice common to most museums. Exhibitions are the content generators raising key issues and the public programme provides a platform for discussion and debate. The public programme provides different modes of engagement with design practice and design practitioners through a range of discursive events such as lectures, talks, performances, workshops, film screenings, panel discussions, symposia and conferences. These discursive platforms have generated new audiences for museums and, in turn, created new roles for the curator. The new frameworks offer a more hybrid space for social practice and public engagement and can give greater visibility to research and thinking around global issues. The outcome is rarely an exhibition; in fact the exhibition is just a

---

[3]Irit Rogoff, 'Turning', *e-flux journal*, Issue 00 (2008): E1–E10.
[4]O'Neill, 'The Curatorial Turn: From Practice to Discourse':13–28.
[5]Sally Tallant, 'Experiments in Integrated Programming', Tate Papers no. 11 (2009): 1–6. Available at https://www.tate.org.uk/research/publications/tate-papers/11/experiments-in-integrated-prog ramming (accessed 3 March 2019).
[6]Ibid.: 2.

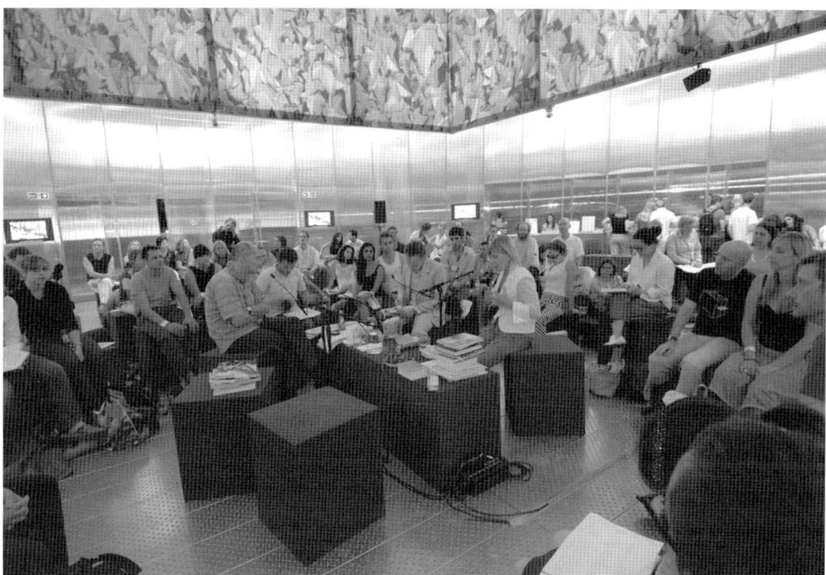

FIGURE 2.3 *Leading artists, writers, musicians and directors taking part in the Serpentine's first 24-hour* Interview Marathon *in the park, 28 July 6pm–29 July 6pm 2006.* © *Mark Blower.*

starting point for a broader conversation which can be enhanced by discursive events around it, such as talks, performances and workshops.

The impact of this shift towards new forms of public engagement can be seen at a number of London-based institutions. The Serpentine Galleries have been pioneering in introducing new discursive curatorial formats and frameworks that bring in a range of voices. In 2005 curator Hans Ulrich Obrist initiated the Marathon at the Serpentine Galleries to provide a discursive space in which to debate areas of contemporary practice (Figure 2.3). Over an intensive programming period of twenty-four hours, specialist audiences came together to take part in a programme that moved between live talks, film screenings, performances and panel discussions. Each year the focus changed to reflect research that defined the previous twelve months. Themes have included transformations, memory, gardens, maps, extinction and artificial intelligence. The formats could be written, spoken or performed and have included up to fifty practitioners with academics, activists, architects, anthropologists, politicians, poets, scientists and urbanists contributing to the debates.[7] Lucia Pietroiusti was curator of live programmes at the Serpentine Galleries between 2013 and

---

[7]'The Serpentine's Annual Festival of Ideas', Serpentine Galleries website. Available at: https://www.serpentinegalleries.org/whats-on/explore/marathon/page/2/ (accessed 3 March 2019).

2018. She has observed how the public programme provided a more discursive space in which to debate areas of contemporary practice. It also achieved a holistic approach to programming in museums, creating a more integrated environment with exhibitions and learning teams working much more closely together.[8]

The public programme is now integrated into the programmes of many institutions. The Institute of Contemporary Arts (ICA) delivers a programme of talks, performances and events inviting international theorists, designers, academics, philosophers and poets to contribute.[9] RIBA Public Programmes offer a series of engaging and thought-provoking public-facing talks, events and displays for both a specialist audience and the broader public. Events are programmed alongside the major exhibition seasons, and themed programmes encourage public engagement with architects and architecture.[10]

The Design Museum, London, recruited its first public programme curator in 2017. Historically, this activity had been managed by the learning team with a programme that consisted largely of talks given by designers featured in the museum's exhibitions. The Design Museum public programme was designed to be an autonomous programme that brought together different voices to discuss the nature and role of design practice. Sumitra Upham, the first senior curator of public programmes at the Design Museum, has described her role as to work closely with exhibition curators and to think about design in new and unexpected ways. She views the public programme as a means of extending content outside the exhibition and expanding on the questions and themes posed in the exhibition. This could be through a talk or an intervention in the gallery space. The public programme is an important means of generating research, promoting new ideas and giving space to the many voices and narratives that shape design.[11]

A further, highly popular strand of public programming has been the evening and night-time events known as Lates, which have become a feature of UK museums and galleries. The initiative derived from a decision taken by the Royal Academy (RA) in 1999 to open round-the-clock on a single day on the occasion of its exhibition, *Monet in the 20th Century*. The RA became the first British gallery to open for twenty-four hours. In 2001 the V&A started a Friday Lates programme, which was to have a significant impact on the wider museum sector. In 2005 other national museums developed after-hours

---

[8]Presentation by Lucia Pietroiusti, Curator of Live Programmes at the Serpentine Galleries, to MA CCD students at the Design Museum, 21 November 2017.

[9]The Institute of Contemporary Arts website. Available at: https://www.ica.art/ (accessed 3 March 2019).

[10]RIBA website. Available at: https://www.architecture.com/whats-on/ (accessed 3 March 2019).

[11]Presentation by Sumitra Upham, Curator of Public Programmes at the Design Museum, to MA CCD students at the Design Museum, 14 November 2017.

programming under the banner of *Museums at Night*, a nationwide festival forming part of the Campaign for Museums' Museums and Galleries Month.[12]

The V&A Lates, originally curated by the V&A contemporary team, celebrate all aspects of contemporary visual culture and design in society. The programme engages audiences with leading and emerging artists and designers through live performance, film, installation, DJ sets, debate and late-night exhibition openings. The Lates are designed to provide something different from a daytime visit to the museum. They offer a shared social experience and an element of theatrical experience that takes place within the museum space.

A report commissioned in 2018 by the Arts Council into the role of UK museum Lates highlighted them as a distinct strand of museum practice. The research shows how the events enabled museums and galleries to reach untapped demand, creating new and increased income streams and attracting new audiences into their spaces. The report suggested that they offered an alternative to the blockbuster, high-impact loan exhibitions which were often criticized as being difficult to access and for being overcrowded. Late events can be viewed as a more accessible, social, experiential and affordable alternative to visiting an exhibition. As the report authors claim, 'over the next fifteen years, if the sector is supported, it could be as normal to walk through the doors of a museum at night as it is to enter a theatre'.[13]

---

[12]See Museums at Night. Available at: http://museumsatnight.org.uk/ (accessed 3 March 2019).
[13]'A Culture of Lates', Report commissioned by the Arts Council England and Culture24, 2018: 2.

2.4

The Experiential Turn in Museums

As museums responded to new pressures in the sector to attract visitors and generate income, they started to look towards their competition. During the early 2000s, the cultural sector was influenced by a more general shift towards an experience economy as a way to attract, engage and retain customers. The experience economy is a theory that underpins the understanding of customer experience. Although the concept was initially focused on business, it has crossed into many other areas including retail, leisure and the cultural sector.

The term was first proposed by a Harvard business text published in 2011, *The Experience Economy*, in which the authors B. Joseph Pine II and James H. Gilmore explore how today's economy has developed from one based on the exchange of goods and services to one that is driven by the exchange of experiences:

> So let us be most clear: goods and service are no longer enough to foster economic growth, create new jobs and maintain economic prosperity. To realise revenue growth and increased employment, the staging of experiences must be pursued as a distinct form of economic output. Indeed, in a world saturated with largely undifferentiated goods and services the greatest opportunity for value creation resides in staging experiences.[1]

For Pine and Gilmore, consumers are attracted not only by the goods sold but also by the quality of the store experience. Providers of services are under increasing pressure to stage compelling experiences in order to guide

---

[1] Joseph B. Pine and James H. Gilmore, *The Experience Economy*, Boston, MA: Harvard Business Review Press, 2011: ix.

vital transformations for their customers. Crucially, an experience needs to be memorable. Pine and Gilmore's suggestion of two dimensions of the experience are particularly interesting: those of 'customer participation' and 'connection', which encompass both absorption and immersion.

Pine and Gilmore suggest that there are many examples of staged experiences in the entertainment industry. Staging an experience is not simply about entertaining a customer but about engaging them. An experience may engage on any number of dimensions from passive to active. The authors offer a model of 'experience realms', which they list as entertainment, education, escape and aestheticism. All are mutually compatible domains that often merge to perform uniquely personal encounters. A combination of all four dimensions is seen to achieve optimum engagement. Pine and Gilmore interpret the exhibition as having the potential to offer all four experience realms, allowing a connection with the visitor on both an intellectual and emotional level.[2] The research revealed that this idea had been circulating since the 1950s with the proliferation of theme parks and experience-centred initiatives such as Disneyland, which they cite as an example of an orchestrated and staged customer experience.[3]

Pine and Gilmore's research has implications for the contemporary museum and, in many ways, reflects changes in the way in which design exhibitions were conceived and presented during the 2000s. In an era when culture is consumed by a wider public than ever before, and when museums are competing for their audiences with other experience realms, they are no longer perceived as merely repositories for objects but as active sites of experience.

In 1994, educational theorist Eilean Hooper-Greenhill identified this shift when she suggested that a new role had to be found for museums as they entered a new and rapidly growing world, that of the leisure and tourism industry dedicated to pleasure and consumerism. In a series of studies about the changing relationship between museums and their audiences, Hooper-Greenhill argues that, with the development of a varied and professional leisure industry, it was possible to rearticulate a purpose for museums and galleries:

> If museums are now clearly placed within the leisure industry, the public sees the form of leisure that museums represent as closely connected to learning, and linked to worthwhile and valuable experiences rather than trivial short-term thrills.[4]

---

[2] Ibid.: x.
[3] Ibid.: x.
[4] Hooper-Greenhill, *Museums and Their Visitors*: 2.

She identifies a clear and consistent demand for a close and active encounter with objects and exhibits and a physical experience using all the senses. Visitors were understood to desire explicitly designed and promoted experiences, the more memorable the better. This idea filtered down to the museum experience which started to offer a new kind of encounter, in which visitors were exposed to highly designed encounters, often incorporating performative and theatrical presentations.

During the 2000s, a number of exhibitions and installations at museums and galleries were notable in the way they created experiences which often brought the exhibition closer to a piece of immersive theatre. In 2004 the Turbine Hall at Tate Modern, London was transformed into a public space in which artist Olafur Eliasson presented an installation that created an extraordinary optical illusion (Figure 2.4). *The Weather Project* was the fourth in a series of commissions for the Hall supported by Unilever. It took the subject of the weather as the basis for exploring ideas about experience, mediation and representation. At one end of the hall was fixed a vast, semicircular disc made up of hundreds of mono-frequency lamps, with yellow and black as the only colours visible. This form was reflected upwards in hundreds of small mirrors that were hung from the ceiling to give the impression of an entire sphere of extraordinary luminosity. Each mirror was offset fractionally so that the upper edges of the form appeared blurred, tricking the eye into thinking that the effect was related to the light or the heat. The boundary between real and fictive space was further eroded by means of a fine mist that permeated the space, which seemed to be seeping in from the nearby River Thames. As visitors wandered through the space, they were compelled to sit or lie flat on the floor, either alone or with friends, in order to engage more fully with the experience.[5]

In 2012, *Rain Room* at the Barbican Centre, London offered visitors a similar weather-related experience, a simulation of real rainfal. The exhibition was created by Hannes Koch, Florian Ortkrass and Stuart Wood, three design graduates from the Royal College of Art, London, who went on to establish their own design studio, Random International. In the Barbican's exhibition space known as The Curve, viewers of the exhibition walked through a 100-square metre space of pouring rainfall, which operated through a digital simulation of the sounds, humidity and visual experience of rainfall but without getting wet – the installation's sensors shut off flow when they detected bodies below them. The audience's response becomes a crucial part of the

---

[5]'The Unilever Series: Olafur Eliasson: The Weather Project', Tate website. Available at: https://www.tate.org.uk/whats-on/tate-modern/exhibition/unilever-series/unilever-series-olafur-eliasson-weather-project/ (accessed 15 May 2019).

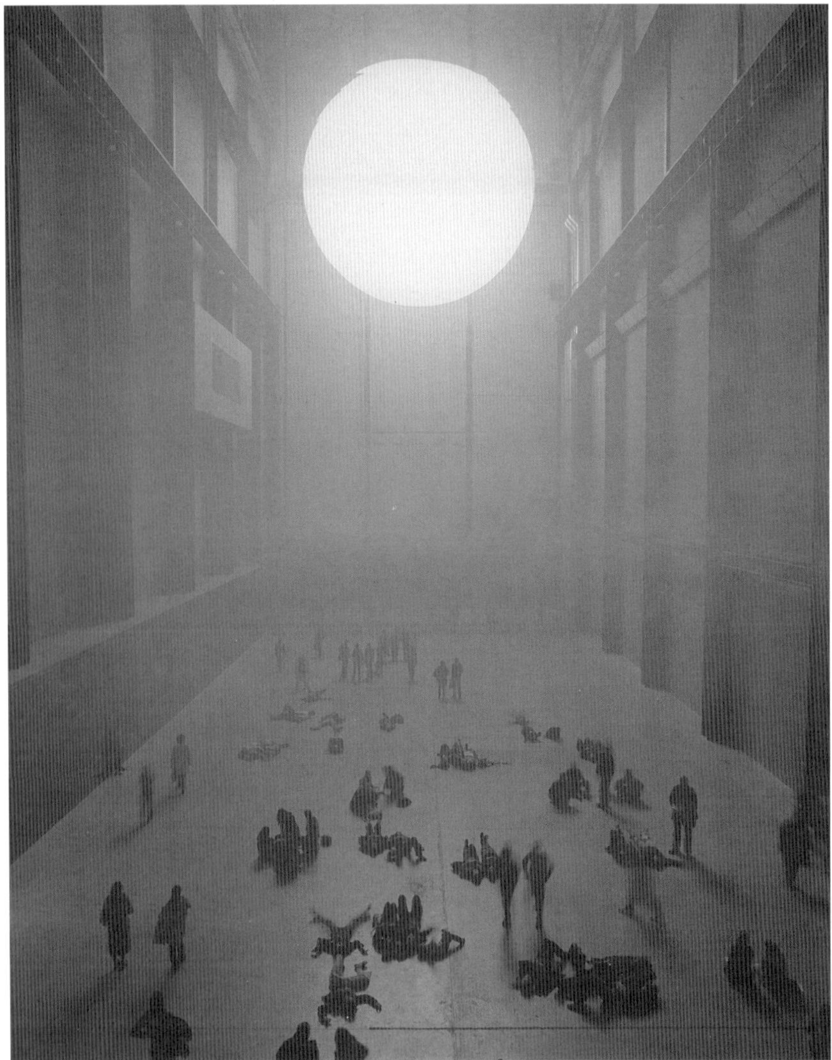

FIGURE 2.4 *Olafur Eliasson,* The Weather Project, *Monofrequency lights, projection foil, haze machines, mirror foil, aluminium, scaffolding, 26.7 × 22.3 × 155.44 m, Installation view: Tate Modern, London, 2003. Photo: Olafur Eliasson Courtesy of the artist; neugerriemschneider, Berlin; Tanya Bonakdar Gallery, New York / Los Angeles 2003 Olafur Eliasson.*

installation. As the rainfall responded to their reactions through motorized mirrors, the audience became the subject of the artwork.[6]

---

[6]'Rain Room, Random International', Barbican website. Available at: https://www.barbican.org.uk/read-watch-listen/random-international-rain-room (accessed 15 May 2019)

The exhibition prompted unprecedented interest from the media, with one critic describing it as an example of 'how the role of digital technology is taking audience participation, response and interaction to the next level within the world of art'.[7] *Rain Room* had a powerful social media presence, with more than thirty thousand images and videos posted on Instagram with the hashtag #rainroom. The exhibition subsequently toured to New York's Museum of Modern Art (MoMA) and the Los Angeles County Museum of Art, where tickets completely sold out.

In an article for *Art Forum* in 2013 Felicity Scott, professor of art and architecture history at Columbia University, suggested that the popularity of *Rain Room* was due to its ability to 'harness and reflect a contemporary desire for seemingly direct participation and spectacular forms of exposure'.[8] Other commentators also noted this shift towards accessibility and questioned whether smartphone photography was preventing people from looking and thinking about the art in front of them. Philip Kennicott, art critic for the *Washington Post*, commented that such exhibitions invite visitors to treat them superficially because they are looking at the art through their phones, rather than through conscious, in-person deliberation. Critic Ken Johnson writing for the *New York Times* remarked that *Rain Room* seems 'little more than a gimmicky diversion'.[9]

Installations such as *The Weather Project* and *Rain Room* show how increasingly exhibitions that encompassed spectacular, immersive experiences were changing the museum experience. They offered a communal experience and a personal one. They also translated into immediate photo opportunities on social media. The increasing desire by visitors to take photographs of artworks and upload them on Instagram or Snapchat can be interpreted as a way for people to want to share what is important and meaningful to them.[10] The installations are also examples of exhibitions that are participatory in the sense that, through sound and movement, visitors are able to engage more closely with an artwork. They serve to demonstrate

---

[7]Lucia Ruggiero, 'Rain Room at London's Barbican', *Digital Meets Culture*, 2012. Available at: http://www.digitalmeetsculture.net/article/rain-room-at-londons-barbican/ (accessed 12 May 2019).

[8]Felicity Scott, 'Limits of Control: Rain Room and Immersive Environments', *Art Forum*, September 2013. Available at: https://www.artforum.com/print/201307/limits-of-control-rain-room-and-immersive-environments-42636 (accessed 12 May 2019).

[9]Philip Kennicott, 'Newly Scrubbed Renwick Gallery Opens Friday', *Washington Post*, 12 November 2015. Available at: https://www.washingtonpost.com/entertainment/museums/newly-scrubbed-renwick-gallery-opens-friday/2015/11/12/cd486116-88ad-11e5-9a07-453018f9a0ec_story.html (accessed 12 May 2019).

[10]Ken Johnson, 'The Natural World: Here, It's Had Work', *New York Times*, 30 May 2013. Available at: https://www.nytimes.com/2013/05/31/arts/design/expo-1-new-york-at-moma-ps1-and-other-sites.html (accessed 12 May 2019).

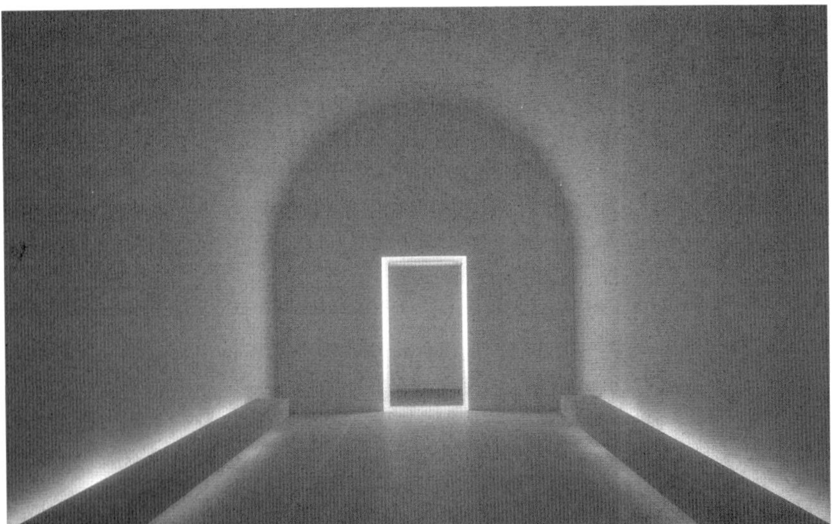

FIGURE 2.5 *1:1 installation in* John Pawson: Plain Space, *the Design Museum, London, 22 September 2010–30 January 2011.* © *Luke Hayes.*

how the conditions of a given space can provide the impetus for creating immersive experiences.

In 2010 an exhibition on the work of British architect and designer John Pawson opened at the Design Museum, London. Curated by Gemma Curtin, *John Pawson: Plain Space* (22 September 2010–30 January 2011) celebrated Pawson's career with models, film, photographs and architectural elements relating to some of his most important projects. Often described as a 'minimalist', Pawson is known for a rigorous process of reduction that creates designs of simplicity, grace and visual clarity.[11] As well as the more conventional curated content of an architectural show, the design incorporated subtle changes to the gallery space itself to create an overall atmosphere that communicated Pawson's aesthetic (Figure 2.5). In an interview for *Dezeen* shortly before the opening of the exhibition, Pawson explained: 'Through the exhibition the viewer will get an in-depth look at my design process – from sketches and study models right through to a full scale installation.' At the heart of the exhibition was a site-specific 1:1 full-sized installation designed by Pawson which offered a direct 'experience' of his work, the first such installation at the museum.[12]

---

[11]Design Museum website. Available at: https://designmuseum.org/designers/john-pawson/ (accessed 20 June 2019).

[12]Rose Etherington, 'John Pawson: Plain Space at the Design Museum', *Dezeen*, 16 September 2010. Available at: https://designmuseum.org/designers/john-pawson/ (accessed 20 June 2019).

The exhibition attracted praise from reviewers for the way in which the museum had attempted to solve the perennial problem of exhibiting architecture in a museum. But for one reviewer the experience of being confronted by a blank white space with a barrel-vaulted ceiling fell short: 'Its gauzy diffused light creates a cone of silence for introspection, but that falls apart when you sit on the benches. What are we supposed to do here? Stare at the person opposite you? Stare at the ground?'[13]

These new interventions in the museum and gallery space represent a new approach to curating exhibitions. Art critic Boris Groys has discussed how art installations can be interpreted as Gesamtkunstwerks that are experienced only from within. The term, 'Gesamtkunstwerk', meaning a total work of art, was first introduced by the German composer, Richard Wagner in 1849.[14] As Groys comments, this idea can be applied to the experience of being within an installation that 'erases the border between stage and audience'. It transforms the viewer from being the 'viewer' to being a part of the installation itself. The viewer experiences the piece from within, rather than experiencing the piece from the outside looking in.[15] The new interventions also reference a broader shift by museums towards an experience economy as a way to engage and retain their visitors, and as a way to reach new audiences. As Lisa Roberts has argued, they represent the notion that entertainment is not simply a stepping stone to education but a progenitor of the receptive state required for authentic learning to occur.[16] The curator is actively constructing experiences that promote engagement and which generate personal connections between the visitor and the content of an exhibition.

---

[13]Jennifer Kabat, 'Reviews: John Pawson', *Frieze*, 1 January 2011. Available at: https://frieze.com/arti cle/john-pawson/ (accessed 20 June 2019).

[14]Boris Groys, 'Entering the Flow: Museum between Archive and Gesamtkunstwerk', *e-flux Journal*, Issue 50 (December 2013). Available at: https://www.e-flux.com/journal/50/59974/enter ing-the-flow-museum-between-archive-and-gesamtkunstwerk/ (accessed 20 October 2019).

[15]Ibid.

[16]Roberts, *From Knowledge to Narrative*: 79.

2.5

Designing Exhibitions as Narrative Space

As curators reached a new understanding of the ways in which their audiences learn in exhibitions, they applied this understanding to the construction of appropriate visitor experiences. These visitor experiences were influenced by a shift towards employing a narrative approach, as a way to enhance the ways in which visitors engage with spaces, concepts and objects.[1] This approach has become a powerful and persistent idea for many curators working in museums and has influenced approaches to curating design exhibitions.

In her study published in 1997, *From Knowledge to Narrative: Educators and the Changing Museum*, Lisa Roberts explores how museum educators have become central figures in shaping exhibitions and displays. They construct narratives based less on explaining objects and more on interpreting objects, which are determined as much by what is meaningful to the visitor as by the curatorial intention. Roberts discusses museum education in relation to entertainment, which in her view can be understood as 'a tool of empowerment, as a shaper of experience and as an ethical responsibility'.[2]

This approach derives from a simple idea that humans are natural storytellers. Psychologist and educator Jerome Bruner has argued that, since ancient times, humans have used stories that represent an event or series of events as ways to learn.[3] He suggests that humans employ two modes of thought,

---

[1] Key texts include Roberts, *From Knowledge to Narrative*; Suzanne Macleod, Laura Hourston Hanks and Jonathan Hale (eds), *Museum Making: Narratives, Architectures, Exhibitions*, London: Routledge, 2012; John H. Falk and Lynn D. Dierking, *Learning from Museums: Visitor Experiences and the Making of Meaning*, Lanham, MD: Altamira Press, 2000.
[2] Roberts, *From Knowledge to Narrative*: 79.
[3] Jerome Bruner, *Actual Minds, Possible Worlds*, Cambridge, MA: Harvard University Press, 1986: 11–14.

each providing distinctive ways of ordering experience and constructing reality: paradigmatic and narrative. He recognizes imaginative narrative as leading to 'good stories, gripping drama and believable historical accounts. It deals in human or human-like intention and action and the vicissitudes and consequences that mark their course, and strives to locate the experience in time and place'.[4] Philosopher and literary theorist Roland Barthes suggests that stories are an integral part of our experience as human beings. For Barthes, narrative 'is present at all times, in all places, in all societies; indeed narrative starts with the very history of mankind; there is not, there has never been anywhere, any people without narratives; all classes, all human groups have their stories'.[5]

A number of museum theorists have identified this idea as being pertinent to museums. In *Museum Making: Narratives, Architectures, Exhibitions*, Laura Hourston Hanks, Jonathan Hale and Suzanne Macleod argue that what unites many curators' approaches is an attempt to create what might be called 'narrative environments', experiences which integrate objects, spaces and stories of people and places as part of a process of storytelling that speaks of the experience of everyday and a sense of self:

> Whereas storytelling in literature is determined and confined by the linear arrangement of text on a page; in cinema to visual images on a screen; and in traditional theatre to the static audience with its singular perspective, the museum represents a fully embodied experience of objects and media in three-dimensional space, unfolding in a potentially free-flowing temporal sequence.[6]

In the years leading up to the millennium, museum professionals spoke increasingly of the need to contextualize the objects on display for visitors. In 1997 Nicholas Serota, who was director of Tate between 1988 and 2017, suggested that the new museums of the future would seek to promote different modes and levels of interpretation by subtle juxtapositions of experience explored by visitors according to their particular interests and sensibilities: 'In the new museum each of us, curators and viewers alike, will have to become more willing to chart our own path … rather than following a single path laid down by a curator.'[7]

---

[4]Ibid.

[5]Roland Barthes, 'An Introduction to the Structural Analysis of Narrative', *New Literary History*, Vol. 6, No. 2 (1975): 237.

[6]Macleod,Hourston Hanks and Hale (eds), *Museum Making*: xxi.

[7]Nicholas Serota, *Experience or Interpretation: Dilemma of Museums of Modern Art*, London: Thames & Hudson, 2000: 55.

In 2001 museum consultant *Leslie Bedford* advocated narrative as a powerful way for museums to engage their visitors with content. Bedford examined the ways in which the narrative or story form can generate personal connections between visitors and content. Through a discussion of case studies of exhibitions, public programmes and outreach to schools, she argues that stories aid humans in defining their values and beliefs and allow the visitor to make connections between museum objects and their own lives and memories:

> Stories are the most fundamental way we learn. They have a beginning, a middle, and an end. They teach without preaching, encouraging both personal reflection and public discussion. Stories inspire wonder and awe; they allow a listener to imagine another time and place, to find the universal in the particular, and to feel empathy for others. They preserve individual and collective memory and speak to both the adult and the child.[8]

Bedford proposes that narratives are key to the process of memorizing, retrieving and retelling knowledge. This is particularly important for the educative role of the museum as John Falk and Lynn Dierking also suggest: 'Universally, people mentally organise information effectively if it is recounted to them in a story or narrative form.'[9]

The traditional image of museums as repositories of artefacts characterized by a linear, encyclopaedic display has gradually given way to a narrative structure devised by the curator working with an exhibition designer brought in to create varied rhythms and levels of intensity. Art and media theorists Anna-Sophie Springer and Boris Groys have likened the role of the curator to that of a cartographer. Like maps, curatorial projects are social constructions, or 'narrative spaces', that shape an understanding of place and space:

> Every exhibition tells a story by directing the viewer through the exhibition in a particular order; the exhibition space is always a narrative space.[10]

The concept of narrative has extended into the museum as an interpretation strategy and as a means of creating links between the subject of an exhibition and the audience. As a number of educational theorists have served to highlight, while interest and curiosity may first attract a museum visitor to

---

[8]Leslie Bedford, 'Storytelling: The Real Work of Museums', *Curator*, Vol. 44, No. 1 (2001): 33.
[9]Falk and Dierking, *Learning from Museums*: 51.
[10]Boris Groys quoted in Anna-Sophie Springer, 'The Museum as Archipelago', *Scapegoat: Landscape, Architecture, Political Economy*, Vol. 05 (Summer/Fall 2013): 247.

an exhibit, the interaction with the exhibit has to be intrinsically rewarding in order to enable positive emotional or intellectual changes to occur. For the design exhibition, the idea of narrative alludes to the power of stories as structured experiences unfolding in space and time in which visitors are encouraged to participate and construct their own learning. An interaction is structured around stories, rather than objects, and the narrative is essential in the meaning-making, understanding and remembering of the messages, content and information presented.

The concept of narrative space has influenced a further area of practice over the last decade: the field of exhibition design. David Dernie has identified how narrative has become central to exhibition design. In his view, the sector has become a varied, media-rich, highly interpretive landscape. Exhibitions engage with the clarity and persuasive techniques that once belonged to the world of advertising, reaching out to a broader range of visitors:

> The emphasis on narrative space that has characterised modern exhibition practice has recently refocused, as museums and galleries respond to an increasingly sophisticated and competitive leisure market. What is now fundamental to contemporary exhibition design is the creation of an 'experience' that is engaging, multi-sensory and rewarding.[11]

Many ideas have influenced the development of exhibition design as an essential component of curatorial practice. The relationship between the curator and the exhibition designer can be understood as a legacy from the Bauhaus and the experimental approaches to exhibition design developed by designers such as Herbert Bayer (1900–85), first as a student and then a teacher of advertising, design and typography at the design school. Writing in 1937, Bayer accorded exhibition design a new status:

> Exhibition design has evolved as a new discipline, as an apex of all media and powers of communication and of collective efforts and effects. The combined means of visual communication constitutes a remarkable complexity: language as visible printing or as sound, pictures as symbols, paintings and photographs, sculptural media, materials and surfaces, colour, light, movement, films, diagrams and charts. The total application of all plastic and psychological means makes exhibition design an intensified and new language.[12]

---

[11]David Dernie, *Exhibition Design*, London: Laurence King, 2006: 13.
[12]Herbert Bayer, 'Fundamentals of Exhibition Design', *PM*, Vol. 6, No. 2 (December 1939–January 1940): 17.

He argued that every aspect of design, from graphic to lighting to interiors, should be brought to bear on an exhibition's design and that the creation of a rich visual and physical relationship between the viewer and the works on display encouraged engagement. The theme should not retain its distance from the spectator, but that it should be brought close, to penetrate and leave an impression.

Bayer's approach is cited as one of the foremost influences on the early years of temporary exhibitions at MoMA in New York. Art historian Mary Anne Staniszewski has shown how installation design and practices, such as viewer interactivity and site specificity alongside multimedia, electronic and installation-based work, can be found in the exhibitions at MoMA in the early twentieth century.[13] In *The Power of Display: A History of Exhibition Installations at the Museum of Modern Art*, Staniszewski asserts that visuality, display and narrative are central to any curated exhibition, with display understood as the core of exhibiting.[14] Staniszewski emphasizes the influential part played by artists, designers and curators such as Alfred H. Barr, Herbert Bayer, Frederick Kiesler, László Moholy-Nagy and William Sandberg in contributing to this discipline.

More recently, curator Zoë Ryan has singled out exhibitions at MoMA such as *Modern Architecture: International Exhibition* (1932) and *Machine Art* (1934), where each of the installation designs were particularly influential with display methods designed to engage and provoke the visitor. The exhibition design for *Machine Art* was very carefully conceived by its curator Philip Johnson. A press release for the show explicitly stated that, for the first time, the museum was giving as much importance to the installation as to the exhibition itself.[15]

Over the last two decades, museums have changed the way in which they communicate with their visitors through an increasingly diverse range of interpretive tools. Many writers have documented the shift away from curating as an administrative, caring, mediating activity towards that of curating as a creative activity more aligned to a form of artistic practice. Jonathan Watkins has suggested that, in curated exhibitions, the display or exhibition is aided by the curator's manipulation of the environment, the lighting, the labels, the placement of other works of art.[16] Mary Anne Staniszewski argues that

---

[13] Mary Anne Staniszewski, *The Power of Display: A History of Exhibition Installation at the Museum of Modern Art*, Cambridge, MA: MIT Press, 1998: xxii–xxiii.

[14] Ibid.: xxi.

[15] Philip Johnson cited in Zoë Ryan (ed.), *As Seen: Exhibitions That Made Architecture and Design History*, The Art Institute of Chicago, New Haven, CT: Yale University Press, 2017: 18.

[16] Jonathan Watkins cited by Paul O'Neill in 'The Co-Dependent Curator', *Art Monthly*, Vol. 291 (November 2005). Available at: https://www.artmonthly.co.uk/magazine/site/article/the-co-depend ent-curator-by-paul-oneill-november-2005/ (accessed 2 September 2019).

visual effect, display and narrative are central to any exhibition and stresses the important functions of 'curating, exhibition design and spatially arranged exhibition forms'.[17]

A substantial proportion of museum visitor research in recent years has been directed towards the impact of exhibition design. Studies that explore how visitors interact with exhibitions have shown that the designed spaces of exhibition galleries can have the greatest influence on the visitor experience. Falk and Dierking, in their research on the nature, quality and impact of museum experiences, have drawn attention to the fact that too many exhibitions are designed with the assumption that the museum, rather than the visitor, controls the experience.[18] They argue that exhibitions are, and should be, designed to engage the visitor in a learning experience that involves them stopping, looking and making sense of the information presented. This research has led to a shift towards exhibition design as now explicitly audience-focused with the aim of creating a relationship between the visitor, the space and the object. Exhibition design operates as an interpretation tool and provides a framework that brings the concept and content of an exhibition alive. Dinah Casson, co-founder of exhibition design company, Casson Mann, has described exhibition design as 'an invisible craft, its creative merit is often overlooked yet its power to bring objects and ideas to life is tangible. Remember what solemn and inaccessible places museums and galleries used to be?' She explains that the skill of the designer is to plan and balance the experience, tempting the visitor with sensorial pleasure, encouraging thoughtful contemplation, developing a journey through the subject and piquing and rewarding curiosity. Like theatre design, exhibition design plays a supportive role but one that has the potential to elevate an experience from the ordinary to the extraordinary.[19]

This shift has also brought about a review of the role of exhibition graphics as an interpretive device in the exhibition. In the early years of the museum, exhibitions presented collections for public view and communicated the voice of the specialist curator. Labels and other interpretive materials were often verbose and highly technical. New interpretation methods introduced in the 1990s attempted to bring the world of the expert and the world of the visitor closer together. New guidelines for labelling were introduced that aimed to achieve a balance between accuracy and intelligibility. In 1999 the Campaign for Museums (CFM), supported by the Museums Association and the Department for Education and Employment, launched a new initiative. *Design*

---

[17]Staniszewski, *The Power of Display*: xxi.

[18]Falk and Dierking (eds), *The Museum Experience Revisited*: 105.

[19]'Dinah Casson in Guardian Culture', 13 November 2013. Available at: https://cassonmann.wordpr ess.com/2013/11/13/dinah-casson-in-guardian-culture/ (accessed 20 September 2019).

a Label aimed to generate a debate about labelling and interpretation while at the same time offering practical information for museums and galleries to make labels easier to read and understand by visitors.[20]

Such initiatives resulted in the development of new writing styles, with labels written in a language that was short, simple and direct. Many museums introduced a hierarchy of information that distinguished between general and specialist information. Standards were established regarding type size and layout, placement, background contrast and other design issues – all to improve legibility. The guidelines extended beyond the text on walls to more visual presentations such as signage and interpretive graphics.

The inherently spatial character of narrative and storytelling has influenced not only curatorial approaches in museums but also at many other different types of cultural venues such as visitor centres, historic sites, entertainment venues and retail destinations. This narrative approach can also engender a highly collaborative approach with distinct disciplines contributing to the narrative process in an exhibition. A project team for an exhibition will invariably include curators, architects, 3D designers, 2D designers, communication designers, interaction designers, time-based media designers, scenographers, writers, retailers and project managers.[21]

---

[20]*Design a Label: Guidelines on Labelling for Museums*, Museums Association and The Campaign for Museums, May 1999: 1–8.
[21]MA Narrative Environments Degree Show Catalogue, Central Saint Martins, London, 2015–17: 4–5.

2.6

Curating Narrative and Experiential Environments

Over the last two decades, a narrative and experiential approach to curating exhibitions has influenced curating practice at a range of institutions. Educational theorists such as Falk and Dierking have drawn attention to the fact that most visitors are drawn to exhibitions that are both visually compelling and intrinsically interesting to them on a personal level. Education and entertainment are intrinsic ingredients of the museum experience.

The education versus entertainment debate has been a long-running debate in the museum sector. For curators they are two ideologically laden terms, as Falk and Dierking have noted: 'To the academic, education connotes importance and quality, while entertainment suggests vacuousness and frivolity.' They argue that the area has been something of an epistemological blind spot for some curators who continue to treat the two variables as if they were mutually exclusive instead of complementary aspects of a complex leisure experience.[1]

Supporting this argument has been research undertaken into alternative modes of spectatorship, in particular immersive and interactive ways of experiencing visual spectacle and not usually considered part of the canon of design exhibitions.[2] The research has assisted in fostering an understanding of the nature of immersive spectacle and the role of theatricality, performance and illusion in shaping the visitor experience. As more exhibitions are studied intensively, many of the traditional perceptions of how visitors use museums are coming into question, such as a lack of engagement with interactive exhibits or with reading text and graphic panels. As Alison Griffiths has noted,

---

[1] Falk and Dierking (eds), *The Museum Experience Revisited*: 114.
[2] Research has been undertaken by Alison Griffiths published as *Shivers down Your Spine: Cinema, Museums & the Immersive View*, New York: Columbia University Press, 2013.

'the search for innovative methods of immersing spectators in exhibit spaces has been something of a holy grail for museum curators'.[3]

In *Shivers down Your Spine: Cinema, Museums & the Immersive View*, Griffiths explains how museums have always relied upon technologies of vision and sound, such as photography, recorded sound, cinema and electronic images to heighten the gallery experience and to enhance learning and understanding through sensory and emotional appeal. She examines less obvious exhibition sites such as the medieval cathedral, the panorama, the planetarium, the IMAX theatre and the science museum as exemplary spaces of immersion and interactivity.

Writing within the context of film spectatorship, she argues that spectators first encountered immersive ways of experiencing the world within these environments. By so doing, she reveals the antecedents of modern media forms that suggest a deep-seated desire in the spectator to become immersed in a virtual world. Griffiths's research marks out the museum as the perfect institutional venue for drawing these ideas into sharp relief. For Griffiths, there is a strong sense of déjà vu in contemporary debates about new media in the museum and the role of immersive and interactive environments. Immersive and interactive display techniques, reconstructed environments and touch screen computer technology have redefined the museum space.[4] She argues that it is not possible to talk about the immersive view without talking about museums. A great many of the themes uniting immersive spaces are all mobilized in the museum:

> I use the term immersion … to explain the sense of entering a space that immediately identifies itself as somehow separate from the world and that eschews conventional modes of spectatorship in favour of a more bodily participation in the experience, including allowing the spectator to move freely around the viewing space.[5]

Over the last two decades, rapid advances in digital and interactive technology have enabled museums to explore a wide range of methods and subject matter to engage with their audiences. Visitors are no longer considered to be passive readers of an exhibition but an active voyager in the exhibition space. In order to enhance visitor experiences, curators now embrace more spatial interventions such as interior architecture and theatrical installations to transform the exhibition space into an immersive environment.

---

[3]Ibid.: 250.
[4]'An Interview with Alison Griffiths', New York: Colombia University Press, 2013. Available at: https://cup.columbia.edu/author-interviews/griffiths-shivers-down-your-spine/ (accessed 20 September 2019).
[5]Griffiths, *Shivers down Your Spine*: 2.

Designed exhibition spaces become a stage for dramatic and theatrical effects. As Judith Barry has noted,

> increasingly, [there is a] sway of another kind of exhibition design, one designed not simply for display, but specifically for consumption, to cause an active response in the consumer, to create an exchange.[6]

This approach has influenced curators and designers working outside the context of the museum. In 2008 interior stylist and designer Faye Toogood founded Studio Toogood with the aim of creating environments and experiences that immerse the viewer and communicate concepts through commanding all of the senses. The studio's commercial projects have included interior retail environments such as the redesign of Dover Street Market, Liberty's window displays and Tom Dixon's London showroom. The studio has had an international presence at design fairs including the Salone del Mobile and London Design Festival. In an interview, Toogood explained the concept behind her work:

> I think there is obviously a time and a place for the 'white cube' approach, but I feel that it's often an overused method, adopted by many, in the hope it will elevate a product and its design credentials beyond its worth. It's very easy to stick something on a white plinth in a gallery-like environment and hope for the best. Each project that we work on is entirely different and we try to find ways of communicating the value of what is being presented by creating an experience around it – without overpowering it. This approach isn't about competing with the products but more about inspiring people to poke them, pick them up, sit on them, wear them, walk off with them or simply stare at them.[7]

In 2012 Toogood created a series of installations for the Salone del Mobile in Milan (Figure 2.6). The installation was conceived as a visual antidote to the chaos of the Salone. *La Cura* was conceived as a hospital for the senses in which visitors were invited to rebalance through a series of intimate performances. Participants were seated on a circle of bandaged chairs around a central pavilion where figures in white tended a garden of clay sculptures. They were offered an 'elixir' created by food designers Arrabeschi di Latte before being presented with an enamel dish and ball of clay to mould. The 'caretakers' collected each clay sculpture in turn and committed them to

---

[6] Judith Barry, 'Dissenting Spaces', in Reesa Greenberg, Bruce W. Ferguson and Sandy Nairn (eds), *Thinking about Exhibitions*, London: Routledge, 1996: 311.

[7] '2 or 3 Questions for Studio Toogood', *Moco Loco* web archive, 2012. Available at: https://mocol oco.com/2-or-3-questions-for-studio-toogood/ (accessed XX).

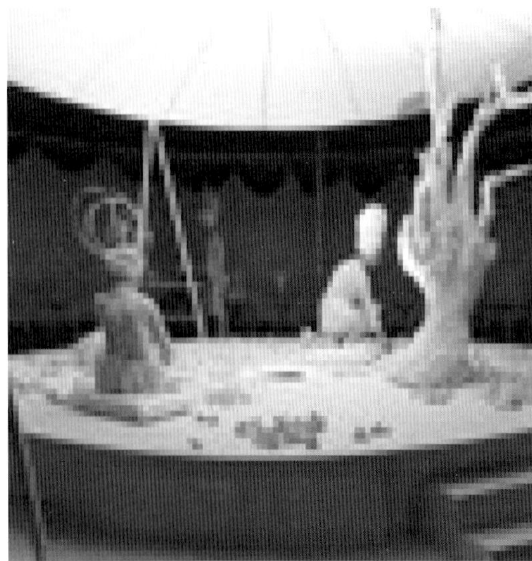

FIGURE 2.6 La Cura, *Installation curated by Studio Toogood, Salone del Mobile, Milan, 2012.* © *Studio Toogood.*

the central pavilion where they became part of a collaborative sculpture that expanded as the week progressed.

Projects like *La Cura* represent a new form of exhibition practice which combines a site-specific installation and a designed environment to promote a deeper engagement with the visitor and enhance understanding of the ideas presented. They can also act as sites for experimentation where a new understanding of the work can be created through the interaction of the visitor which, in turn, feeds back into the practice of the designer.

This new approach to the visitor experience determines a curatorial process radically different from the conventional 'historical' or object-driven mode of display where objects are presented as design pieces without any context or story. It looks to the creation of different visitor experiences where the visitor determines relationships between exhibits and makes sense of what is on display. The curator offers multiple modes of engagement to inspire an understanding of design concepts and practices, an approach supported by Paula Marincola:

A well-curated show, in fact, is that it seemingly elevates and enriches our experience of all the art that it presents. It provides lesser works with a setting in which they shine, and in which they're most interesting.[8]

[8]Paula Marincola (ed.), *What Makes a Great Exhibition?*, Philadelphia, PA: Philadelphia Exhibitions Press, 2006: 44.

Since the late 1990s, exhibitions that have exemplified this new approach were often described as 'blockbusters', a term more commonly applied to films and not usually associated with art exhibitions. Blockbuster exhibitions were large-scale, popular, income-generating showcases that delivered a powerful impact. They have become important sources of revenue for museums and create visibility and prestige for museums both nationally and internationally. In the early 2000s, the rise of the so-called blockbuster exhibition was characterized at the V&A by a series of large-scale international exhibitions that demonstrated this new approach. The exhibition, *Art Nouveau 1890–1914* (6 April–30 July 2000) began a series of style exhibitions that included *Art Deco 1910–1939* (27 March–20 July 2003); *Modernism: Designing a New World 1914–1939* (6 April–23 July 2006); *Cold War Modern: Design 1945–70* (25 September 2008–11 January 2009) and *Post Modernism: Style and Subversion 1970–1990* (24 September 2011–8 January 2012).

In 2013 the V&A staged a retrospective exhibition of the musician David Bowie, *David Bowie Is …* (23 March–11 August 2013). The museum had previously curated exhibitions of living musicians but the Bowie exhibition was singled out by reviewers for its innovative interpretive approach. In media interviews, the curators Victoria Broackes and Geoffrey Marsh explained that, rather than presenting a traditional chronological exhibition, they had wanted to examine Bowie's creative process through lateral associations and position him as a figure who was hugely influential in art, design, music, pop culture and society.[9] The curators had direct access to Bowie's personal archive and the exhibition featured a broad range of material that included stage costumes, original handwritten lyrics, album covers and film. A number of different creative techniques were deployed in the exhibition to achieve an immersive effect. Headphones were issued to every visitor who was able to listen to Bowie soundtracks, which changed as they walked though the installation. Huge inverted set designs and high-impact video projections integrated objects and themes into a theatrical environment that was intended to capture the excitement of a live performance.[10]

The success of the curatorial interpretation was confirmed by reviewers of the exhibition:

Then, in the final room, you encounter the apotheosis of Bowie, the musician. On huge screens, five times life sized, film of legendary

---

[9]'David Bowie Is – an Interview with V&A Curator Geoffrey Marsh', *Phaidon* web archive, 18 March 2013. Available at: http://uk.phaidon.com/agenda/art/articles/2013/march/18/david-bowie-is-an-interview-with-the-vanda-curator/ (accessed 14 June 2018).

[10]Lauren Field, 'A Portrait in Flesh: An Interview with the Assistant Curator of David Bowie Is', *Un-Making Things*, 2013. Available at: http://unmakingthings.rca.ac.uk/2013/david-bowie-is-an-interview-with-the-assistant-curator/ (accessed 14 June 2018).

performances plays, with the costumes glittering through the gauze. The sheer grandeur brought tears to my eyes ... I can't believe you will walk away from this stunning exhibition without understanding a little of why he inspired those of us who love him.[11]

Helen Charman, director of learning at the V&A, observed a similar strategy at the Design Museum with fashion exhibitions that include *Hussein Chalayan: From Fashion and Back* (22 January–17 May 2009), *Christian Louboutin* (1 May–9 July 2012) and *Hello, My Name Is Paul Smith* (15 November 2013–9 March 2014) which toured to eleven international venues.[12] In her view, each of these exhibitions created an immersive environment that brought the designer and their process closer to the visitor. The approach differentiated and distinguished design curating from Brian O'Doherty's description of the 'white cube' gallery environment, in which 'everything but the work itself is expunged in order to provide an unadulterated pure visual engagement with art'.[13]

The last two decades have witnessed significant changes in the operating landscape for museums in the UK, resulting in a rapidly shifting landscape for curatorial practice. It has marked out the emergence of new discourses surrounding the design exhibition. Fluctuating budgets, advances in digital technologies and evolving audience expectations have presented not only new challenges but also opportunities for contemporary curators. In the present moment, the field is being influenced by a multitude of cross-cultural and global conversations which are opening up new definitions, processes and ways of working. One of the most significant discussions has been how institutions can more successfully interact and engage with their audiences. Contemporary curatorial approaches are now informed by a sophisticated understanding of the motivations for visiting an exhibition and the devices available to foster direct engagement with its content. The shift towards highly designed environments, adopting approaches common to the leisure and retail industries, has extended into the design exhibition. Education and entertainment are related and complementary aspects of the museum experience.[14]

---

[11]Sarah Crompton, 'David Bowie: The Show Goes On at the V&A', *The Telegraph*, 18 March 2013. Available at: https://www.telegraph.co.uk/culture/music/rockandpopmusic/9937804/David-Bowi e-the-show-goes-on-at-the-VandA.html (accessed 14 September 2019).

[12]Helen Charman, 'Just What Is It That Makes Curating Design So Different, So Appealing?', in Liz Farrelly and Joanna Weddell (eds), *Design Objects and the Museum*, London: Bloomsbury, 2012: 144.

[13]Brian O'Doherty, *Inside the White Cube: The Ideology of the Gallery Space*, Berkeley: University of California Press, 1976.

[14]Educational theories include Eilean Hooper-Greenhill, *The Educational Role of the Museum*, London: Routledge, 1999; Falk and Dierking (eds), *The Museum Experience Revisited*.

Deyan Sudjic, formerly director of the Design Museum, London, has commented on how the role of the curator is to mediate and to explain, to tell an effective and engaging story in as few words as possible and to bring together images and objects that can evoke or provoke. In his view, the curator's task is to select and be selective. To do so, the curator needs to understand the gap between curatorial intentions and the impact that a display has on an audience.[15] For him, there is something about a design exhibition that, when it works, will persuade many more people to pay for the experience who would invest the same amount in a book or magazine:

> An engaging physical exhibition … does indeed offer a richer, more immersive experience that speaks to more people than any depiction in a book or magazine. In the same way that live performances continue to flourish, even as sales of recorded music have been decimated, so the primary shared physical experience that an exhibition offers has a future.[16]

Sudjic's use of the terms 'immersive' and 'experience' reflects a more general shift in museums away from linear, object-focused displays in favour of experiential exhibition environments that have the potential to offer a more personal and rewarding visitor experience.

[15]Penny Sparke and Deyan Sudjic, *Representing Architecture: New Discussions – Ideologies, Techniques, Curation*, London: Design Museum, 2008: 21.
[16]Deyan Sudjic, *B Is for Bauhaus*, London: Penguin Books, 2014: 60.

PART THREE

Interviews with Eight International Design Curators

To understand what the curator does is to understand what you are looking at in an exhibition.

– SETH SIEGELAUB (2012)[1]

---

[1]Seth Siegelaub cited in Paul O'Neill, *The Culture of Curating and the Curating of Culture(s)*, Cambridge, MA: MIT, 2012: 19.

3.1

The Reflective Practitioner

In 1990, art critic Seth Siegelaub suggested that 'demystification' was one of the most pertinent issues in curatorial discourse. The term described a process in which curators and artists attempted to understand and be conscious of their actions, and to make clear what they and others were doing. Siegelaub advocated an urgent need to expose the processes behind the art exhibition. In his view, making curatorial procedures more visible and exposing the various decision-making processes through which exhibitions are produced demonstrate what is disseminated as art and how information about art is mediated.[1] In 2012, curator Joshua Decter revealed a similar concern when he commented:

> Cultural institutions and museums would prefer that 'invisible' forces of contemporary art exhibitions remain precisely that – invisible. So much of what happens inside cultural institutions remains hidden from the public's view, and, often, even from the eyes of the specialised art crowd.[2]

Terry Smith has also noted that it is rare for curators to reflect, in a sustained way, in print, on their professional practice.[3] For Smith, by revealing the ways in which the curator has chosen to initiate, organize, display and interpret material is to think about how art is framed, how it is spoken about and how it is expressed by those responsible for its conceptualization and production. The process of documenting and critically reflecting on the practice also contributes to an evolving history of curating. The issues identified by

---

[1] Ibid.: 32.

[2] Joshua Decter cited in Paul O'Neill, *The Culture of Curating and the Curating of Culture(s)*, Cambridge, MA: MIT, 2012: 32.

[3] Terry Smith, *Thinking Contemporary Curating*, New York: Independent Curators International, 2012: 179.

Siegelaub, Decter and Smith are discussed in relation to art curating. They are also applicable to design curating, even more so, because the practice remains largely underexplored.

The final section of this book sets out to 'demystify' the practice and expose the processes behind curating design by inviting eight international design curators to reflect on their practice. At a time of unprecedented interest in curating, and during a rapidly changing landscape for design curating, it seems both necessary and urgent to reflect on the practice. The interviews undertaken for this book attempt to contextualize the ideas, theories and processes behind curating design. The interviews not only reflect and build on the more recent shifts in curating practice discussed in Parts One and Two but they also signpost future directions for curatorial practice.

The conceptual methodology of the reflective practitioner influenced the approach to the interviews. This mode of investigation pioneered by social scientist Donald A. Schön provokes a process of self-questioning into practice.[4] As Schön argues, the reflective practitioner engages in reflective conversations with their situations by reflecting on their patterns of action, on the situations in which they are performing and on the know-how implicit in their performance. Schön argues that it is necessary to demystify professional knowledge, a view supported by curator and writer Paul O'Neill some thirty years later when he notes that demystification is now widely accepted within curatorial discourse as a method of defining and representing a curatorial position.[5]

Interviews have regularly been employed in creative practice as a research tool. The interview format facilitates the gathering of information about particular designers, exhibitions, publications and events generating first-hand responses to key issues, often in areas which have little critical material published. In a study published in 2013, *Oral History in the Visual Arts*, Linda Sandino and Matthew Partington explain how oral history has become an established, global and reflexive methodology. The term is wide-ranging and encompasses the in-depth interview, recorded memoir, life story, life narrative, taped memories, life review, self-report, personal narrative and oral biography. As Sandino and Partington state, the interview has become a dominant research method, as 'history' and as a means to gain insights, first-hand narratives and experience, not available by other means.

A further influential approach has been the work of curator Hans Ulrich Obrist. From the beginning of his career, Obrist has undertaken an ongoing, expansive project to interview artists and creatives. The collection of

---

[4]Donald A. Schön, *The Reflective Practitioner: How Professionals Think In Action*, New York: Basic Books, 1983: 265.
[5]O'Neill, *The Culture of Curating and the Curating of Culture(s)*: 34.

interviews, known as *The Interview Project*, consists of over two thousand hours of interviews representing the cultural figures that have defined modern life. When asked how he approached his conversations with artists, Obrist responded:

> For me, it's never predictable how a conversation will go. In order to prepare for a conversation, I read a lot, and I start with a single question. There are a few questions that I always return to when I have a conversation with an artist. The first is 'How did it all begin?' It is fascinating to learn what brings an artist to make art. Similarly, I ask 'What was the beginning of the group?' 'Who brought them together and how did they meet?' We start at the beginning.[6]

The interviews for this book were conducted over the course of three months, and in the middle of a global pandemic. Because of the restrictions imposed by the pandemic, the interviews could not be face-to-face and took place through the video-conferencing platform, Zoom. The intention was to invite curators working in different spaces and contexts in the UK and internationally. The interviews followed a common structure with questions organized around five key areas: curatorial training and early career, influences, individual practice, design curating as an expanded field and the future for the practice, with advice for those seeking a career in the field. There were also questions that were more specific to each curator's role in order to understand the reality of their day-to-day activities, the opportunities and the challenges they faced. By asking curators to critically reflect upon their own practice, and making that practice explicitly visible, the interviews explore the intellectual convictions and personal visions that inform each curator's practice. They foster an understanding of their roles and responsibilities, experiences and motivations. The interviews are designed to reveal what is so often concealed: how design exhibitions are curated and the distinctive role of the design curator.

The curators interviewed for the book have been working in the field over the last two decades. Some curators hail from the new curatorial training programmes discussed earlier in the book. Others have come to curating by way of a practice background, such as architecture or journalism. This is a generation that has worked outside traditional museum structures as much as within them. They have gained experience through the new institutions and curatorial models that have emerged in the past two decades. Some curators are working within the context of a decorative arts museum or a design museum. These curators are, in the course of their work, navigating

---

[6]Hans Ulrich Obrist, *A Brief History of Curating*, Zurich: JRP/Ringier, 2008 and *Everything You Always Wanted to Know about Curating*, Berlin: Sternberg Press, 2011.

institutional politics and diverse audiences. Some curators are working independently and occupying other spaces such as the design gallery, the design festival and the design biennial. Others extend their practice into the very public arenas of the hotel or the cruise liner. Each curator is practising in the physical space but increasingly occupying virtual spaces and actively experimenting with different formats for presenting design. These curators are interpreting and communicating a rapidly changing landscape of contemporary design. They are also actively shaping the new discipline of design curating and contributing to its growing historiography.

Each curator provides a perspective on the more recent developments in design curating as practice and discourse, in the museum and outside of it. What does curating design represent in the current moment and how might the practice look in the future? Considered together, the interviews provide a fascinating insight into the work and thought processes of some of the most creative individuals shaping the way we experience design today.

3.2

The Interviews

- Corinna Gardner
- Andrea Lipps
- Riya Patel
- Sumitra Upham
- Renata Becerril
- Fleur Watson
- Wilhelm Finger and Melita Skamnaki

Corinna Gardner

Senior Curator of Design and Digital, Victoria & Albert Museum, London, UK
Interview: 30 November 2020

DONNA LOVEDAY: How did you become a curator? How did it all start?

CORINNA GARDNER: I have always enjoyed ideas and been very curious about objects. And so rather than go into academia or study for a PhD, I came to curating by way of putting objects into conversation with people. My undergraduate study was initially in Italian and Design at UCL and The Bartlett. I then changed course to study Art History at the University of East Anglia. Design has, since early childhood, always been a strong interest and, as a way to get back to it, I studied for a masters in the History of Design at the Royal College of Art, London, with the V&A. This MA programme offered the opportunity to work within a museum and to see that there are objects as well as words, things to touch, study and explore as well as books to read and essays to write, and that is how I got here.

DL: What was the first exhibition or project you curated?

CG: Again, an interesting question for me. I studied Design and Technology at A-level and, at that age, I was absolutely determined to become a designer. During my study, I worked on a project which combined a practical/making element with a more reflective research project. My research-based project was about museum displays. The creative project was inspired by my own collection of paper bags, which I still have. I'm not sure that I understood them as examples of graphic design at the time but I liked them and decided to make a storage and display case for the bags. The project encouraged me to think about how I might conceive a space of display and encounter. I went off to university and after dropping out, my direct contact with the practice of design waned. But it was a discovery of the making side of curatorial practice during my MA that got me to what I do now.

At the V&A, I started working with Christopher Wilk, who is Keeper of Furniture, Textiles and Fashion. I was first involved with data entry for the exhibition, *Modernism: Designing for a New World*. I worked hard to make myself useful and my role expanded to assistant curator. I ended up staying with the exhibition through to its opening at the V&A in 2006 and then for its international tour. I was immensely fortunate to work on a project that covered such an important period of design history, and it was also an incredible opportunity to work with a world-class collection and a brilliantly ambitious curatorial team. As a result, I benefited from a very good curatorial training early in my career. Of course, thereafter my own exhibitions took on a smaller scale but then I moved from the V&A to Barbican Art Gallery, also in London. The first project I worked on here was *The Martian Museum of Terrestrial Art* in 2008. The exhibition presented contemporary artworks under the fictional guise of a museum collection conceived and designed for extraterrestrials who had come to earth and were working to decipher the meaning of art in the twenty-first century. For a curator whose training was in design history, it was a brilliant way to cut through the artspeak, to learn about the field and to open it up to fresh interpretations. At the Barbican I worked primarily on architecture and design exhibitions, but I also had the opportunity to collaborate on fashion, photography and art exhibitions, and this very much broadened my perspective and understanding of the wider creative world. I was also able to explore what it means to exhibit design and architecture, in contrast to photography or contemporary art.

DL: Have certain curators, exhibitions or encounters been decisive for you? What or who has influenced your involvement in design?

CG: At school in Coventry I had a brilliant Design and Technology teacher, Mr Grundy, and it was very much his attitude of enablement that made thinking about design possible for me. I was the only girl at my school to study A-level Design and Technology (D&T) and it was both brilliant and challenging. I vividly remember moments when my pencils were put through the sander or books were replaced by blocks of wood so that, in the next class I wouldn't have the right materials with me. Studying A-level D&T was both an act of creative intent and one of resilience. I come from a family of academics and going to museums was always part of my childhood and perhaps, despite my best efforts at the time, it exerted a strong influence on me. But then somehow, I have ended up here at the V&A. Other much more recent influences have been shows that have opened my mind to the possibilities of exhibitions. At the Barbican, there was an exhibition in 2016 of the work of Ragnar Kjartansson, who is an Icelandic artist. It was an entirely transportative experience integrating sound, vision and the collective moment. In terms of people who have influenced me, early on, I can't help but think of Paola Antonelli as a woman in the field with a steely and creative determination to bring design exhibitions and collections to a public audience. I have German family, and spending time in the German museum world where the federal states have their own design collections was also an important influence. I wouldn't say that there is any one design exhibition that has been particularly influential. Design for me was more a study of objects, as opposed to thinking about the medium of the exhibition. Now I am very clear that the curator needs to be a public intellectual with a deep expertise about objects and the clear ability to communicate that expertise broadly and make it meaningful in diverse contexts. This is what I look for in design exhibitions, and this is what motivates me.

DL: How would you define your practice? What is the motivation behind your work?

CG: At the V&A, I am in the privileged position of being an acquiring curator as well as an exhibiting curator. There is as much work and opportunity in collections as there is in putting objects on display. Rapid Response Collecting has been a huge part of my role over the last few years. It is a collecting programme that is about enabling a broader understanding of design. It reaches beyond the professions to the world, and to objects that stand as evidence of economic, social and manufacturing change. As a programme of acquisition, it sits in compliment to my wider curatorial responsibilities and the work of designers who create objects with a conceived context and a narrative. To me both are equally important aspects of the designed world, and together they strike towards an expanded definition of the field. This is where I would situate my interest: how objects are embedded in the political, economic, technological, social and political fabric.

At the moment I am working with my colleague, Johanna Agerman Ross, to redisplay our twentieth-century and contemporary design collections. As a curator, that sense of being a cultural listener and looking out to the world to the pressing questions of today is what motivates me. We negotiate our place in the world through designed things and it is this that I seek to investigate, give context to and bring to a broad audience through the collections and their display. It is a way of working that depends on reactive contemporary knowledge that is not necessarily my own. I don't think that curators have a monopoly on expertise. Our role is to be that interloper between expertise and broad interest. We enable the visitor to seek an encounter with objects and the world, but also to have an encounter with themselves within the context of the exhibition or the permanent gallery.

DL: As Senior Curator of Design and Digital at the V&A, can you explain what your role entails? What have been your greatest achievements, but also challenges?

CG: As Senior Curator of Design and Digital, I sit within the Design, Architecture and Digital department and take responsibility for contemporary product, industrial and digital design. Those categories are forever changing. I work with a team of curators who have specialisms in digital, product and furniture design. Between us, we acquire objects into the collection and consider ourselves to be a public resource in terms of knowledge and expertise. It's about setting the work that we do into a public context, be that through talking about the acquisitions we make, putting our objects on display, teaching or any other moment of public engagement. We also communicate our research through publications or peer review journals. In terms of acquisitions, that means bringing objects from different areas of creative practice into the collection, but it is also Rapid Response Collecting.

I work with my colleague responsible for digital design, Natalie Kane, to think about how we acquire complex digital objects into the museum's collection. Design is digital in the twenty-first century, and we have a clear and important responsibility to capture this new and fast-growing area of practice. It is important to help define what this practice is and to enable those who are working in digital design to understand how they might want to keep a record of their work for the future. We are also reflecting on how, in an institution with a national collection, there can be a conversation about what it means to collect digital contemporary practice. That could be thinking about how a studio ceramicist might be using digital tools to think through what they make, through to videogames or Apps which are the means by which we orchestrate our lives. Another part of my role is responding to public enquiries which at the moment are particularly interesting in the context of the global corona virus pandemic and the heightened importance of the Black Lives Matter movement. Both pose the challenge of how we might think about objects that, through their design, enable us to ask the bigger questions about contemporary society. Another area on which I spend time is thinking through how we operate as a design museum in the twenty-first century. For a contemporary design historian, that becomes interesting when you think about the distinctions between design history and social history, particularly if you are reaching beyond the design professions in the way that you look at the designed world. What do you collect? How do you seek to capture and communicate the contexts of an object's design, manufacture, consumption and use for the visitor today and into the future?

In my role, one of my greatest achievements is the establishment of the Rapid Response Collecting programme and being able to set it in motion within an organization where there is a clear appetite for change, but where the ability to push it through is sometimes more challenging. At every stage of the process, there was a task of persuasion. It is deeply encouraging that this has developed into a contemporary collecting programme that is recognized across the world, both in terms of what it does for the understanding of design and how the contemporary has the potential to energize and reframe the historic. Rapid Response Collecting works for the visitor who has limited or no familiarity with design, who might see an object in the gallery that they otherwise carry in their pocket and be prompted to think about it differently. Working with the programme over time, I have learned that many school and university students who visit the museum engage with the programme and see it as a call to action. It promotes an understanding of what it is to be a designer, how we think about design as a practice and how it is shaping our future and the choices we make.

I think at a national museum like the V&A, with millions of objects, it is important to have a contemporary voice, in the sense of a design museum as a public, civic space. I have the great fortune as a contemporary design curator to be able to work with living, working designers and with objects that are familiar to the public, and to interrogate the challenges of the here and now. The museum is still a privileged environment and to think about that as a constant point of discourse and conversation is vital. The other big challenge is working with digital design and the complexity of those objects and practice. An artist will very often work with you as the curator to suggest what comes into the collection, how it might be exhibited and even how it should be preserved and stored. With design, that becomes much trickier because an object is defined so much by its user, but who is the user that you want to capture in your act of acquisition? How many of those voices and points of interaction is it possible to define, when preserving and exhibiting this type of object? For example, we have the social media platform WeChat in the collection. We had the opportunity to work with the Chinese technology company, Tencent, to help us navigate the huge challenges of privacy and intellectual property around such objects. Digital objects only become meaningful when they are switched on and interacted with. Both of those aspects are difficult within the context of a museum collection, display or exhibition. It is a challenge that is shared by museums across the world. I think so often institutions are, understandably, risk-averse particularly when dealing with digital practice. For example, when introducing Rapid Response Collecting, there was a strong encouragement by one sector of the V&A to have a five-year time frame in order to decide whether objects should enter the collection. The digital object then becomes an historic object. So much of contemporary practice is going to pass away, without institutions like the V&A engaging directly and immediately with the digital.

DL: Do you have plans to develop the Rapid Response Collecting programme?

CG: Rapid Response Collecting is a programme of acquisition that the V&A introduced in 2014, shortly after the Design, Architecture and Digital department was established. The intention was to bring objects of design into the museum at the time when they were subject to public discourse and debate, whether that was positive or negative. Contemporary design history needs to be told in the round, through objects whose story can be as sinister as it is beautiful. I don't aspire to be comprehensive in my choices; it is about selecting objects that enable a wider understanding of design. As a curator, I work to capture the here and now for tomorrow, and I feel a clear and direct responsibility for that. The redisplay of the twentieth-century and contemporary design collections, which has been delayed due to the Covid-19 pandemic, opens in 2021. It is the first opportunity to reconsider how we display the Rapid Response Collection. It is critical that every object and the reason for acquisition are made clear to the visitor at the point of entry into the collection. It is taking what we have learned in the first five years and putting that into practice in a new way in the gallery. It has become clear that Rapid Response Collecting is of considerable appeal beyond the walls of the museum. We are fortunate that it is covered by the specialist design press, but also has a broader media interest. We have sought to redesign the display of the object in the gallery and to make clear, whether the visitor is looking at the object in the museum space or via a social media feed, that they understand it as part of the Rapid Response Collecting programme. Currently we have twelve objects displayed together but inevitably, as a set of twelve objects, they begin to surface and tell their own story about today's world. In the new galleries the twelve objects will be distributed throughout the collection displays. The interplay between the collection and Rapid Response will be much more direct and I am curious to know whether that will diffuse or strengthen the message behind those objects.

Rapid Response Collecting is not new, and I would not want to say that the V&A has reinvented the wheel. But in breaking down that commonly held notion that the museum decides the objects that enter the collection and, by inviting in the expertise of others to suggest objects, visitors can more readily identify with Rapid Response Collecting. Over the last very challenging twelve months, what has been so striking to me is how the term, Rapid Response Collecting, is found in museum practice and discourse, whether it's in the newspaper or in peer review journals across the world. In the UK, New Zealand, the United States and Argentina there are peers and colleagues working to acquire the pandemic through a system or a practice that is termed Rapid Response Collecting. Again it comes back to the idea of the curator as a cultural listener, taking a measure or temperature of the world and thinking about those objects that enable us to talk about or mediate challenging times. But also to think about how design practice has changed though craft, community and organization. What has become clear is the ability of individuals or small groups to make a difference through the designed object. That sense of industry to repurpose and innovate is a game changer in terms of thinking about mass manufacture. The political and social side of the pandemic has come through contemporary acquisition programmes. For me it is important as a design curator to think about how the world understands what design is, and how that has shifted at a time of global crisis.

DL: As one of the lead curators for the new twentieth- and twenty-first-century galleries at the V&A, how did this project start and how did you decide on a curatorial narrative for the new display?

CG: The Design, Architecture and Digital department came into being in 2013. At the time, there was an institutional recognition that the practice of design had changed and that the collections and related curatorial expertise needed to reflect that better. There was a renewed interest at the museum in architecture and urbanism, product and digital design. The Twentieth Century Gallery, as it was known, had not been reconceived for decades, and there was an acceptance that change was needed. I lead the project together with my colleague, Johanna Agerman Ross. We have been working collaboratively on the project for the last four years, and it has taken that period of time because we have been delayed by a pandemic but also because galleries take a long time to happen. We have therefore had some time to think about how we could redisplay the twentieth-century and contemporary design collections. Johanna's responsibilities are across twentieth-century and twenty-first-century design. I come at it from an entirely contemporary perspective, in terms of the social, political, technological and manufacturing impact of design. In 2019 every department in the V&A reviewed and updated its collection development policy, and that sense of the connectedness of objects to society is very clearly articulated within our own departmental policy. When we started to think about a curatorial narrative for the galleries, it was clear to Johanna and I that our visitor wakes up in the twenty-first century. How do we take that shared experience of living in today's world and address the pressing questions that people are facing in the UK and internationally. How does design enable us to understand and grapple with these questions, and how is that understanding informed by the recent past?

We have identified six themes which take a period of time in the last 120 years as a starting point and then expand out into a broader conversation (Figure 3.1). For example, one theme is automation and labour. It starts with a focus on the early decades of the twentieth century and looks to understand the impact of mechanization and how that has been played out in the designed world. The question that you might ask of today is: Will a robot take my job? What's so interesting is that the development of the assembly line and increased automation in the factory setting was of considerable concern in the 1910s and 1920s. How does the experience of those years and our perspective today come into conversation and play? Within this section of the gallery, there are two subsections, one is about the changing nature of work and the other looks at manufacturing for scale. These subjects are addressed across the period the galleries cover. I am hugely excited by that dual opportunity to have a chronological backbone against which you can get an understanding of the designed world in the 1910s and 1920s but then also to see an Amazon robot or an Apple computer next to, and in juxtaposition with, a Chinese Pigeon typewriter which was designed to automate the writing of the immensely complicated Chinese language through the push of a button. Johanna and I wanted to think expansively and more broadly about the possibilities of design but also the challenges and constraints of the designed world. Another section looks at sustainability and subversion in the 1960s and 1970s, which considers the dawning realization of the need to care for the environment. When did that need to consider and protect the natural world emerge and when did designers and architects begin to use their work to frame that discourse? The curatorial narrative for the galleries is really about the issues of today and how they are informed by the issues of the recent past.

DL: There have been a plethora of publications on curating but they have mostly focused on the area of fine art curation, with design curation and the role of the design curator remaining largely underexplored. Why do you think the practice of design curating has been so neglected, despite being a growth area over the last twenty years?

CG: From a collections perspective, it is in part to understand how design in a collection is understood differently from art or another practice. Design institutions, within the wider museum world, are quite new and I think it's

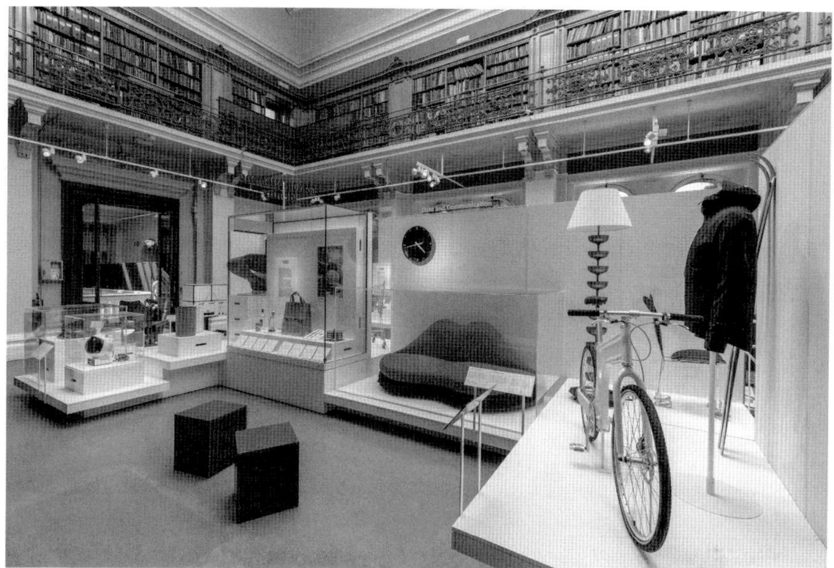

FIGURE 3.1 *Consumption and Identity*, Design 1900–Now, *Rooms 74, 74A &*
76, Victoria and Albert Museum, London, 2021. © Victoria and Albert Museum,
London.

that an accumulation of study and scholarship is only now coming much more to the fore. In the museums world design has played second fiddle to other modes of practice. Even here at the V&A, the world's first design museum, there is a hierarchy of objects and approaches to objects. Here, as elsewhere, the collections and the way they are catalogued still follows an authorial and professions-led model. I think it's a challenge and we need to think about the design exhibition as being different to the art exhibition. It is interesting how architecture is to many an elevated art form, the idea of the singular hand of the great architect, that you find more readily in the structure of the museum and that still so much shapes how institutions engage with architecture and the practice of design. In addition, design history as a subject of research is a young academic field. Art has played so much more of a role in the contemporary imagination but that is changing, particularly in the UK. The creative industries are a major part of our economic landscape and there is a broader interest in how that is reflected in a scholarly or practice-led manner. There are many brilliant practitioners in the field who are communicating design but until recently, it was not seen as an elevated subject of study. It is interesting to think about our go-to texts in the field of curating design. It remains quite a challenging and a limited ask, and I am delighted that is changing.

DL: What is unique about the practice of curating design? What is distinctive about the role of the design curator?

CG: The challenge of the practice of curating design is that an object reflects both the process of making and the object's intended use, and this requires thinking about the object in the broadest of contexts. The critical, analytical aspect of design curating is important and by that I mean the study, acquisition and public display of objects. It comes back to that question of what you understand the role of the curator to be in the twenty-first century and that is as relevant to design as it is to architecture, art, photography or fashion. Curating design is about deepening understanding and heightening expertise, but also broadening understanding of where that expertise sits beyond the scholar and curator and giving broad context to the work of the designer or architect. I am always interested in how we capture those ideas in the collection but also in exhibitions. For me, one of the most magical examples of this was when we were in the process of opening Rapid Response Collecting and we were in the unusual position of putting twelve objects on display at one time. We had paper cut-outs of the different objects taped onto the front of the showcases so that our technicians would know which objects went where. We had a paper cut-out of a mobile phone showing the game, *Flappy Bird*. We brought this game into the collection because it was an example of design that was intended to irritate but that also indicated the potential of mobile phone-based gaming. It was part of a popular discourse because, at the time, the Vietnam-based designer was receiving death threats because his design induced such anger. On the back of this, he withdrew the game from Apple- and android-download opportunities. The object became part of a broader context of how we understand gaming and game design, both in how games are played and that their creation can be the work of one individual, not just vast studios. Here interaction between player and designer had direct personal impact. All of this was captured in this one object, *Flappy Bird*. We had a colour photocopy of a mobile phone taped to the front of a showcase and a group of schoolboys who must have been about twelve or thirteen raced up to that piece of paper and started to have a conversation about what mobile gaming meant to them. The space of the museum enabled them to think differently about what they do in their everyday lives. For me, that is one of the unique opportunities of working in the field of design. It is an immense privilege and a responsibility that we as curators need to take seriously.

DL: What do you feel are the essential components of a good design exhibition?

CG: A well-designed exhibition that reflects a strong collaboration between the curator, the 3D and the 2D designer. A well-written exhibition text that is broad in its perspective and inclusive. There are so many ways to make good exhibitions but for me situating the design object in its broader context of use, that reaches beyond the heroization of the maker is key. I think increasingly, and particularly in the contemporary field, the experience of the exhibition, its pace and atmosphere have become an essential and integral part of its narrative arc. Exhibitions are conceived experiences as soon as you walk through the entrance up until the time you walk into the exhibition shop at the end. The context of an exhibition needs to be as creative as its content. A good design exhibition needs to have a transformative effect, which the visitor takes away with them into the wider world.

DL: Is there an exhibition that you have seen that fulfils a lot of the aspects that you talk about?

CG: An exhibition that brought the visitor experience and the encounter to the fore was *The Glass Room*, convened by Berlin-based NGO Tactical Tech. It was shown in a number of cities across the world, and in 2017 it took place in a new retail space on Charing Cross Road, London. The space hadn't been let, so you were entering into what appeared to be a new and flashy shop that had something of the Apple-store vibe to it. The exhibition was an encounter with the digital world and the question of privacy, and how it is reshaping our lives. The use of a shop and a retail environment in which to encounter beautiful product-like exhibits, but which made you think afresh about the question of privacy and the digital public sphere, was brilliant. A richness of experience became possible in that type of environment. It is not a museum, it was shop-like but precious and object-focused, and the quality of that encounter was very special. It's interesting to think about how that type of engagement can be enabled within the context of a museum and how the museum can take its content beyond its walls to create such provocative encounters. This is a conversation that has been transformed by the pandemic, when public museums cannot invite visitors into their physical spaces. How can the digital encounter be made meaningful, and that's an exciting and challenging opportunity for the museum of the twenty-first century. Projects such as *The Glass Room* are the ones that I keep coming back to, in how they can inform my work, particularly in my focus on product and digital design.

DL: How can design curators and design institutions more successfully interact and engage with their audiences?

CG: Engaging with the design world in a democratic and global sense and from a breadth of perspectives is vital. I think relevance is as important as interaction because it brings a different audience. If the sofa that you see in the museum is forever going to exceed your monthly salary, the design field is going to pass the majority of people by. As curators and exhibition makers we need to think about the voice that we use in our spaces and the experiences we create. How objects are discussed, interpreted, exhibited and for whom, are the big questions of today. These are the questions that design curators need to be asking of those objects that sit within our responsibilities and which have a colonial past or legacy. The challenge is ensuring that we forge a record of our time that is truly inclusive and open. And that extends to the type of objects we acquire and the communities and practitioners that we engage with. We need to think about how we bring those voices into the institution so that their expertise is recognized and enabled in the same manner as so much of the expertise that is already richly exhibited within the V&A. I remember in 2015 when the artist Bob and Roberta Smith created a series of screen prints as an open letter to Michael Gove, then Secretary of State for Education, in which he stated, 'All people have culture. There are not people who have culture and those who don't. We must value all voices. Audiences must look like tax payers and programmes must look like the people of the world.' It's a call to action and in my opinion if we address those issues, we will make better exhibitions and we will have a better understanding of the designed world.

DL: What are the key shifts that have influenced design curating practice over the last two decades?

CG: A key shift has been a growing confidence in design as a field of study and research in its own right. Design exhibitions are popular and draw an audience; they are important arenas of learning and encounter. I think that the design of exhibitions has become a much stronger point of discussion and recognition. It has certainly heightened our understanding of the possibilities of exhibition design, which has been of huge benefit when grappling with design within the context of the museum. There is much talk of the immersive experience as an essential aspect of good exhibition-making today. I think immersive experiences have always been there but how they are understood, studied and considered in the museum and gallery context has changed. The investment that goes into making an exhibition, beyond the display of the object, is an important shift. The 2018 exhibition *Videogames: Design/Play*

Disrupt at the V&A was a good example in which the design of the show was inspired by what was exhibited. Greyboxing is a means of testing game-level layouts while in development and the transference of this approach to the gallery space meant the real experience aped the virtual. As such it was a draw for the expert and lay visitor alike. Audiovisual opportunities have clearly transformed the field of exhibition design too. If you look beyond institutions such as the V&A, there is a brilliance of practice that has taken place over the last two decades that has certainly forced institutions such as my own to think differently and more broadly about the practice of exhibition-making. London examples of this include *Secret Cinema*, *Punch Drunk* and projects such as *The Infinite Mix* staged at 180 The Strand.

DL: How have these developments impacted your own practice?

CG: The more discursive approach of the design festival and the biennial has helped to build a confidence in the contemporary as a subject. I am fascinated how some museum collection policies still think of the twentieth century as the space of the contemporary. Time moves on but institutions move more slowly. Festivals, exhibitions and trade fairs are places of innovation and experimental thinking. This innovative, probing, more reflective thinking about our designed world is vital. Companies and brands increasingly seek to use the civic, public and independent platform of the museum as a mode of validation. The exchange is twofold; museums need industry as a way of remaining contemporary but the nature of that relationship has become more complex. To create the experiences expected today, funding is often part of the collaboration and this can lead to tensions about how stories are told. Museums are sought out because they are spaces of independent expertise, and yet it is this very quality that is so often challenged in these collaborations. Certainly, at the V&A, a more critical engagement with contemporary design practice has taken place. In collecting terms, Rapid Response is a lead example, as are exhibitions including *The Future Starts Here* (2018) and *Disobedient Objects* (2014).

DL: What do you feel are the key debates driving design at this moment to which curators must respond?

CG: In the twenty-first century, design is confronting many issues. One of the greatest challenges across the world is heightening inequality. Design is one of many tools which can address that challenge, both on a small scale but also at a larger, more global scale. If the last twelve months are taken as an example, how can we create and enable meaningful encounters in a world of sudden distance? That is a huge design ask and one that also confronts me directly as a curator responsible for furthering public conversation. Another big question is at what scale can change be enabled? This might be the design and technology workshop at a local school creating 3D-printed visors or a group of women bringing out their sewing machines to sew scrubs, both at a time of shortage. It could also be a huge industrial competitor such as Ford or Mercedes putting their expertise together to enable the retooling and manufacture of ventilator parts at a moment of global crisis. These are questions shaped by the pandemic. If we think about urban design, for whom are we making spaces? Creating cleaner greener neighbourhoods is hugely important but how is the streetscape or public space experienced by different individuals? The experience of a young Black man walking along an empty street is very different to that of a middle-aged white man or woman. It is this sensitivity to different lived experiences that is one of the great challenges for design as a practice today, but also for curators in how we use the collection and exhibitions to reflect on those questions. How can we capture that diversity of perspective that shapes the design process but also the experience of design?

DL: **What advice would you give to a young curator entering the field today? What is the skill set that the design curator of the future will need to have?**

CG: In terms of skill sets, I think a literacy with objects is really important and a consideration of what advantage the material fact of the object gives you as a curator. What does it enable, particularly when so many objects are virtual and intangible. Locating and understanding what stories can be drawn out from the object and its design is a skill set that is critical. If I were looking to forge a career as a curator today, it would be important to have a clear sense of what I bring to the field, having taken advantage of the opportunities to make that public for myself either by submitting articles to a magazine, having a well-developed Instagram feed or establishing my own small collection and making it public. It is the ability to show that you have the ambition and desire to communicate through objects and to demonstrate the radical possibilities of your own curiosity.

Andrea Lipps

Associate Curator of Contemporary Design, Cooper Hewitt, Smithsonian Design Museum, New York, USA
Interview: 20 October 2020

DONNA LOVEDAY: **How did you become a curator? How did it all start?**

ANDREA LIPPS: It started with graduate school. In 2005 I began studying for a masters degree in the History of Decorative Arts and Design offered by Parsons in conjunction with Cooper Hewitt, Smithsonian Design Museum, New York. I was interested in studying design and at the time the programme had a strong emphasis on historical design and decorative arts. I have always been very focused on the contemporary. So in many ways I had to forge my own path through my studies and define my own classes, because at that point contemporary design was not really a subject for study. In 2007 as I was finishing my studies, I had the good fortune to secure an internship at Cooper Hewitt. I worked with curator Cynthia Smith on the exhibition *Design for the Other 90%* (2007), which centred on low-cost solutions for the majority of the world's population who are typically underserved by design. That was the first exhibition I worked on and following that, I had the opportunity to work with the senior curator of architecture and design at MoMA, Paola Antonelli, as a research assistant on the exhibition *Design and the Elastic Mind* (2008). I often say that I really cut my teeth on that show. It was huge and ambitious, and sought to share highly contemporary and cutting-edge design with a general public. It was a seminal show on many levels and particularly for me as a young curator starting my career. It expanded my understanding and appreciation of design's reach and expansiveness. I stayed on at MoMA and worked on

Home Delivery: Fabricating the Modern Dwelling (2008), an exhibition that examined prefabricated housing as architectural invention. I then got a call from Cooper Hewitt, who were recruiting a curatorial assistant to join the team on their next Design Triennial. That was October 2008 and I am still at Cooper Hewitt, almost twelve years later.

DL: What was the first exhibition or project you curated?

AL: After Cooper Hewitt reopened following its renovation, the first exhibition that I curated was *Beauty: Cooper Hewitt Design Triennial* (2016) with Ellen Lupton, senior curator of contemporary design. As a Design Triennial, the show featured work from boundary-pushing designers created in the prior three years that explored ideas of beauty, a nebulous yet visceral concept. It was a rewarding show to curate in that we delved deeply into historical and philosophical texts about beauty and emerged to discover that, at that moment in history (2016), designers were feeling exuberant and hopeful, if transgressive, in reconfiguring ideas about beauty.

DL: How would you define your practice? What is the motivation behind your work?

AL: As design curators, we are first and foremost advocates for design and designers. We synthesize designers' work and provide a portrait to audiences about why design is so important and deserves to be seen, studied and understood. There are varying and complementary modes to curatorial practice: exhibition-making, writing and collecting. Exhibitions are visual theses. Curators construct a narrative and tell a story through objects. I always hope that visitors leave the galleries having learned something new or shifted their thinking or piqued their curiosity to explore an idea further.

Exhibitions and collecting are as much about sharing and preserving knowledge as about stimulating new ideas. At the same time, I often say that as curators of contemporary design, we are mediators to the past as much as we are witnesses to the present. An important facet of a critical curatorial practice is to situate the contemporary moment within the continuum of history. We need a solid understanding of design history in order to most effectively work in the present. Currently my output is most apparent in the major exhibitions and books I have curated and written. Yet for years I have been quietly undertaking research and building my expertise in collecting born-digital design, design which is created and exists digitally. I have spearheaded the museum's efforts to collect digital design in a meaningful way.

DL: In your role at the Cooper Hewitt, you collect digital works for the collection. How would you define the museum's policy towards digital collecting?

AL: Cooper Hewitt was interested in collecting born-digital works and had undertaken a couple of digital acquisitions in the early teens that were initiated by staff outside the curatorial department. Those acquisitions got us started, but we did not have a comprehensive approach about how to collect digital work responsibly and strategically with an eye towards preservation and stewardship. In 2017 the museum was awarded a major Collections Care and Preservation Grant to evaluate our collection holdings for digital work, which primarily included computers and consumer electronics in our Product Design and Decorative Arts department. The project was dubbed the Digital Collection Materials Project, or DCMP. We singled out digital materials as especially vulnerable to the effects of technological obsolescence and decay, which can lead to inaccessibility and information loss, responding to an urgent need to address the conservation needs of digital materials in the collection. The project enabled us to define the landscape of digital design in our existing collection and to develop conservation case studies around a subset of objects in order to mitigate risk and clarify best practices for future acquisitions.

While this work was being undertaken on the digital conservation side of our existing collection and centred on consumer electronics, a number of us at the museum began meeting informally to discuss collecting digital design. In 2017 we formalized this with the creation of the Digital Acquisitions Working Group (DAWG), which included a registrar, a conservator, a digital experience gallery technician and me. As critical as my contributions are to intellectually frame and drive this work forward, it is a highly collaborative effort that sits at the sweet spot between our respective interdisciplinary areas of expertise, tackling not just what we collect digitally, but how. At the outset we conducted extensive research and outreach, attended conferences, met with computer scientists, IP lawyers, historians and our museum colleagues at sister institutions and developed a digital acquisitions workflow modelled on what we were learning. It was informed by what was being discovered in the Digital Collection Materials Project, and which became key in educating other Cooper Hewitt staff about the complexity of collecting this type of work. As we have discovered, the hurdles to collecting digital work are not just its inherent complexity, but a deep and systemic lack of institutional understanding about what this work is, the resources needed to collect it and how we need to treat it.

We launched a 'DAWG lunch club' in which we invite colleagues to an informal meeting to learn more about their activities and research and to share what we're up to. We have developed methods and systems that guide our digital acquisitions, which we have begun to implement. We have systematized our cataloguing and have developed strategies for caring for and displaying our digital collection. And of course we recognize that this is a constant work in progress. As we gain new insights, we update our procedures. As internal staff members express interest in joining our working group, we welcome them. Nothing is ever final. And while we have learned a lot from our colleagues at art museums who have spearheaded best practices in collecting and caring for works of time-based media, we have needed to consider and telegraph how design is different. At this stage, the museum recognizes the importance of collecting digital design and has made a commitment to doing so; it is one of the four priority collecting goals identified in our updated Collections Plan.

DL: In your view, how should museums curate digital objects?

AL: It's a good question. Once we identify a work of digital design we'd like to potentially acquire, the process begins by considering what the actual work is and in what form it is intended to live in the world. Frankly, this is something that changes with almost every digital piece. We take a multi-tiered collection strategy both to accommodate future display but also to address future preservation issues. For example, for a work we recently acquired, *Visualizing the Cosmic Web* by Kim Albrecht and the Barabasi Lab, the primary acquisition was the code for the browser-based visualization. We also acquired three digital files of static moments from the visualization that could be printed, following the designer's specifications, for exhibition display at a later date. Supplemental to this, we gathered an explanatory video and generated video documentation via screen recordings of the visualization, should we one day be unable to access the visualization itself.

DL: What are the challenges for the digital curator?

AL: Collecting is one of the primary challenges. Collecting digital design is still unknown and unexplored territory and suggests a totally different way of approaching collecting. We are often making it up as we go along. I have a fantastic team of intellectually curious conservators that I am fortunate to work with and the community of curators who are collecting in this space are very open to sharing knowledge and learning from one another. There is a collective, collaborative and collegial shared experience around this work. At the same time, because this is a completely new field of collecting, it requires buy-in from the very top in order to get the resources and support needed. I have delivered a lot of education internally for our senior leadership in order to help them understand exactly what it means to acquire born-digital work and the inherent complexities to accomplish that.

Another challenge is that digital works obsolesce more quickly than physical objects. The digital ecosystem is constantly evolving, software, operating systems, hardware, meaning that efforts to preserve the work need to happen more regularly. We talk about digital works almost as living objects.

And finally when curating an exhibition that includes digital work, it's critical to calibrate the immersion and experience in which to share this work with the public, so visitors are not simply passing by a wall of monitors or screens. How can the digital object have its own presence within the gallery space?

DL: There have been a plethora of publications on curating but they have mostly focused on the area of fine art curation, with design curation and the role of the design curator remaining largely unexplored. Why do you think the practice of design curating has been so neglected, despite being a growth area over the last twenty years?

AL: Despite the fact that design is perhaps among the most ancient and definitive pursuits that make us human, design as a discipline and area of academic study is relatively young. As design scholarship grows, design will continue to have a more visible presence, amplifying the practice.

DL: What is unique about the practice of curating design? What is distinctive about the role of the design curator?

AL: Design starts from a place of use or function. It is not about finding something in the world and putting it to use, but shaping something to optimize function, and here it is important to think expansively about function. When we curate design, we are curating objects and experiences that were intended for use, to be held and touched. And while exhibitions of design often privilege looking at objects under vitrines and behind stanchions, design is activated by our whole bodies. In many ways, users give objects and the built environment significance through our embodied experience with them. Products, spaces and media are static things until they are activated by us as users. How can we convey this information in exhibitions? How can we reanimate the potential of contemporary design by recasting objects as dynamic sensorial experiences? How can we ensure that diverse and inclusive narratives around objects are conveyed? How can we create various entry points to access information?

DL: What do you feel are the essential components of a good design exhibition?

AL: Every exhibition needs a clear thesis. What is the show about? Why is it important? A clarity of narrative is very important. I previously mentioned that exhibitions are visual theses, using objects and the experiences within the gallery space to tell a story. Thus the rigour of selecting work is critical to pushing forward the narrative.

Exhibition design is also critically important. It not only immerses and engages an audience, but frames their experience and guides them through a space. Really good exhibition design is an experiential synthesis of an exhibition's concept (Figure 3.2).

DL: How can design curators and design institutions more successfully interact and engage with their audiences?

AL: Most importantly, and I say this five months into the pandemic and lockdown, I think curators and museums need to meet their audiences where they are. Many of our audiences are online and communicating through social media and at the moment, it is the only way for them to access the museum. For better or worse, these are the places we need to be.

Museums are not the most nimble and agile of institutions. We are effectively eighteenth-century institutions that have stumbled our way into the twenty-first century. The Covid-19 pandemic has quickly pushed all of us into virtual spaces. When people return to museums and galleries in full numbers, the emphasis on virtual spaces and digital experiences will remain important and something we need to plan for with every exhibition and programme that we curate.

DL: What are the key shifts that have influenced design curating practice over the last two decades?

AL: I have witnessed an increasing interest in contemporary design practice over the past fifteen years. In 2005 when I started my studies, I was a bit of an outlier because of my interest in contemporary practice. Over this period, the design field itself and design practice expanded. Technology and new modes, formats, materials and means for designers to create and produce work have broadened the field. The porosity of design practice, in which designers are collaborating with those from other disciplines or are even dabbling in new areas themselves, has led to new innovations and directions in design. The emphasis on addressing the climate crisis and meeting the needs of underserved communities has given a renewed energy and emphasis to the importance of design. Critical and speculative design

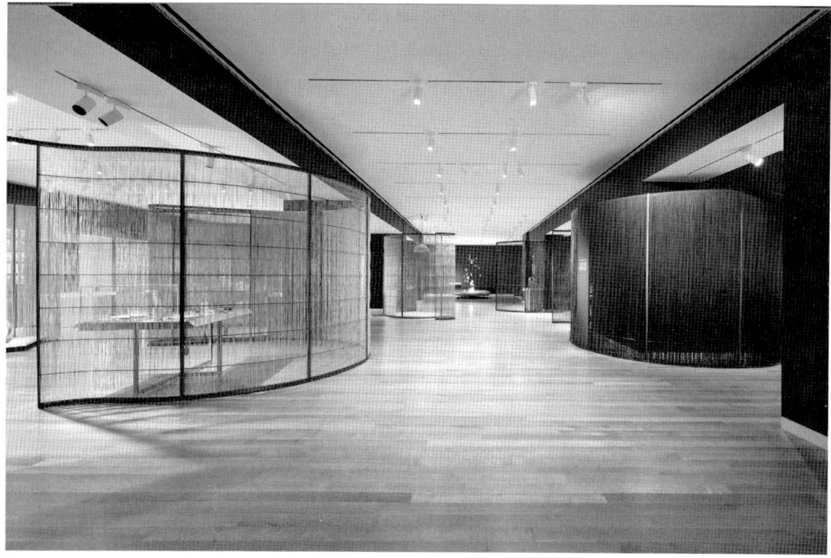

FIGURE 3.2 The Senses: Design beyond Vision, *Cooper Hewitt, Smithsonian Design Museum, New York, 2018. © Thomas Loof.*

practice, as established by Anthony Dunne and Fiona Raby in the RCA's Design Interactions programme in the 2000s, broadened the role of design at the outset of the twenty-first century. Curation is often a balance of distilling and synthesizing what's happening in design, so it has been an exciting time to be a contemporary design curator.

DL: What do you feel are the key debates driving design at this moment to which curators must respond?

AL: It's not necessarily a debate, but more of a reckoning; we need to decentre whiteness in design. So much of our training in design and art history is centred around white, European, American and colonialist ideas of design and design history. We learn about the normative, hegemonic and dominant histories, which are reinforced in most museum collections. How can we decolonize design? How can we make space for our own research and learn to tell more inclusive and nuanced narratives? How can we welcome more voices and practitioners into our field?

DL: What advice would you give to a young curator entering the field today? What skill set will the design curator of the future need to have?

AL: A boundless, intellectual curiosity is so essential to our field. Communication, both written and verbal, is also key. As curators, we constantly share information with diverse audiences across a range of platforms. Within the creative process of curating, we only benefit from being open to collaboration and to other people's contributions. Exhibitions and collections are always better when they include, and reflect, other voices.

Riya Patel

Design and Architecture Curator and Writer
Curator, The Aram Gallery, London, UK (2015–20)
Interview: 19 August 2020

DONNA LOVEDAY: How did you become a curator? How did it all start?

RIYA PATEL: I studied Architecture at Cardiff University and graduated in 2008. From there I went to work in journalism with an internship at the *Architects' Journal*, and later a junior editor position at *ICON* magazine. I wasn't very fulfilled by the work I was doing as an architecture graduate, and found publishing more exciting. When I was ready to move on from journalism, I wanted a role where I could use my design knowledge and contacts in a new way, not necessarily working for another magazine, but in a different space. *ICON* is a monthly magazine, and I found that I didn't get a lot of time for research and to explore a subject in depth, before moving on to the next issue. When I took up the role at The Aram Gallery, it was about adapting the knowledge and experience I had gained from education and working in magazines to this new role as a curator. The gallery staged five exhibitions a year, and although that's quite a fast pace, it offered more time to research subjects and that was appealing to me.

DL: What was the first exhibition or project you curated?

RP: It was called *Extra-Ordinary*, in July 2015. I wanted to look at designers who were using materials that had a previous, often mundane existence and turning them into something more interesting. The show focused on the question: How can we transform once-used materials into something totally unrecognizable, either as a product or another useful material? The outcomes explored properties of materials that were often unseen or not known about. Some designers ended up designing entire new systems for design. To give an example, Odd Matter, a Dutch design studio, presented a project that started with granules of recycled plastic. They didn't just design a product with it, they designed a whole system where the user buys the granules which are moulded into one piece of furniture and, when the piece of furniture becomes redundant, it is disintegrated and moulded into something else. It was a whole new system for consuming design. The exhibition was more than I would have ended up writing about as a magazine editor, because there was the opportunity, the time and the space to achieve so much more.

DL: Have certain curators, exhibitions or encounters been decisive for you? What or who influenced your involvement in design?

RP: I knew little about design before I went to work for *ICON* magazine. My background was architecture. At the magazine, I was working closely with the deputy editor, Johanna Agerman Ross, who is now curator of twentieth century and contemporary furniture and product design at the V&A. She introduced me to the field of design and when she left *ICON*, I became interested in the areas that she had been writing about for the magazine. In a curating context, an important influence was Daniel Charny. As founding curator of The Aram Gallery, he set up the whole ethos. He found a new way of existing as a design gallery. At the time, he developed quite a punky way of presenting design which really appealed to me. The Aram Gallery doesn't have to sell tickets, it doesn't have to count visitors; so it has the freedom to do things completely differently. It was very refreshing to see the way that Daniel started with that ethos but was also able to keep that momentum going. He established an identity for The Aram Gallery and gave it a foothold in the London gallery scene.

DL: How would you define your practice? What is the motivation behind your work?

RP: I guess what took me from journalism into curation is the idea of supporting designers at an early stage of their careers. When I was working at *ICON*, my interest was in writing profiles on young and emerging designers and identifying that talent before it rose to the surface. I think that is really what drives me. It also connects with what Zeev Aram, founder of the Aram Store, had been doing for a long time with his graduate summer shows. He had this amazing track record of discovering talent, like Thomas Heatherwick and Martino Gamper, right at the start of their careers and giving them a space to show their work. There is really no other platform than the gallery for designers who are at that first stage in their careers. They have their graduation show, one chance to exhibit their work, but they don't have the means or the opportunity to stage a solo show until much later, if at all. They are somehow inbetween these spaces and I find that really interesting and exciting. As the gallery does not have to adhere to any institutional remit, we are very free as to what we present. It's about identifying what's interesting and what fits the programme at the time. Design is a continually evolving subject and I am always looking for ways to keep things flexible and adaptable. When you work with designers who are in their early careers, they don't always have a fixed idea of how they want to present themselves. Every exhibition is therefore a collaboration, to find out what a designer wants from the exhibition, but also what I want to achieve as the curator.

DL: The early 2000s saw the opening of a number of independently curated spaces for design that exhibited the work of contemporary designers at the start of their careers. The Aram Gallery is one such example. Why do you think there was a need for these spaces?

RP: I think the decline in manufacturing in Europe saw more designers turning their attention to another way of working: making collectable work and editions as a way to express their creativity. This was the time of Design Art in the 1990s with superstar designers like Philippe Starck and Marcel Wanders. Where a young designer might have previously dreamed of going to work for a company like Braun, it suddenly became exciting to work under your own signature. I'm not sure there was a need for spaces like these, but places like The Aram Gallery which opened in 2003 became a natural home for those working experimentally. You could say that the designers whose work is shown at the gallery have a process closer to art than design. I think what's necessary about showing design in a gallery context is that the curator can be a lot more responsive to change, more so than a museum or larger cultural institution. The Aram Gallery can respond much more quickly to topics, before they become irrelevant. It doesn't have to worry about finding buyers for the works. It can just say, look here's something or somebody interesting, without that pressure. Maybe that's why the whole scene flourished in the early 2000s because design itself became more diverse and interesting at that time.

Design encompasses so many things now. It can be a toothbrush, but it can also be a very expensive vase. It was the first time design was being seen, not just in the form of everyday mass-produced products, but as something radical and boundary-pushing in terms of material and form. Design could be put on a pedestal and admired like art.

DL: The gallery is located above the Aram store selling designed objects. How far does that influence the exhibition programme and what you decide to show in the gallery?

RP: It's purposefully kept quite separate. We are not obliged to sell what we present in the gallery. Only occasionally are there crossovers because it's a space that is not income-generating and the store has to support the gallery. I think the real strength of the space is that it's a counterpoint to the commercial store. The gallery provides the context for the finished products you see in the store. It promotes understanding of contemporary design by showing process and prototypes (Figure 3.3). For example, behind the design for a beautiful chair is a rigorous process of testing and experimenting. The gallery also contributes to the idea of the store as a destination. There is a reason to visit the building, to buy something but to also learn something. This is very much in line with the ethos that Zeev Aram had for the gallery in the beginning. He has two things that he wants me to bear in mind for every exhibition: shows are to be as accessible as possible and that the space is always free to visitors. It's a public space; so anyone should be able to walk in, whether they know a lot about design or very little, and be enlightened in some way. That's a really wide remit for putting together the shows because they can appeal to both an expert and a layman. They work on lots of different levels and everything I plan for the gallery adheres to those core values.

DL: Your background is in design journalism. How has this influenced your work as a curator?

RP: Both jobs are really about analysing information, thinking critically and providing interpretation. When researching a subject, you have to be quite strict in not following too many divergent paths. You have to keep coming back to the main subject and a sense of narrative in the exhibition. Our exhibitions run for five weeks, and with five shows a year, you can't ever go into too much depth. The skills of editing, so important in journalism, are useful to me on a daily basis. To be able to say that's interesting, but if it doesn't really fit with what we are trying to say, then it shouldn't be in the exhibition. And then there is the network and the knowledge about the industry that I gained from journalism. Visiting studios and workshops, seeing what designers do, what they care about and what they're talking about is really valuable. Designers themselves don't always have an overview of what's happening more broadly in the industry, which you do have as an editor or a curator. That's crucial, to be able to identify and pull together themes. So on a practical level, I use the skills of being able to research, edit and present information clearly every day.

DL: There have been a plethora of publications on curating but they have mostly focused on the area of fine art curation, with design curation and the role of the design curator remaining largely unexplored. Why do you think the practice of design curating has been so neglected, despite being a growth area over the last twenty years?

RP: I think one reason is because design doesn't have the profile of architecture, fashion or art, in terms of commercial interest. These are much bigger fields than design with a stronger culture of criticism. I also think that, for many people, design is a harder subject to understand. It's an industrial pursuit connected to manufacture, but also to craft and luxury. I think that perhaps this is more of a UK problem. We don't really have the design culture of other countries, such as Italy or Scandinavia, where there is a more general consciousness about the value of design. There is a recognition as to why it is important to have good design in your home and why it is important to go and look at objects in museums that have been well designed. Design is also a fast-changing subject. The term has come to encompass so many things in the last few decades. It is not just about objects but services, experiences, the virtual and the digital. It is such a huge subject that you almost have to define it for yourself before you begin to curate. Those elements make the design curator part of a very small pool of people and make it quite a specific thing to do; so perhaps that's also why it has been underexplored as a practice. But I think it's a fascinating area to work in because of those reasons.

DL: What is unique about the practice of curating design? What is distinctive about the role of the design curator?

RP: For me, what is unique about curating design is that you communicate the process as well as present the final product. We are not always dealing with things that are immediately seen as precious; so we have to reveal the value of design in other ways. I don't think that is asked so much of other practices. There have been some exceptional fashion exhibitions on process, such as *Pheobe English* at NOW Gallery in May 2015, or Burberry's *Makers House* series, but they tend to appear a long time after the collection and certain elements have to be kept under wraps. You might see a designer's preparatory sketches but you rarely get a sense of the making and the finished object at the same time, as you do with design. Barber Osgerby's exhibition at the Design Museum in 2014, *In the Making*, was really interesting. We are familiar with everyday objects like a tennis ball, but then to see the sheet of felt that the ball is cut from is not something you would normally engage with. I think it's our job as curators to reveal things about our everyday life that might have gone unnoticed or underappreciated.

DL: What do you feel are the essential components of a good design exhibition?

RP: For me, the best exhibitions are relatable and work on a number of levels. They are interesting to the expert but also to the person who knows very little about design. Design touches everybody's life in a way that high fashion or art doesn't; so right there you have an accessible route into the subject. The best exhibitions have been those that are about unexpected acts of design. I remember seeing an exhibition, *Tu nais, tuning, tu meurs*, at the 2015 St Etienne Biennale about people who 'souped up' their cars by applying go-faster stripes, adding lights or creating shiny iridescent surfaces which are all acts of design. We all design our lives, whether we are conscious of doing it or not. Exhibitions that take design out of a rarified context are the ones which are most interesting for me. And also exhibitions that challenge. I am purposefully quite light with the labelling in exhibitions in the gallery.

Sometimes there are no labels at all, because with design you already have some sense of what an object is and does. The visitor doesn't need to be told what a chair or a vase is. It's more about inviting someone into a space, giving them a few clues as to why these objects are together, and giving them the space to make their own connections and form their own opinions.

DL: How can design curators and design institutions more successfully interact and engage with their audiences?

RP: As curators we need to consider whose voices we are representing. We need to make selections to ensure that exhibitions reach different audiences. I like to engage our visitors with surprise. You shouldn't come to the gallery expecting to see something specific; it should always be different. We don't ever want visitors to say, 'That's not what The Aram Gallery does, that's not the kind of show they do'. There is no type of show that we wouldn't consider. So I think to continually evaluate what you are showing, and why you are showing it, is vital. I think exhibitions that encourage wider accessibility and involve more voices are important. Design exhibitions need to come out of the institutional context to engage with more people. That is what's great about festivals where interventions are happening at street level. People are not having to go and seek out a design exhibition experience; they are encountering it on the street or on the underground. I think as curators we have to work harder to stay relevant and interesting. Historic buildings and large institutions can be intimidating for many people. Perhaps we need to come out of our buildings more and interject into daily life, in order to reach wider audiences.

DL: What are the key shifts that have influenced design curating practice over the last two decades?

RP: I think our environmental responsibility is a huge one in terms of subject matter but also how we present exhibitions. There is more of a consciousness around what we're showing and why. I try to ask myself: What is the benefit of having a physical exhibit in the space? What can you learn from being in a room with that object that you wouldn't necessarily learn from a book or seeing it online? Because we work with such a tiny budget in the gallery we reuse a lot of display material and we don't believe in a lot of visual support for the exhibits. We have a beautiful space; so we can put a few objects on the floor and that can make for a simple but effective exhibition. I think that, moving forward, exhibition design is going to become leaner, not just in galleries like ours, but across the board because we are all thinking about how much material we use for such temporary projects.

Another shift is the amount of soul-searching taking place in museums that were set up centuries ago. They were intended as repositories of the best examples of craft and manufacture, holding them up for the world to see. Now we have a very different view of what a museum should be, what constitutes an exhibit, and we are continually trying to understand what exhibition-making should be and who it should be for. So developing a greater critical consciousness around our exhibitions is key, to ask ourselves what kind of values are we upholding within design curation and the design exhibitions that we present?

We are also battling with the role of physical space in design curation. With many of the exhibitions at the gallery, visitors come in, snap everything on their phones, leave and then post the images on social media. It can be really challenging to get people to engage beyond that, or even stay in the space for long. So how can we make an exhibition work in various dimensions, both digitally and physically? The challenge for the future will be to maintain the practice of exhibition-making but adding these strands so the gallery stays relevant. As curators, we need to continually ask ourselves those bigger questions. Who are we making exhibitions for? Who are they reaching? What are we trying to say?

DL: How have these developments impacted your own practice?

RP: From an environmental perspective I try to constantly evaluate our reasons for making physical exhibitions and the amount of resources they require. When working with a tiny budget you have to justify why you are spending money to transport an object to be physically present in the gallery. We did an edition of the *Prototypes and Experiments* exhibition series on architectural models in August 2018. Roz Barr Architects showed a large 1:10 model of a part of a church. It is pretty amazing to be looking at an architectural detail on that scale. It is also rare for an architect to make a model to that scale because of the difficulty in transporting and storing the work. What was important about bringing it into the gallery was that visitors were able to see a fragment of that building and experience it as closely as possible to the real thing. In some cases, the object really does need to be physically experienced in order to be understood.

DL: What do you feel are the key debates driving design at this moment to which curators must respond?

RP: The big one is environmental responsibility. Should we still be making exhibitions about stuff? As a gallery, we are not selling objects but we are still making objects desirable. We are contributing to this cycle. How can we reconcile that part of our role which is to promote the idea of looking at and buying design. More recently, non-commercial exhibitions have tended to draw a lot of interest because they focus on anonymous and purely functional design. I am thinking of *U-Joints*, an exhibition about screws and bolts at Milan Design Week in 2018, or *Typology: An Ongoing Study of Everyday Items* at Vitra Design Museum in 2019. I think

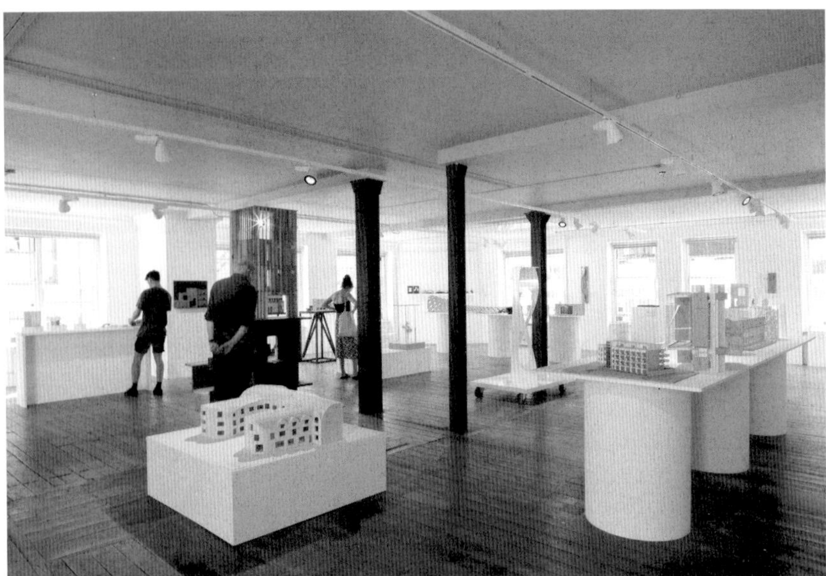

FIGURE 3.3 Prototypes and Experiments 10, *The Aram Gallery, London, 2018* © *Agnese Sanvito.*

as curators we have to ensure that we aren't so much promoting the idea of creating new products, but lending value to the quality of good design; buy less but better. And our role in that is to show what better is. So environmental responsibility is important and also diversity. Design itself isn't the most accessible subject to people from all walks of life. Are we being representative of all the different people that are affected by design? That's a huge debate that every curator has to grapple with for every exhibition. Are we being fairly representative and are we reaching beyond our networks? We need to work harder to be inclusive and not so reliant on the usual sources.

DL: **What advice would you give to a young curator entering the field today? What skill set will the design curator of the future need to have?**

RP: What has served me well in my career is an ability to be flexible. Not having a fixed mindset of what a curator does or what a curator should be. Curation doesn't just take place in museums and galleries, it takes place at festivals, online, it can be creating a project with a community. A curator needs to be flexible, adaptable and to keep an open mind about what design can encompass. They also need to be responsive. I am working alone in the gallery and the programme could easily end up being what I am personally interested in. It would be very easy for me to present designers that I like or in whom I have a personal interest. So it is important that I keep educating myself about the wider context for design and to keep coming back to the wider reasons for curating exhibitions. Traditionally curating was about caring for collections. I don't work in a museum and I don't have access to a collection. The whole world, and everything in it, is our collection and that's what's so exciting about being a curator now; everything is your material.

Sumitra Upham

Head of Public Programmes, the Crafts Council, London, UK
Senior Curator of Public Programmes, the Design Museum, London, UK
(2017–21)
Curator of Programmes for the 5th Istanbul Design Biennial (2019–21)
Interview: 30 October 2020

DONNA LOVEDAY: How did you become a curator? How did it all start?

SUMITRA UPHAM: I studied a BA in Performance and Visual Cultures at Brighton University. I then went on to study an MA in Curating Contemporary Design at Kingston University with the Design Museum. But I guess my big break was when I got a job at White Cube, which was my first permanent role in the arts. White Cube is a commercial gallery where curators in the traditional sense don't really exist. Artists have a dominant role in the conceptualization and execution of exhibitions and artist liaisons play more of a mediatory role. Witnessing the evolution of exhibitions at White Cube sparked my interest in curating. At the start, I was working at the Hoxton Square site but I also oversaw the development and move of the gallery to Bermondsey in a converted south London warehouse redesigned by architects Casper Mueller Kneer, which is the gallery's main base today. I was working for the director of exhibitions, Tim Marlow, who is now director of the Design Museum, London. At that time, the vision for Bermondsey was to showcase major exhibitions by the gallery's impressive rostra of leading international artists, but also to have space for more experimental programming through their 9x9x9 gallery. This included a younger generation of artists not represented by the gallery. It was a new direction for White Cube which involved having more curatorial input from the exhibitions and artist liaison teams, who had more freedom to develop thematics and critical ideas for shows. This process intrigued me and opened my eyes to the potential of curating as a profession.

A further turning point was when we developed a learning programme for the gallery. This included talks and other discursive events with artists, curators and academics. I enjoyed the opportunity to experiment with new formats for presenting practice and new thinking. My involvement in that programme definitely played a role in shaping my interest in the discursive side of curating and how education can inform curatorial practice. Possibly the most valuable outcome from this period was being part of a new network of curators and artists who were very engaged and connected to the contemporary art scene in London. We would go to shows and events at least three times a week, which opened my eyes to new types of curatorial practice.

My next role after White Cube was associate curator of learning at the Institute of Contemporary Arts (ICA), which was my first job as a curator. There I worked collaboratively with artists and academics to develop experimental outreach, research and display programmes that placed radical learning and pedagogy at the centre of its enquiry.

DL: What was the first exhibition or project you curated?

SU: Prior to joining White Cube, I carried out an internship in the United States working for a company called Creative Time, who were a commissioning agency for public art. While I was there, I assisted on the curation of a project by the British artist Jeremy Deller. It was a project called *It Is What It Is: Conversations about Iraq*. It was a discursive project but also a piece of public art. The artist drove a car that had been blown up in the Iraq war, all the way through the United States down to the Southern states, interviewing war veterans along the way and recording those conversations. It was an extremely powerful project which opened my eyes to the value of working in the public realm, outside of a gallery context, and the power of using art as a tool to activate conversation and engagement with local people. It showed me how art can have more of a direct impact on people's lives, interjecting into everyday environments in a way that is powerful and responsive, but also respectful.

DL: Have certain curators, exhibitions or encounters been decisive for you? What or who has influenced your involvement in design?

SU   My entry into the field of design was mainly through my studies on the MA in Curating Contemporary Design at Kingston University, but shortly after I graduated, I landed a job in the art world which took me in a different direction. So much of my professional experience has been working within an art context, but the projects that I have worked on have been driven by design and architecture in some way. As a young curator I was reading people like Irit Rogoff, Charles Esche, Markus Miessen and Claire Bishop, who were writing about the social turn, participation and spatial practice, and the potential of implementing education into curatorial practice. I think that period was a really interesting time for curating, shifting attention beyond the four walls of the gallery space and thinking about new areas that curatorial practice could occupy, whether it was the public realm, or the atrium or corridors of galleries.

I was interested in questions like: What happens if you open up the gallery space to not include a traditional display of objects? What happens if you hand over the space to a group of activists or urbanists to take up residency in the gallery and create a learning programme? How does that create new forms of engagement for the public? The Serpentine Galleries were doing interesting work at that time. I was following the work of Dr Janna Graham, who now teaches at Goldsmiths, University of London, but who at the time was a project curator at the Serpentine leading research and outreach projects. She initiated the Centre for Possible Studies, which was an off-site curatorial site and programme of residencies, events and exhibitions that initiated collaborations between artists and local people to celebrate the rich history and cultures of communities in the neighbourhood of Edgware Road in west London. There was also the Serpentine Marathon, which I would never miss. I think the Serpentine was an interesting model in terms of pioneering new discursive curatorial formats and frameworks. It brought in academics, activists and urbanists to have conversations with artists and architects. I found that pluralistic way of working, and the dissolving of traditional hierarchies within institutions, really inspiring. It was a space that I was keen to occupy and learn more about.

Raven Row was also an exhibition space that I would visit a lot. They were programming exhibitions about forgotten cultural histories and exhibition formats and theories. For a curator, it was interesting to observe how things had been done previously and what we can take from these typologies when building new curatorial practices for the future. In relation to design, I was following Paola Antonelli's programme at MoMA. Her shows have fundamentally changed the way in which design curators think about the impact of design on society. I was reading people like Mark Fisher and Donna Haraway, who opened my mind to ideas around more-than-human politics and curating from different perspectives. When I was starting out, the biennial model was expanding. Witnessing the evolution of these new global, experimental platforms for curating, such as *Documenta* and *Manifesta*, were fundamental in the development of my understanding of what curating could do, its urban transformative capacity and its ability to inform and engage a spectrum of people.

DL: How would you define your practice? What is the motivation behind your work?

SU: Working on the 5th Istanbul Design Biennial has encouraged me to think more about this than ever before. I am not a traditional exhibitions curator. Of course, I love exhibitions and they inspire me, but exhibitions in the traditional sense have not always been the format that I wanted to work within. I am more interested in working within this hybrid space between social practice, public engagement and research. I'm interested in different typologies and formats and how, as curators, we can design new frameworks for work to exist within. What interests me is how art, design and technology can be used to challenge existing forms of public engagement and give visibility to urgent research and thinking around social justice and inclusivity. The outcome of my work is rarely an exhibition, but often something more performative and discursive. It could be a series of workshops that engage local citizens, activists and researchers in conversations with architects, urbanists and artists about their local high street, or performances that activate forgotten sites in urban settings. I am interested in collaborative formats, often driven by research, that address the role of art and design in creating social change.

DL: You were the first curator of public programmes at the Design Museum. What prompted you to apply for this role and how have you been able to develop this strand of the museum's programming?

SU: I have had a long-standing relationship with the Design Museum. I did the collaborative MA and had followed the programme from afar for a long time but had never worked there. When the museum opened at its new home in Kensington, there was a distinct shift in the direction of the programme to address more social, political and ecological issues that, in my view, had been overlooked in the past. For example, the museum's first exhibition at Kensington, *Fear and Love*, felt like more of a biennial show made up of new commissions by artists and designers whose work demonstrated design's role in helping us navigate through complex issues and parameters. This was curated by Justin McGuirk, who had recently been appointed as chief curator of the museum, and whose work I had followed a little.

Having worked as a curator within learning and non-traditional programming contexts, I had developed a level of professionalism within a certain field of curating. This type of curatorial practice was familiar and flourishing within a contemporary art context, but for design it was less common. I was intrigued that the museum has decided to recruit for a role like this, acknowledging public programming as a form of curatorial practice. The fact that it was a new role was also interesting for me, as there was space to shape and propose a new direction for the programme.

DL: How have you been able to develop the programme while you have been at the museum? What do you feel you have been able to achieve?

SU: It has been challenging. Whenever you take on a new role, there is often a perception that you have the power to do anything you want to. The reality is often that you spend time trying to justify your ideas, actions and new ways of working. This is often the case in institutions that have been running for a long time and are reluctant to change. When I started the role, my vision was to develop a programme that was, first and foremost, critical and self-reflective and driven by research. A programme that would underpin the exhibitions and expand on the questions and themes that they posed, but also act as an independent space outside the exhibitions, to respond to what's happening in the world right now.

Museum exhibition curators can be working on a show for three years and by the time it opens, the main narratives may have evolved. I'm not saying that exhibitions are less urgent than other forms of programming, but the focus on the final outcome can be limiting and doesn't allow space to present research in the process. The public programme has the agility to be outwardly, unashamedly responsive in its framework and in the topics and questions that it addresses. So for the Design Museum, the public programme was an important new platform that would allow the museum to be responsive and at the heart of design debate, and that's what we set out to do. We run an interdisciplinary programme of lectures, discussions, salons and symposia, along with performances, screenings, online and off-site projects. The programme seeks to unearth urgent topics, form collaborative relationships and provide a platform for new voices doing incredible work in pushing the boundaries of what design is and who it's for. Due to the often insular nature of the design industry, these practitioners and thinkers aren't always given a platform, particularly if their work is critical of accepted practices and knowledge. Where possible, I try to use the public programme as a home for these types of voices.

DL: Can you give me an example of an individual to whom you have given a platform to showcase their thinking and research?

SU: In 2018 I worked with Justin McGuirk on a project called *Convivial Tools*. This was a curatorial programme of events exploring the work of the late Ivan Illich. Illich was a social philosopher, polymath and priest whose perceptive critical views on education and industrialized society have come back into currency in recent years and inspired the work of many curators, including Jan Boelen's *School of Schools* programme for the 4th Istanbul Design Biennial. *Convivial Tools* was a programme of talks, workshops and a curated dinner that culminated in a symposium at the museum exploring the legacy of Illich's concept of conviviality in contemporary society. Because Illich's work has inspired so many creative thinkers and practitioners, we were able to invite a range of artists, designers and technologists to reflect on his practice. This included established voices like Joseph Grima, the creative director of Design Academy Eindhoven and co-founder of the design research studio, Space Caviar, the writer and technologist Adam Greenfield and the co-founder of design practice Public Works, Torange Khonsari. The programme also included other progressive thinkers, less known within design, like Ruth Catlow, curator and founder of Furtherfield Gallery, the designer, writer and activist Eleanor Saitta and the philosopher Nina Power. We tried our best to create a democratic platform for discussion and debate that encouraged social integration and collaboration.

More recently, I started a collaboration with London Festival of Architecture called *Manifestos: Architecture for a New Generation*, which is something that I am particularly proud of. It started as a small project that invited ten established architects and urbanists in London to nominate ten emerging practitioners who are changing the landscape of London. These were people who were developing new manifestos for the city that were more inclusive and relevant to a younger generation. The project has become an annual event and each year we provide a platform for ten architects to present their manifestos in different forms. In 2019 it culminated in a talk and debate at the Design Museum as part of the Friday Lates programme. In 2020, it fell in the middle of the Covid-19 pandemic; so instead we commissioned ten three-minute films for social media in which each architect presented their manifesto. The participants included Ibiye Camp, a graduate of architecture from the RCA whose work explores how augmented realities reveal hidden narratives that deconstruct dominant geopolitical biases, and Jayden Ali, an architect who teaches at Central Saint Martins, whose work explores engagement and diversity in public space, often through film.

In the same way that biennials stand to present work by a new generation, I'm interested in using this strand as a platform that carves out space for emerging designers to present their refreshing ideas to a mass audience. That feels like a very valuable thing. The curating part of it is working with those architects and designers to think about how best to present those manifestos in a meaningful way. I'm interested in curating new spatial typologies to shape and present new ideas. The manifesto, as a design framework, interests me in that respect.

DL: You have curated the programme for the 5th Istanbul Design Biennial. A visible shift in curatorial practice over the last decade has been the proliferation of Biennials on a worldwide scale. Why do you think the Biennial as an exhibition structure has become so important?

SU: I think firstly, and building on what we have just been talking about, the biennial is important as a platform to review new work. I think for journalists, writers and curators, the biennial has become a repository of new knowledge and practice where you can get a sense of what's happening globally, not just in your city. There is also the professional network and peer-to-peer learning that you gain from attending biennials, mostly in the opening week. However, increasingly I think the biennial has become more about the role of the curator. The themes, questions and new frameworks proposed by biennial curators are shaping curatorial practice. The themes directly address urgent global issues and demonstrate how art and design is responding.

DL: What were your aims in curating the programme for the 5th Istanbul Design Biennial? What were some of the challenges you faced but also opportunities?

SU: Our theme for the biennial was *Empathy Revisited: Designs for More than One.* The biennial was led by the brilliant Mariana Pestana, a Portuguese curator and architect who has been a constant source of inspiration to me curatorially. She built the team around it, which included myself and the writer, Billie Muraben. The aim of the biennial was to bring together ideas and projects that seek to define a new role for design based on empathy. As a mediator of emotions and feelings, design is presented as a practice that regards care as its main purpose. Of course, the biennial took place amidst a global pandemic, which presented many challenges, but also a unique opportunity to question the role of the biennial in this very moment. I think what's interesting about Mariana, Billie and myself as curators is that we have very different practices but we share an interest in ideas around participation and social engagement. The programme aimed to dissolve traditional curatorial hierarchies and develop more democratic formats for engaging audiences more directly.

The pandemic changed what we could do physically. Of course, we weren't able to make any visits to the city, until the installation began. The fact that we couldn't get there, and neither could the designers and artists, meant that we had to radically reshape the programme but also the ways that we work as curators in this very moment. We were limited to Zoom and other similar means of communication, which was challenging, particularly when developing relationships and trust.

We ended up with a programme that comprises four key strands. One is a programme called *Civic Rituals*, which is a series of interventions that invite visitors to reimagine the role of the citizen in the city through new encounters. These public encounters were created by designers, architects and artists but hosted by different community groups in the city, who take ownership of the works. Virtually all of the works will live on past the biennial and become permanent works in the city for the people, maintained by these groups. For example, we have a work called the Revolution Stove, which is an outdoor woodstove designed by a Beirut-based design collective called Bits to Atoms (Figure 3.4). It can be manufactured from an open-source CAD file and is easy to assemble. During the revolution in the city (2019–ongoing) the stove provided heat and the means to warm up food for protestors at night and during the cold winter months. We approached Bits to Atoms to create a new stove for Istanbul and we have installed it at Karaköy Pier, which is an area where many homeless people congregate. It is our hope that the stove will provide warmth to the homeless community and enable them to heat food and cook on the stove. The project has been developed by Urban.koop, a local community group.

Our research programme is called *The Library of Land and Sea*. We have worked in collaboration with ten designers and cultural activists who were engaged in research around the Mediterranean. Each of them was working in different regions to challenge or reimagine the geographical boundaries of the Mediterranean through engaging with our relationship to land and sea. This could be from the soil that we grow our food from, or the land that we build architecture onto, right through to the water that connects us to different territories. Some of the initial research is presented in the library which has just opened in Istanbul. The idea is that this research continues to grow over the next six months with the support of the biennial. In spring 2021, each project will produce a legacy outcome that will give back in some way to the region or the context in which each project is working.

And then we have *The Critical Cooking Show*. This is a series of eighteen episodes directed and produced by practitioners working in different parts of the world, re-engaging with their local contexts in this stationary period. Each episode takes an ingredient or a recipe as a starting point for thinking more broadly about social, ecological or geopolitical issues. For example, the Chilean architect Linda Schilling takes avocado toast, the quintessential middle-class bite, as a starting point for talking about resource extraction and the impact of the expansion of avocado growth on the landscape of Chile. The programme is presented online every Sunday via e-flux Architecture.

The concept of localism was important to us in this period. The biennial model is often critiqued as being extremely wasteful and extractive with a disregard for the local context. People jump on flights across the world to

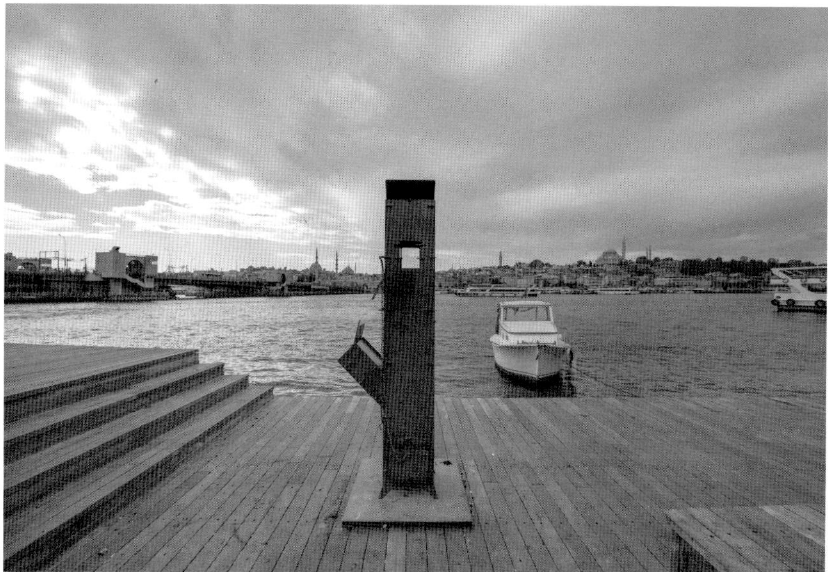

FIGURE 3.4 The Revolution Woodstove/*Devrimin Sobasi, Bits to Atoms +
BeirutMakers/Sobya't Thawra, at* The Library of Land and Sea *for the 5th Istanbul
Design Biennial, 2020 © Kayhan Kaygusuz.*

see an exhibition that lasts for only three weeks. We wanted to address
that critically and to create a programme that was locally produced and that
has a meaningful legacy. We were less interested in having these 'peak'
moments, for example, when an international, influential crowd travels to
the biennial for the opening week and all resources go into that moment.
Instead, we developed a programme that engages with people over a
longer period of time, six months, and at a more intimate and local level.
The *Civic Rituals* are for the local people of Istanbul first and foremost. The
research programme engages people at a regional level, inviting them to
understand Istanbul within the wider context of the Mediterranean. *The
Critical Cooking Show* is a digital programme and accessible to international
audiences, but it invites viewers to re-engage with their local environment
wherever they are.

Because of the pandemic, we are all engaging with our local environments
in different ways: going on the same daily walk, talking more frequently to our
neighbours and shopping at our local shops. I think the pandemic presented
us with an opportunity to champion localism as a theme, but also as a practice.

On the one hand, we have a programme that has been locally produced,
but on the other, we have a programme that has been developed in dialogue
with the local citizens of Istanbul and other communities around the world
who are re-engaging with their local environment in this present moment.

In terms of the legacy, the intention is that the research projects continue to grow beyond the biennial and the installations in the city will become permanent sites that continue to support everyday life in the city, long after the biennial closes. The *Critical Cooking Show* will live online as a repository of knowledge that will be a reminder of how work was conceived in this unprecedented moment. But first and foremost, the programme provides some much-needed online entertainment. In all of these programmes food is presented as a serious design subject. Our proposition is that if we use food as a design tool, then perhaps we will find answers to some of the world's most pressing problems.

DL: **There have been a plethora of publications on curating but they have mostly focused on the area of fine art curation, with design curation and the role of the design curator remaining largely unexplored. Why do you think the practice of design curating has been so neglected, despite being a growth area over the last twenty years?**

SU: Such a good question. This is an obvious answer, but I think first and foremost, there are not enough design institutions or spaces. It's incomparable to contemporary art and that's a reason why I think the practice hasn't expanded to the same extent that art has. If I may be critical, I think it has taken a long time for the practice to change. The practice has been safe and not as ambitious or experimental in the way that contemporary art curation has been, particularly in developing new formats and delving into very politicized issues. Today, we are in the midst of an ecological crisis and levels of inequality are growing across the world. I think it is unavoidable and naive for design curators to shy away from addressing these issues, particularly when design plays a fundamental role in shaping them. Politics is engrained in design and design is engrained in politics, and we as curators have a duty to present design as a political tool with agency. I do think that design exhibitions are now doing this, but, as you have recognized in your book, we have only really seen this shift in the last decade.

DL: **What is unique about the practice of curating design? What is distinctive about the role of the design curator?**

SU: What interests me about design curating over other forms of curating is the idea of design as a democratic practice and process. Design pervades all aspects of life and directly engages with it, human and non-human. As a design curator you have the ability to reflect that democracy, and the subjects and objects that you present have a direct engagement with the lives of everyday people. I am interested in designing curatorial experiences and exploring how, as curators, we can develop new ways of engaging audiences more democratically. I'm not just talking about the exhibition design and building plinths or designing VR experiences, but designing active social experiences between objects and people.

DL: What do you feel are the essential components of a good design exhibition?

SU: Good design exhibitions in my opinion are those in which you see design presented in its natural habitat. Whilst I never get tired of seeing an exhibition on Le Corbusier or seeing an Eames chair or a Charlotte Perriand table, they are almost always presented on plinths as very precious objects. I'm less interested in these types of curatorial formats when it comes to design, and more drawn towards formats that promote accessibility and direct engagement. I find exhibitions that give a subject back into the hands of the user and the visitor very inspiring.

DL: How can design curators and design institutions more successfully interact and engage with their audiences?

SU: Today audiences are consuming content and knowledge online more than ever before, and particularly in this moment during a pandemic when we are all glued to our phones and our laptops. Communications teams in institutions are constantly thinking about how to engage audiences online but it isn't just the responsibility of the Comms teams anymore. Curators need to be occupying this space and reflecting on online audiences as just as valuable and important as audiences that visit exhibitions. We need to be engaging with the TikTok generation, just as much as the Charlotte Perriand enthusiasts. I think after the pandemic, we are going to see a huge shift in museums prioritizing local audiences. With people not travelling, I hope we will start to see curators coming out of their institutions and into the environments of different communities, to build relationships with people and to attempt to understand their contexts.

Rather than constantly striving to produce never-seen-before content, how can we re-engage with existing material and knowledge to present new ideas? This is what we need to start asking ourselves. Museums are already starting to find new ways of activating their collections because of a lack of resources available to produce blockbuster exhibitions right now.

DL: What are the key shifts that have influenced design curating practice over the last two decades?

SU: More politicized design curatorial practices have brought immense value to our field. I also think that the boundaries between art and design have become ever more fluid. It is difficult to talk about these subjects as separate things because there is so much that brings them together. We have seen this shift acknowledged in art institutions engaging with design in recent years. In 2019 the ICA hosted a solo show by the Dutch design practice Metahaven and another by Forensic Architecture, who went on to win the Turner prize.

The Serpentine Galleries now have a design programme and in 2020 presented an exhibition of work by Formafantasma. I think that in contemporary art there is now an acknowledgement and appetite for design and architecture as critical subjects and investigative tools. Design is seen as intrinsic to contemporary art practice. I guess some design museums and curators would probably find it frustrating that contemporary art institutions are occupying this space, but I think it brings value in helping to elevate design to different and larger audiences. There has also been a rise in the status of the design curator. Early on in my career, there was Paola Antonelli but not many other design curators that you would religiously follow. Now we have curators like Joseph Grima, Jan Boelen, Marina Otera, Yesomi Umolu and Mariana Pestana, who exist within this hybrid field of contemporary art, design, architecture and pedagogy. They are undertaking research and curating large-scale biennials, where design sits alongside many other disciplines. The other key shift is technology and how it has transformed the way in which we view and experience design. Technology has also created new ways of presenting physical, interactive experiences in museums and galleries. It has enabled curatorial practice to expand in ways that were not possible previously.

DL: How have these developments impacted your own practice?

SU: My background is in art as well as design. As a result, I have developed an interdisciplinary practice which has expanded because of this greater fluidity between disciplines. In my own practice I work with a range of practitioners that include artists, architects and urbanists, as well as writers and philosophers. Seeing design curators exist within different social and cultural contexts, and witnessing design research becoming a more serious subject, has had a big impact on my work and the areas that I aspire to work within.

DL: What do you feel are the key debates driving design at this moment to which curators must respond?

SU: We are in the midst of an environmental crisis that is unavoidable and underpins everything that we do. I don't think we need to constantly have shows that are about waste or the Anthropocene, but I do think the game has shifted and these kinds of politics need to be inherent and infused in the content that we are platforming. The other aspect is race. I think the world, and more specifically the cultural sector, is beginning to recognize the drastic levels of inequality that exist in our museums, our collections, our programmes and our ways of working. Curators have a duty to reflect on their practice and to think about how they can develop, not only inclusive ways of working, but also more representative narratives and histories that have been overlooked, or deliberately concealed. It is no longer ok to ignore this. It never was, but now it will not be tolerated. In my view, that's very promising, but time will tell as to what changes actually come as a result of this awakening.

Design is a great tool for decolonizing and as design curators, it's up to us to use design to create more inclusive systems and frameworks.

I have seen a rise in the last twelve months, and even prior to the pandemic, in curators engaging with topics like care and empathy. These areas are finally being discussed critically in ways that they haven't been previously. The world is in a complete mess right now and we have to be thinking about what's next and how we can create a better future. Ideas around empathy and care are constantly evolving but, as practices, they feel more urgent than ever and it is right that design is trying to make sense of them. Curators are using biennials and exhibitions as frameworks to understand these emotions.

DL: What advice would you give to a young curator entering the field today? What skill set will the design curator of the future need to have?

SU: Because curating has become a more politicized practice, curators need to have their fingers on the pulse more than ever, in terms of being aware of what's happening in the world socially, economically and ecologically. All of these issues are becoming the topics that we respond to in our practice. If the Design Museum was looking to recruit an assistant curator, we would be looking for someone who has an understanding of these things. I think it's a different landscape from when I started out. I followed a very traditional route to become a curator. I firstly volunteered, which is a privilege that not everyone has, then became an assistant curator and worked my way up. That trajectory is still there but it's not the only way to become a curator. There are different avenues, skill sets and experiences that are super valuable. I think there has been a shift in journalists and writers entering the curatorial field. Most major institutions now have a chief curator or a curator who comes from that background. I'm not one of them but I think that style of curating has changed the game immensely. Exhibitions often have an editorial aspect to them, where important questions or topics are presented in a headline way that's very responsive and reactive to what's happening in the world. While that approach is important in order for institutions to remain relevant, it is still very important to have curators that have an understanding of the more traditional forms of curatorial practice and its processes.

An understanding of audiences and the actual mechanics of what it takes to put on an exhibition, from researching objects and developing narratives, to managing the installation. It's important to find ways of gaining those experiences. I think you can learn some of those skills on the job but it's important to have a fundamental understanding and respect of what it means to be a curator before you embark on this career. Understanding contemporary audiences is what young curators can bring to the game right now, particularly millennials who have grown up online and understand those audiences in ways that I and my peers don't fully understand. This knowledge is going to become invaluable for museums and institutions in the future, in understanding how to develop content that is relevant. I think there is a real opportunity for young, aspiring curators who want to develop new formats for those audiences to enter the field and to shake things up. Increasingly museums will be looking for those types of people in the future.

Renata Becerril

Design Curator and Critic
Founding Director of the International Design Festival, Abierto Mexicano de Diseño, Mexico City, Mexico
Interview: 10 October 2020

DONNA LOVEDAY: **How did you become a curator? How did it all start?**

RENATA BECERRIL: I was finishing my Architecture diploma in Querétaro City at the beginning of 2001. The director of the course had met Federico Zanco who was working on an exhibition for Vitra Design Museum. A colleague and I were invited to develop a research project for the exhibition. We presented our research to the curator, Mathias Schwarzt-Clauss, who really liked it and offered us the opportunity to work on the project. The exhibition, *Living in Motion: Design and Architecture for Flexible Dwelling*, opened at Vitra Design Museum in 2002. Undertaking this research opened my mind to the possibilities of design. I then went to France to work on the museum's summer workshops at Domaine de Boisbuchet. The workshops were run by internationally recognized artists, designers and architects. I was working alongside Ingo Maurer, Daniel Charny and Roberto Feo. The Bourroulec brothers and Matali Crasset were also there. For me, it was a very valuable experience. Following that period, I went to the museum in Germany to focus on the exhibition. Working with Mathias, I was contacting designers like Hella Jongerius to request objects for the exhibition and meeting with Alexander von Vegesack, the director of the museum. I was also spending a lot of time researching in the museum's archive, which became my second home. So for me that was the starting point. And then I moved to London. It was while working as an architect for a small practice in Hampstead that I came across the masters course in Curating Contemporary Design at Kingston University with the Design Museum, and I decided to apply. It was while studying that I realized that working as an architect, I had enjoyed being able to research a subject in depth and then think about how to explain that subject to a wider audience. I resolved that curating would allow me to do that. At that time, living and studying in London and visiting museums two or three times a week offered so many possibilities. I felt that curating was what I wanted to do. So yes, that was the starting point for everything.

DL: What was the first exhibition or project you curated?

RB: While doing research for the exhibition at Vitra Design Museum, I began to realize the importance of research to connect thoughts and ideas. I was interested in connecting my academic knowledge with the realities of today's word, so for me research was a way to further understand the areas I was interested in: design and exhibitions. This interest really comes from my childhood. My father was a politician, historian and philosopher. As a child I was surrounded by books; so knowledge was an emotional connection to my father. Before I decided to study architecture, I had thought about studying either graphic, industrial or fashion design. I like objects and creating things. But I realized that it didn't provide a strong enough theoretical basis for me. Architecture was a way forward in that respect but I discovered that curating took this further. The first exhibition I curated was an exhibition presented by the Mexican Embassy at RIBA as part of the London Festival of Architecture in 2008. The British Council had invited me to participate as part of their embassies programme. It was the first time the festival had included other countries. The exhibition was called *mAxico: Architectures from Mexico*. I commissioned five emergent architects based in Mexico City to create a work that could represent an important aspect of Mexico City but without using any reference to the usual architectural formats like drawings, models or photographs. I wanted to move away from the way architecture has been presented historically in the exhibition space. The brief also stipulated that the work needed to fit within a wooden crate of specific dimensions, so that it could be shipped inside the crate and used as part of the exhibit. This exhibition allowed me to expand my interest in research and also in design and architecture exhibition formats. My intention, through the project, was to communicate my reflections on these themes to the architects with the resulting works introducing other ways of displaying architecture.

DL: Have certain curators, exhibitions or encounters been decisive for you? What or who influenced your involvement in design?

RB: Firstly it was Vitra Design Museum. It was the first time I became aware of the importance of design in our material and visual landscape and the role of the curator. It was also my first face-to-face encounter with important figures related to design, which had a great impact on me. Other influences have been theorists and practitioners in the art and philosophy field, such as Nicolas Bourriaud, the French art historian and curator. His critical thinking and concepts such as relational aesthetics and post-production have shaped my thinking and my practice. I have also been influenced by Rem Koolhaas, the Dutch architect, whose architecture connects multiple perspectives that are drawn from politics, economics, culture and social interaction. There is extensive research behind each of his projects which can sometimes take more than a decade to realize. This rigorous approach to research exerted a huge influence on me. Another influential concept was put forward by Kristin Feireiss, a former director of the NAI in the Netherlands. She edited a book, *The Art of Architecture Exhibitions* (NAI, 2001). All the exhibitions featured in the book were created when she was directing the institute and came from the idea of raising awareness about the built environment. That for me was important, the potential of the exhibition to raise awareness.

DL: How would you define your practice? What is the motivation behind your work?

RB: At the core of my practice is research to understand what is behind everything conceptually. Certain writers have been crucial in building my knowledge, for example, the French philosopher and cultural theorist, Jean Baudrillard and his critical theory related to materialism. Also Louise Shouwenberg, who writes about the Dutch designer Hella Jongerius and how design connects us emotionally. This has guided my work as a curator and a consultant and helped to define my practice in raising awareness of our material and visual world, in order to better respond to it. I believe that the more we understand what's around us, the better choices we make in our everyday lives. I teach and write about design; so I try to raise awareness in every aspect of my work. I also see myself as a mediator between designers and the public. When I work with designers, I try to help them to solidify the theoretical and conceptual basis behind their production so that what they create can be more meaningful and long-lasting.

DL: You are the founding director of the international design festival, Abierto Mexicano de Diseño, the first of its type in Latin America. What prompted you to start the festival in 2013?

RB: It was a very organic process. Many of my friends are designers and architects who are helping to shape the cultural scene in Mexico. It was over dinner one evening that we said we needed to do more to help the design scene in Mexico and create a platform for everything that was happening in the city. There was a design week already taking place in Mexico City but it was more commercial and for established designers and international brands. We decided that we needed to create a new platform. So we started having weekly meetings and over the course of three months, we discussed how we could shape this platform. We didn't know exactly what form it would take but we knew that it was going to be a design festival. It would be a democratic platform for people connected to design, whether emerging designers or students, and would bring together international designers. But more importantly, we wanted a design event not created by designers for designers. We wanted to bring design to the broadest audience and connect design to the general public. In order to do that, we needed a space that was democratic and inclusive. We decided that it should be Mexico City's historic centre.

Mexico City comprises a series of neighbourhoods that are divided by social class. But the downtown area concentrates everyone. Everybody feels they have a connection to it, because it is where they buy their groceries but also where they go to see the opera. It also has the largest number of museums in Mexico City and in Latin America. The area is known as the city of palaces with almost fifty museums concentrated in a single area. We wanted to connect to those museums but also, more importantly, use the public space to connect audiences with design. It could be their first encounter with design that would not require the need for previous knowledge. We wanted people to almost stumble across works and be amazed by what they were seeing, which would then arouse a curiosity to find out what was behind the work. That for me is the first layer of curating, a visual layer, which then presents an opportunity to delve deeper. For the design festival in October 2015, we commissioned installations for the public square by designers such as Ultimo Grito, Kengo Kuma, Azuma Makoto, Morag Myerscough and Moritz Waldemeyer. We felt that people would find these spaces more accessible, than going to a museum to see an exhibition.

In Zocalo square, the most significant public space in Mexico City, Morag Myerscough and Luke Morgan created an installation that encouraged local people and passers-by to consider their surroundings. *Mira y Ver* (Ways of

Seeing) was a monumental, building-sized camera obscura where visitors could enter a colourful chamber through a large portal situated on a scaffold-supported structure (Figure 3.5). This raised platform allowed visitors to view the familiar plaza in perspectives and angles never before experienced. Once inside the dark room, the camera obscura effect worked to create an upside-down, two-dimensional projection of the outside environment. The phrase 'look & see' on the top of the installation, together with a giant eye, reiterated the artists' appeal to visitors to appreciate the sights and sounds around them. Similarly, a series of swings fixed underneath the platform allowed people to stop and rest within the plaza, while simultaneously participating in an enjoyable activity. By sharing this unexpected view, the artists hoped that local people and passers-by would see things they would normally ignore and enjoy the landscape of the city. An encounter with these works would then hopefully inspire people to attend a public talk with Stefan Sagmeister or take part in a workshop with Lance Wyman. We curated a talks programme that took place in the oldest and largest public park in Latin America. The talks attracted a wide audience, including homeless people who joined the talks and asked questions. Over time, we realized how important this idea of public space had become. For me, it has been a real discovery and a concept that I have actively developed

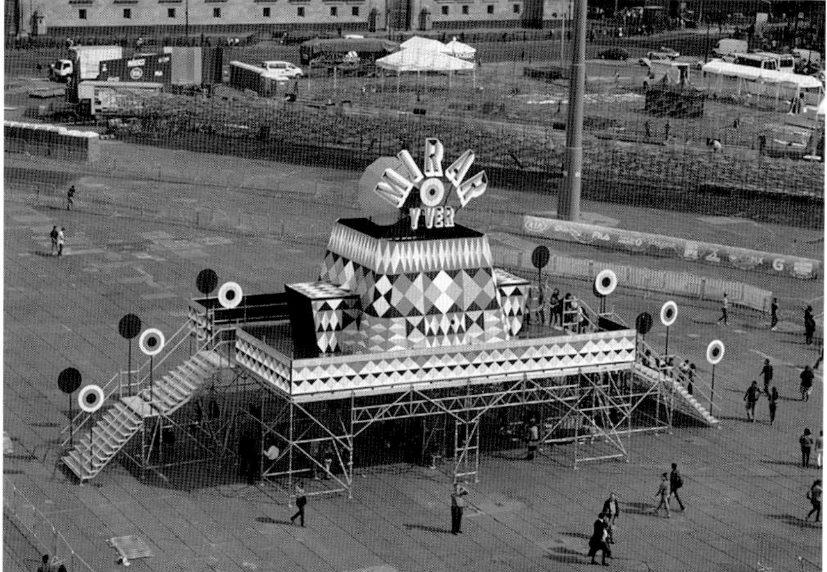

FIGURE 3.5 Mirar y Ver *(Ways of Seeing)*, *Morag Myerscough and Luke Morgan, commissioned by AMD for Zocalo Square, Mexico City, 2015.* © AMD/ *Alex Mejía.*

in my practice. I am involved with consultancy work for the government to develop a public space in the north of Mexico. The task is to bring people to a neglected Riverwalk which ten years ago underwent a major renovation project that did not consider the community. We are approaching it through what it is known as 'Placemaking', so using the existing assets and putting the community at the centre of the decisions in order to create a sense of place and belonging with the minimum of physical interventions.

DL: Can you describe the audience and market for design in Latin America?

RB: Mexico represents what is happening in Latin America on a larger scale. The market and the audience for design is quite niche because culture in Latin America is not democratic, especially in Mexico City. The audience is quite small but it has been broadening thanks to events like the design festival and the design week. There is also La Lonja MX, a local bazaar and pop-up market, where designers and makers sell new creations. The designers talk to the public about their work and that has really opened up the market for design in Mexico City. We have designers who work with artisans in rural communities or urban spaces, who create shoes, leather works or guitars. There are endless possibilities for a designer in Mexico, possibilities which make the creations quite unique and attract an international market.

DL: How has the design festival evolved since 2013?

RB: It has evolved in a really positive way. I directed the festival for five years from 2013 up until 2017 and I am now a member of the board. I have seen the festival programme expand but what has really changed is the quality of the exhibitions and projects. Since the beginning, we said that we would not be judges of the work, so we let in almost every proposal and the bad-quality projects will either become better or disappear altogether. And that is exactly what has happened. Now the quality of work is very high and always innovative. Since the first year we have created a pavilion for universities. We have seen a significant improvement in student projects, and some universities now include the festival as part of their teaching programme to develop festival projects. We have had many interesting collaborations and exhibitions, especially with ECAL in Switzerland. We have also seen how the festival has become a platform for designers and their work. In the first year we presented an exhibition of a stool collection by a young practice, La Metropolitana. The project was selected for the exhibition, *Beazley Designs of the Year* in 2014 at the Design Museum, London. Now the practice is ubiquitous across all of Mexico City's famous restaurants and they also created the furniture for Noma, an award-winning restaurant in Copenhagen.

DL: You now direct Capitales, a design consultancy and gallery. What are the aims behind the consultancy?

RB: When I left the festival in 2017, I was offering consultancy to brands. I had long wanted to set up a design gallery and to have a space for experimentation. I wanted a space that would bring together all the knowledge and experience I had accumulated and the new design that I was seeing. Curating exhibitions in a museum was too restrictive for me but having my own gallery gave me the possibility of working with a more experimental format. Then one day, I said I'm going to do it, this is what I'm going to call the gallery and this is the idea behind the gallery. It was one month from that day to the opening of the gallery. My first exhibition, *Artist's Proof*, in November 2018 put forward the idea behind the gallery as a space for thinking, creating and acquiring work. I wanted to work with designers to create meaningful objects and before creating the pieces, to think differently about what is produced. I wanted to promote the idea of collectable design but not in the traditional sense. Collectable design is often seen as expensive objects and this is not the idea. For me collectable design is an object, no matter what its monetary value, that is meaningful to you and your life, that will last forever and that you connect with intellectually and emotionally. I visited designer's studios and workshops and selected prototypes of one-off pieces to present in the gallery, almost as the first materialization of an idea before the object. The exhibition has since become an annual show. The gallery has three or four shows a year and the space reflects my approach to curating. I don't want to work within an institution. I want to have the flexibility to experiment with new frameworks and processes. Following this exhibition in February 2019, I was invited to represent the gallery in the design section of Zona MACA, Latin America's major art fair.

DL: There have been a plethora of publications on curating but they have mostly focused on the area of fine art curation, with design curation and the role of the design curator remaining largely unexplored. Why do you think the practice of design curating has been so neglected, despite being a growth area over the last twenty years?

RB: Design curating is a younger discipline when compared to art curation, which has a much longer history. A theory that may help to explain the more inferior status of design is an idea put forward by Nicolas Bourriaud, the French art historian and curator. He talked about eclectic art forms in which one can place design in relation to other examples of culture. He explains that the Western mentality rejects anything that falls out of the norm or attempts to pull away from the norm. Design doesn't fit into the cultural norm. I think design curating has established itself as a discipline but I don't think it has established itself as a cultural phenomena, as it is still viewed by many as a by-product of the Industrial Revolution. Design is still not seen as a cultural product like art, but rather as a product of industrial production, economics and capitalism. Of course, design feeds into this system but design also contributes in cultural terms.

DL: What is unique about the practice of curating design? What is distinctive about the role of the design curator?

RB: I think the difference between design and art is that design is understood socially, whereas art comes from the spirit of the creator which people don't always understand. But design connects with everyone because it is everywhere. It is an idea that is expressed well by designer and writer Kenya Hara. In his book, *Designing Design* (Lars Muller, 2014), he suggests that design is not art. It will never be art because we all understand what a chair or a vase is, even if it doesn't have a clear function. Designers like Hella Jongerius create objects that make us connect emotionally with our world and reflect on our environment. They can challenge our understanding of the world. I think that is unique about curating design because design expresses what is behind an object and how it is relevant to everyday life. Design exhibitions have the potential to present an object in all its material, aesthetic and intellectual depth. It can address issues that are relevant today so that people can become more aware of the world around them.

DL: What do you feel are the essential components of a good design exhibition?

RB: Exhibitions that go beyond the first visual impressions of an object and delve deeper into where an object comes from, in terms of its materiality but also intellectually. I see design exhibitions or design criticism working as a taxonomy of an object in three scales. The scale is related to the object itself: understanding its technical level, the materials it is made of and its aesthetics. The second scale is related to its context: what connections the object creates with its user whether in terms of its function, the emotional connections or how the object contributes to the design discipline. The third scale is the largest and considers how the object works within a system: how it is used and how it contributes socially, environmentally and economically.

DL: How can design curators and design institutions more successfully interact and engage with their audiences?

RB: I think that institutions need to break down any barriers that prevent a natural connection with audiences, which could be an intimidating building or the high cost of an admission ticket. So for me the public space is the democratic arena where we can connect with any audience. Design exhibitions should express what's behind an object, to convey the technicalities that allow an object or image to come to life. All these things need to be presented in a way that enables people to approach knowledge in an accessible way. For example, architecture exhibitions present architectural plans but many people are not equipped to read plans. As curators we need to find ways of expressing everything that surrounds a project in a way that connects with people. It's important that people can fully take part in an encounter with an object or a project. Exhibitions need to promote curiosity in the visitor. An exhibition is just a starting point; it needs to suggest other possibilities. I see exhibitions as teaching. Good teachers do not only transmit knowledge, they stimulate a quest for knowledge.

DL: What are the key shifts that have influenced design curating practice over the last two decades?

RB: I think there have been many shifts. One key shift is the move away from design as simply beautiful objects and putting forward the idea that design is a discipline that has a positive impact on our world. It is expressed through objects but also through ideas and concepts that help us to navigate our world in a better way. Design deals with the relevant issues of today's world. A number of exhibitions curated at MoMA and the Cooper Hewitt, Smithsonian Design Museum, New York have explored this aspect such as *Design for the Other 90%* in 2007. It was an exhibition that focused on socially responsible objects for those in need and designs that contributed to solve the world's problems. This approach of design thinking in a broader sense connects design to other disciplines. For example, exhibitions like *Formula One: The Great Design Race* that took place at the Design Museum, London in 2006 communicated the importance of design in the process of creating an F1 car. It considered the thinking behind the complex technical solutions to the graphics for a car or a race. Design exhibitions can go beyond objects; they can present the entire context of an object, be it social, economic, cultural, environmental or political. By contrast, art exhibitions have historically tried to detach the object from any context; the concept of the white cube clearly expresses this idea.

DL: How have these developments impacted your own practice?

RB: They have all informed my practice in some way and broadened my understanding of design. I think that the exhibition is just a starting point for a broader conversation which can be enhanced by discursive events around it, such as talks, performances and workshops. Design exhibitions are evolving in the way they present themselves. They create a narrative that explains an object in its broadest context in order to better understand and raise awareness of our world. This idea has probably become the most important in terms of guiding my work, whether it is exhibitions, writing, teaching or consulting.

DL: What do you feel are the key debates driving design at this moment to which curators must respond?

RB: A key debate is how to present design as a force to inform but also influence, to see design as part of a whole structure where it is related to the environment, politics, the economy, culture and society. It is so important for a curator to express to an audience that everything is connected. We need to focus on how we can use design to imagine the future by creating meaningful objects and projects. I also think curators need to envisage new spaces for showing design. The idea of a museum or an institution is perhaps now obsolete, although it is necessary as a repository of knowledge. We still need history books but we also need other ways of connecting with audiences that involve new formats. It comes back to the idea of the public space as a democratic space. I really think that this is the answer to many of the issues we are facing, because this is where we can express concepts democratically. There is now another concept that tries to move away from the idea of public space. The Greek architect and activist, Stavros Stavrides, has said that, because a public space is managed by the government, it is not a truly democratic space. The public space should be renamed as a common space because common space is constructed by the people and it does not require the involvement of an institution or a government. It is not hierarchical.

DL: What advice would you give to a young curator entering the field today? What skill set will the design curator of the future need to have?

RB: My advice to a young curator would be to challenge paradigms. If we don't, then we had better not do anything. And to be utopian in our thinking. In an interview José Mujica, a former president of Uruguay, said that we all need to allow for utopia in our lives, this is what allows a better world to happen, and that has never been more important than it is now. Curators need to have the skills to translate what's happening around them and to communicate it in an accessible way. If you want to work inside a museum or a cultural institution, maybe you don't need to work so broadly. I think if you really want to achieve things you need to talk to everyone, and that includes politicians and industry. You need to build a network and connect with as many people as you can. I think the future role of the design curator is to be a forecaster. They need to be able to read the world, the zeitgeist, to understand what is important today and what will become relevant for the world in the future. They will need to use the exhibition space as a place for reflection and as a platform for conversations between theorists, designers, makers, politicians, industry and society. We need to challenge established ideas and to be open to new ways of presenting work. As curators, if we want a better world and a better future, we need to act differently.

Fleur Watson

Executive Director and Chief Curator
Centre for Architecture Victoria | Open House Melbourne, Australia
Interview: 10 November 2020

DONNA LOVEDAY: How did you become a curator? How did it all start?

FLEUR WATSON: My pathway to curatorial practice has been shaped by a diverse set of experiences with roles across design, editing and expanded cultural production. I originally studied design in Western Australia in the mid-1990s and, through that process, I started to think about how design ideas could be explored in different ways and beyond traditional modes of practice. As a student, I explored critical writing and, after graduating, I did a further qualification in journalism which led to freelance commissions as a design writer. In 2001, I moved from Melbourne to Sydney to take up the editorship of *Monument* magazine and this proved a critical period. The experience and intensity of editing and curating the magazine over a seven-year period was fundamental in shaping my understanding of the diversity of practice, culture and issues that architects and designers were engaged with across Australia. It was a vibrant time for design journals in Australia. In addition to *Monument*, there were another three or four good design publications that all pursued specific angles or agendas, and that diversity created a healthy culture for design publishing at the time. At *Monument* magazine, we were passionate about supporting and amplifying the quality of Australian architecture and placing it firmly in the local and international context. We were also very engaged with publishing as a cultural act; so events, debates and small exhibitions were very important as ways to mediate design beyond the pages of the magazine. In 2006, I moved to London to study a masters in Curating

Contemporary Design at Kingston University and the Design Museum. I was still editor of *Monument* at the time and the MA enabled me to test new ideas within a project-based model. I was able to explore the kind of criticality that I wanted to bring to curating through the lens of collaborative practice and a desire to test ideas in the exhibition space in open exchange with audiences. When I returned to Australia, I was committed to testing these ideas further and pursuing a more porous and open-ended type of practice. I was interested in curating across diverse formats including critical writing, exhibitions, installations, performances and discursive programmes across physical and digital space.

DL:　What was the first exhibition or project you curated?

FW:　When I returned to Australia, I developed a trilogy of small, modest curatorial projects in close collaboration with design practice March Studio, who have since become long-time collaborators and colleagues. It's interesting, because when I look back now, I can see a strong conceptual, curatorial and design thread between all three projects that possibly wasn't so evident to us at the time.

The first project called *After Dark* (2009) was conceived as a late-night discussion club for the State of Design Festival, a government-funded programme that ran from 2008 to 2011. *After Dark* was conceived and curated as an intimate and informal space for local Melbourne-based creative practitioners to meet, exchange ideas and debate their shared concerns. While we celebrated the fact that state money was supporting such a large-scale design event, *After Dark* was an intuitive response to the context of a government-funded festival that generally focused on connecting design with business and industry towards job creation, rather than exploring design as an ideas-driven practice and a cultural pursuit. What we identified was a real lack of opportunity for people coming into Australia from all over the world for the festival to meet and exchange ideas with local practitioners, in a space where that could happen more informally and spontaneously. *After Dark* was conceived as a temporary 'set' for a programme of debates and conversations between international and local practitioners. Working with Aesop, we took over the basement in their warehouse space in Collingwood. The company was quite young and progressive at the time. The installation itself was designed and constructed entirely from yellow trace paper to create a heightened sense of encounter and transformation. Here, we staged a series of presentations by local practitioners and international designers such as Dunne & Raby, Nipa Doshi from Doshi Levien, John Warricker, March Studio, Kovac Studio and others. The intent was to create a kind of scenography and intensity of conditions for new connections to happen and to expose international design leaders to the great work that was happening in Australia at a local level. More than a decade on, it's interesting to see how many of these local practitioners have progressed from emergent design studios to leading practices both in Australia and internationally.

Working integrally with March Studio, I went on to do two more of these very rapid, tight-budget and temporal projects within the design festival context. For the 2009 Melbourne Fashion Festival we produced an installation titled *Figment* in collaboration with the jewellery store, e.g. etal. *Figment* focused on Melbourne's vibrant contemporary jewellery community and examined the generative processes used by a small collective of seven emerging and avant-garde practitioners. The challenge was to subvert the focus on the object itself to reveal the ideas, drawings and tests crucial to the making process. To achieve this inversion, the installation was composed of twenty old overhead projectors in the centre of the space, each with a new work by each artist simply placed or hung on the glass plate of each projector. Through this process of projection and layering, we recognized that something transformative was happening. Lit and glowing from beneath, the objects and their projected shadows, overlaid with the sketches and images that inspired their making, performed to the audience the process that connected the maker to the end-object.

DL: Have certain curators, exhibitions or encounters been decisive for you? What or who has influenced your involvement in design?

FW: There are curators and exhibitions that have resonated deeply or have been influential to my practice over the years. They are often those practitioners or projects which are sited outside of the established museum institution or traditional modes of curatorial practice. My research for a PhD, and now a book with Routledge, was based on the idea of the 'new curator' in relation to exhibiting design ideas, process and research. It's important to be clear that I'm not interested to set up a binary between the old and the new. Nor am I proposing that custodianship, museology and institution-based curatorship is not extremely valuable. However, I am interested in an emergent form of practice that is research-driven, exploratory, porous and investigative. I am interested in the curator's ability to bring critical and sometimes difficult questions into the public realm. Practitioners working within and between the boundaries of curating, design practice and research, such as Marina Otera Verzier, Mimi Zeiger and Beatrice Leanza, come immediately to mind. All of these curators position cultural production and design exhibitions in a sociopolitical context to question or reveal something about design's role in shaping our contemporary life. Then, of course, there are established curators such as Paola Antonelli. Paola continues to be a pivotal influence because of her commitment and dexterity in articulating and mediating nascent design research and critical issues in the exhibition space in a way that is very engaging and accessible for the public yet still pushes the boundaries of the institution. I would also reference Kayoko Ota and Judith Clarke's ability to use modes of research as a way to ask questions and to reveal new ideas that might relate to contemporary life.

I have great respect for the rigour, development and sense of community fostered by the exhibitions and programmes produced by the CCA, Canadian Centre for Architecture, particularly under the directorship of Giovanna Borasi. Their recent publication, *The Museum Is Not Enough* (Sternberg Press, 2019) is very aligned with current curatorial practice and discourse and has influenced my own interest in the exhibition space as a place for critical enquiry and research. There are so many influential exhibitions to cite, but I was completely engaged with *A Stroll through a Fun Palace* curated by Hans Ulrich Obrist with Luis Burkhardt for the Swiss Pavilion exhibition at the Venice Architecture Biennale (2012). For the exhibition, Obrist takes a conceptual leaping-off point from the speculative work of architect Cedric Price to imagine the future of the museum. Together, they draw from Price's quote that 'a 21st century museum will utilise calculated uncertainty and conscious incompleteness to produce a catalyst for invigorating change whilst always producing the harvest of the quiet eye'.[1] A performance envelops Price's and Burckhardt's production, selecting drawings from the archives and re-presenting them, along with the stories of their making, to the public. I think this performative mode, particularly in the context of the frenetic pace of the Biennale, was successful in illustrating how looking back at the past, through interpreting the archive, can be so powerful in reimagining the future.

Closer to home, I have found that working collaboratively with other curators and designers produces the most powerful opportunities to test ideas and create an active exchange with audiences. *Occupied* (2016) at RMIT Design Hub is a good example of this collaborative structure and was co-curated with David Neustein and Grace Morlock of Other Architects (Figure 3.6). The exhibition responded directly to a startling statistic that was receiving much press and radio attention at the time; by 2050, Melbourne is projected to overtake Sydney as Australia's most populous city, with 8 million inhabitants to Sydney's 7.5 million. The exhibition was a fantastic opportunity to bring in approaches from other cities around the world that were grappling with similar issues. As co-curators we posed the question: How can architecture respond to this rapid growth by doing more with less, by retrofitting, adapting and repurposing existing structures

---

[1] Cedric Price in a private interview with Hans Ulrich Obrist (1997), catalogue, *A Stroll through a Fun Palace*, Swiss Pavilion, Venice Architecture Biennale, 2014.

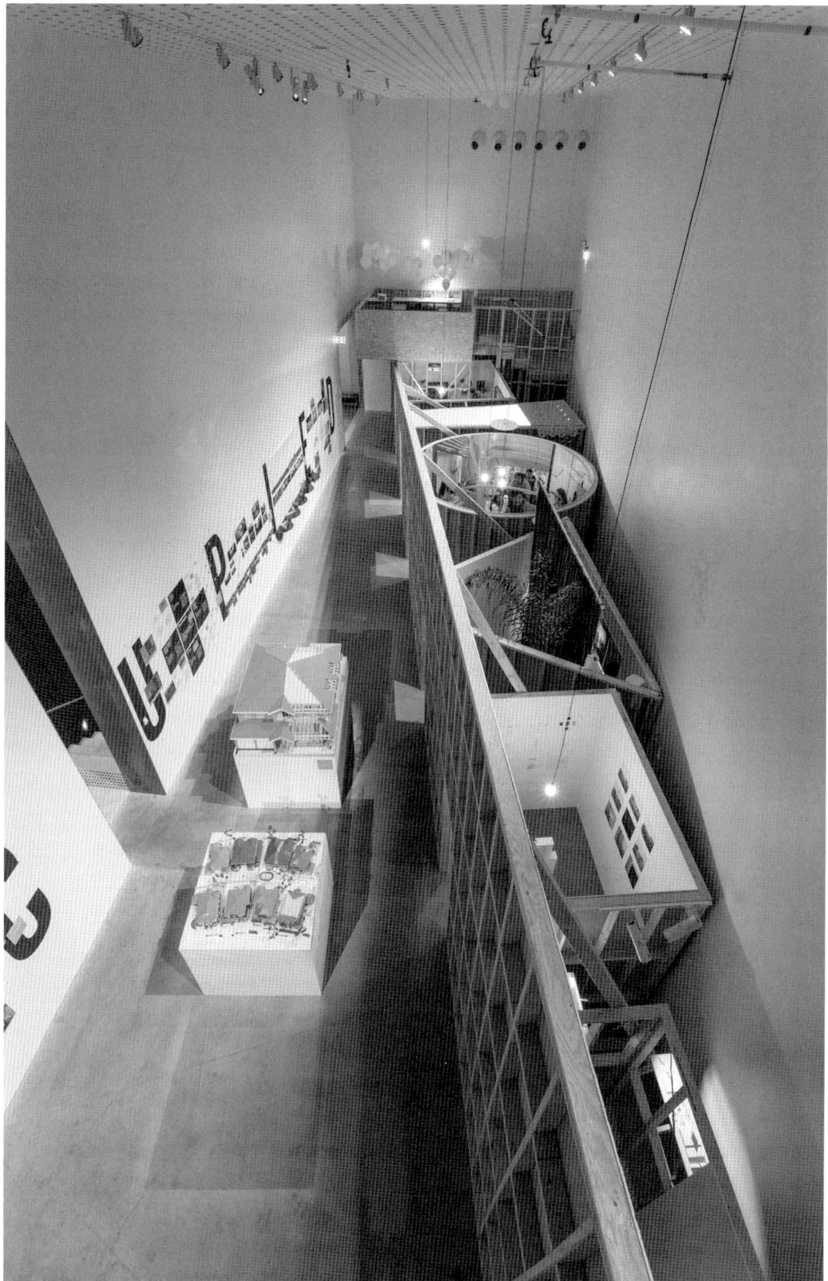

FIGURE 3.6 Occupied, *curated by Fleur Watson with David Neustein and Grace Morlock of Other Architects, RMIT Design Hub, Melbourne, 2016. © Tobias Titz.*

and environments in a way that is both transformative and optimistic? In response to this provocation, we invited twenty-three local and international practitioners to exhibit small-scale, contingent design ideas and projects that operated at the margins of bureaucratic grey zones or emerging economies. The ideas took the form of built and ongoing projects, installation, models, residencies, processes, performances, smartphone apps and collaborative platforms, including an in-situ residency and Airbnb-like space within the exhibition itself. The works created for the exhibition ranged from pragmatism to installation to speculation. We were interested in bringing a diverse mix of people and ideas together to really thrash out these quite complex issues, and by performing the issues of the time inviting direct exchange with the audience.

DL: How would you define your practice? What is the motivation behind your work?

FW: My curatorial practice has focused on exploring, translating and mediating design research and process. I have often worked in spaces outside of the traditional museum or institution. The idea of a responsive, or even rapid, curatorial practice embracing experimentation, live tests and unfinished 'process' works within the exhibition space is interesting to me. A thread running through the collection of projects is an interest in evolving ideas of what might be called a 'performative' practice for architecture and design. Of course, it's not really performative in the context of visual arts or theatre. My intention in using that term is to deliberately reframe the idea of performative as being about mediating and translating a design process in exchange with audiences. In this respect, I'm interested in a more 'open' curatorial hand that is porous and inherently collaborative. In this respect, the curator isn't in the position of expert or custodian but one where there is an intent to reveal or 'tune' into the contemporary condition and make sense of the issues in the world around us, and how design might have agency or respond to that context. The designers that I work with, as well as writers, filmmakers and other creative practitioners, are all embedded into the very beginning of the process so that the final outcome is not something that feels particularly orchestrated. It is a multi-authored, iterative process that builds over time to become a place for active exchange.

DL: From 2012 to 2020, you were curator at Design Hub Gallery and industry fellow at RMIT University where you co-directed an ambitious programme. What initially prompted you to apply for this role and how were you able to develop the gallery's programme?

FW: Curating the exhibition programme at RMIT Design Hub was an extraordinary opportunity because, at the time, it was the largest space dedicated to architecture and design practice in Australia. It was also very deliberately positioned as a project space, or laboratory-like 'hub', with a commitment to exhibiting and translating design research and cross-disciplinary practice across creative disciplines. At the time, there wasn't any such space and opportunity for a progressive form of design curation in Australia. Design Hub Gallery is a public space; it is for everyone and free to experience and actively take part in the exhibitions and programmes. It brings the academy of researchers, lecturers and students together with creative practitioners and the public in one place. As a result, it presented a fantastic opportunity to engage many different people from different perspectives to grapple with the messy, iterative, process-driven realities of design.

At Design Hub, we were interested in experimenting with different formats and methods that could explore design from a diverse set of experiences. We considered how we could develop a programme beyond the traditional exhibition, as an installation, scenography, performance, series of workshops or a debate. We programmed around other events and academic pursuits and resisted the traditional six-to-eight-week turnaround. The programme was multilayered and international from the very beginning. We curated small-scale exhibitions that were experimental in approach. We also curated large-scale exhibitions, working with international institutions such as Mode Museum, Antwerp and the Design Museum, London. There was always an intention within that model to create an exchange with others and bring new knowledge into the public realm. We were able to work within a relatively rapid turnaround time for producing these types of quite ambitious programmes. I think that rapidness is quite important. As I learned, the flip side is a slowness that does allow more of a rigour and depth, but it also has the downside of not being able to be very responsive to the issues of the moment. In addition, the heavy production that sometimes goes with an exhibition in development for a long period of time can bring with it a weight of expectation which can make it difficult to take risks. At Design Hub, we were able to take a risk and to stand by that risk. The most important outcome was that the work generated discussion and debate.

DL: You have recently taken up a new role as executive director and chief curator for the Centre for Architecture Victoria and Open House Melbourne. What ambitions do you have for the organization and in developing the programme?

FW: The sense of goodwill and trust that the Open House Melbourne programme has generated over thirteen years is really quite extraordinary; it is a much-loved cultural event and offering for the city. For the new Centre for Architecture, a new independent and not-for-profit organization, the intent is to build upon that goodwill and trust to create a new meeting place. It will launch digitally through a distributed series of 'in the real' exhibition and programmes with like-minded partners and collaborators. The Centre for Architecture will foster public appreciation for architecture and public engagement in conversations about the future of our cities. Through programmes, exhibitions, conversations, performances and publications, we intend to explore and ask questions about the world around us, making space to imagine, test and risk new ideas. But most of all, I hope that the Centre for Architecture will be an open place for discovery, questioning and experimentation in how quality design in our built environment means that we can all live and work better together.

I think there is a big responsibility here because our cities, regions and communities are facing challenging issues in respect to the built environment and public life. What are the pressing challenges that we need to address in terms of creating a quality built environment for everybody? Some of those issues are challenging but urgent, such as unceded sovereignty and the trauma of Australia's colonial past. We can no longer pretend that our buildings are built on neutral ground; they are not. How do we address ecology being at the centre of everything? How do we address human and non-human life being equal? How do we promote accessibility and inclusiveness? For me the vision is to embrace and amplify the urgent conversations that are going on around us and show how spatial practice has a critical part to play in addressing those issues. The Centre for Architecture is very deliberately named a centre, rather than a museum, gallery or foundation, because it is envisaged as a place where architects, designers, creative practitioners, artists, policymakers, community leaders and the public of Melbourne can meet and come together.

DL: How has your work as a curator, designer, writer and editor been fundamental in shaping the focus of your practice and your academic research?

FW: I think a process of reflection, across different projects, modes and disciplines, can be a very useful way to think about a practice. You start to see what it is that interests you but also what you react against or feel strongly about. That process starts to give you a sense of what your position is and what you want your contribution to be. How can the curator create programmes, exhibitions, debates, performances, publications or podcasts that have a central idea or position that starts to build over time to form a contribution? My research for a PhD definitely helped me to find this space and to connect with many people who are like-minded in their approach to their practice. Exhibitions ask lots of questions but how can you encourage people to really engage with a subject and to feel that they are part of the process of making the exhibition with you? That comes back to the idea of a performative practice and of an active exchange. It is important for me that the ideas in the PhD continue to be tested and to expand, and that it doesn't stop with a thesis. The research led to the commission for a book that looks at these hybrid, collaborative and porous forms of curatorial practice. What do we mean when we talk about a performative practice? What do we mean when we talk about a set of conditions that allow interactions to happen? These questions are important because we have huge issues to face and we have great knowledge around us. How can we bring those elements together to create the kinds of spaces in which we can think about, test, encounter and debate ways in which we can live together in a better way? That is my interest but also where I hope I can make a contribution.

DL: There have been a plethora of publications on curating but they have mostly focused on the area of fine art curation, with design curation and the role of the design curator remaining largely unexplored. Why do you think the practice of design curating has been so neglected, despite being a growth area over the last twenty years?

FW: It's a really interesting question because exhibitions of architecture, particularly of drawings, have a long history. Arguably, exhibitions of design were a response to the modernist movement; Phillip Johnson's *Machine Art* at MoMA (1934) was seminal in this respect and preceded by *Modern Architecture* (1932). One of the major shifts has been a move beyond representation of the architectural or design object to that of curating design as a process or as a contributor to a system. It is a collective move away from understanding architecture as a singular built object in the landscape or a collective or individual practice. I think there is now a great interest in the culture and civic responsibility of architecture and how architects can bring their skills in other ways, beyond designing objects, to contribute to making better spaces in which we can all live and work. I think it's interesting that younger designers and architects are finding different ways of using their education and spatial knowledge, working with communities and local government or contributing to policymaking in advocacy organizations. We need those kinds of skills and ways of thinking.

I think there is a shift in traditional forms of curatorial practice towards a more expansive form of cultural production. I have rarely worked in the kind of traditional museum model where you have very distinct specialized 'departments' such as curatorial, education, public programmes and collections. I think that kind of 'silo' approach is breaking down quite quickly here in Australia. Curators are working in many different kinds of spaces such as digital, publication, public space, local council, community projects or small not-for-profit organizations. They are working independently across art, design and architecture. And whilst I feel there needs to be some specialization around design and architecture, I also see that there are opportunities to allow those boundaries to blur. For me the biggest issue is criticality. How do curators working in a more expanded field of cultural production develop their own position and criticality? In reality they are going to be working with large institutions, government organizations, sponsors, private enterprise, all people that come with a particular agenda. It's so important to learn how to conceptualize, make and then steer a project through that territory, whether it's a podcast, an exhibition, an intervention in public space, a digital project or a publication. I am always optimistic when I see how the next generation of curators, architects and designers around me are so dexterous and determined at managing their way through that noise and spectacle to make good, critical and challenging ideas happen.

DL: **What is unique about the practice of curating design? What is distinctive about the role of the design curator?**

FW: I'm not always convinced that it's useful to try to guard or 'claim ground' for the design curator. As you'll have noted, many of us come from other backgrounds and experiences, many are former editors and journalists who become curators, myself included! I met a curator recently who is an environmental scientist and doing the most incredible work. If you have a critical position, you can extend that into a curatorial format. Saying that, my own experience has been that there is a certain skill in design curation, particularly those people who come to design curation from some form of spatial practice. They seem to be able to spatialize and translate an idea to create a kind of charged environment for encounter and exchange. Those exhibitions are the ones that I personally respond to and that are fundamental to my practice. At Design Hub, we established an 'expression of interest' process for inviting ideas and proposals from our community which was so important in reaching beyond our 'bubble' of usual collaborators. It's an approach that I hope to continue at the Centre for Architecture. I noticed that some of the proposals that come to us are often important ideas that are well formed, thoughtful and critical, but they are not exhibitions. They are a book or a film or maybe a podcast. They are all curatorial projects but not necessarily right for a spatial experience, and often it's quite hard to unlock people from this idea of a physical exhibition. The idea could take a different form, but one which still brings people together around a critical idea or issue. You can bring a curatorial frame to a piece of critical writing or column for a newspaper, for example.

DL: What do you feel are the essential components of a good design exhibition?

FW: That's a difficult question because a good experience of a design exhibition can be something very different to a 'checklist' of what technically makes a good exhibition. Certainly, I have visited a retrospective exhibition of a body of work and really enjoyed it, where I feel I have gained new insights and have been immersed in the experience of encountering that work. However, I am more interested in a different mode of practice, one that is less concerned with the 'canon' or placing a designer or body of work in a historical continuum. I am more interested in a critically reflective exhibition. How does the space, content and opportunities for exchange, both physical or digital, help to position design in relationship to the world that we live in today? How does it reflect or reveal something new that we may not have previously considered or been aware of? In this respect, design exhibitions can open up new ways of thinking about an issue. They can allow us to bring our imaginations, perspective and experience into the mix. In this way, it's a form of social choreography or a setting of the conditions for exchange.

DL: So can the exhibition be a starting point, rather than the end point?

FW: Cultural institutions around the world are under huge pressure at this moment, and it's likely we are all going to have to operate differently in the future. What opportunities are there to instigate or develop part of a curatorial project that might then further develop elsewhere and with others? For example, is it possible to curate a 'chapter' or part of a project that then might evolve further in collaboration with other like-minded organizations or individuals? I find the idea of a distributed curatorial projects exhibition very compelling and it's definitely something I'd like to explore further. I also spoke earlier about the idea of 'layering' within an exhibition. It is an approach where you don't necessarily have to read an exhibition in a linear way; sections can overlap and grow or change through the life of the exhibition itself.

DL: How can design curators and design institutions more successfully interact and engage with their audiences?

FW: Recently, I have been considering the opportunities for curators and cultural producers working within individual organizations, as well as independent curators, to work in a distributed way? How can we create a networked environment where we tackle certain issues, ideas or concepts collectively? Is it possible to think about certain spaces or organizations that lend themselves to a slower, longer and more reflective enquiry? Other spaces might be more 'rapid' and 'pacey' in the way they approach a particular set of ideas to respond to an immediate issue or condition. How might these fast and slow spaces be networked so that they can inform each other, and possibly even layer over each other? Additionally, how might we work within spaces outside the museum, gallery or institution, such as public spaces, community spaces, places of transition and digital spaces? How do you start to connect these spaces, as you might imagine a festival approach, but not linked to a specific time frame or themes? There are certainly small independent cultural producers here in Melbourne who are starting to test the idea of 'disorganizing' the individual organization to create new types of hybrid entities. There is a shared understanding that, collectively, we have more dexterity and an ability to offer our audiences richer and more layered experiences.

DL: What are the key shifts that have influenced design curating practice over the last two decades?

FW: I think there is a distinct shift in how design curation has moved beyond the object or singular building in the landscape, or a monographic or group practice survey, towards an understanding of design as an expanded and cultural practice. Hopefully, we are also seeing a breakdown of the public profile and appeal of the 'starchitect' or celebrity designer. I think we are starting to see a real shift in curatorial practice that considers design within our social, political and environmental context. There is a focus on how we can translate the value of a design process and what design can do to contribute to the collective public good. I have always been interested in working with emerging curators, designers and creative practitioners. I find that there is a very natural intuition to think in a more relational way and to interrogate how design relates to contemporary concerns, such as the ongoing impact of colonialism, rapid destruction of biodiversity, the climate crisis and addressing the need for increased access and inclusivity towards creating better communities, cities and regional centres for everyone.

DL: How have these developments impacted your own practice?

FW: This exploratory, responsive and relational curatorial approach has been central to many of the collaborative projects at RMIT Design Hub. For example, in 2018, along with Naomi Stead and Kate Rhodes, we co-curated an exhibition called *Workaround: Design, Women, Action* (25 July–11 August 2018). *Workaround* identified, assembled and created a platform for an emerging movement of women who were focused on advocacy and activism in design practice. It focused on practitioners working towards positive change in the built environment and its surrounding cultures, and women working outside existing conventions. In this context, the exhibition had an explicitly activist agenda: to reveal and demonstrate tangible examples of practitioners working differently. The exhibition took the form of a performative 'set' of component parts that could be rearranged and configured to 'fit' each exhibitor. Designed by Sibling Architecture, a series of daily 'live in gallery' episodes were produced by each invited exhibitor and included workshops, performances, discussions and participatory programmes. Fourteen daily 'episodes' were performed live within the project spaces and streamed in real time via the Design Hub Gallery website. The events ranged from live conversations, interviews, debates, workshops, readings, writing and cooking sessions, to interactive performances that articulated strategies for workarounds in relation to design activism.

Monash University's XYX Lab held a participatory open workshop which invited groups of young women and girls to explain how they would design cities to be safer using their knowledge and lived experience of fear and actual threat in urban space. DJ and architectural researcher Simona Castricum's episode and live performance of 'What If Safety Was Permanent', interrogated the way that the design of urban spaces, infrastructures and networks regularly manifest as hostile for gender-diverse people. Guest, Riggs (Kate Riggs and Stephanie Guest) explored the notion of 'hasty work' through cooking a meal, and exposing the experience of working in the gaps of time available in the early years of motherhood, temporary workspaces, long commutes and insecure living accommodation. Many of the women who hosted the episodes mentioned that the one aspect they found incredibly difficult to explain or articulate was the form and process of their practice, which was so different to that of conventional design practice. By literally exhibiting the people and their process, rather than works, we were able to communicate the value of this activist work to a wide audience through both the physical performances and the digital platform. It goes back to the earlier comment about exhibitions potentially revealing new ways of working and provoking new connections rather than focusing on interpretation. *Workaround* was incredibly important in revealing and amplifying these activist practices that were operating in the margins.

DL: What do you feel are the key debates driving design at this moment to which curators must respond?

FW: Without doubt, in Australia, we must acknowledge and address the trauma of our colonial past and the impact of that trauma and unceded sovereignty on Indigenous Australians. In relation to design and the built environment, we need to recognize that the land that we are speaking about, engaging with or proposing any kind of design proposition for, is unceded land and that Indigenous People have lived in this country for over sixty thousand years. They have a deep spiritual and cultural connection to the land and incredible knowledge and expertise to share in how we should care for this country.

Of course, the global climate crisis is of utmost urgency. The communities at the frontline of the devastating bushfires of 2019–20 in Australia are still in crisis mode. This situation has only been made more painful by the Covid-19 pandemic, and speaks so clearly to the impact of human-induced climate change. Curatorially, I am interested in the movement towards a 'nature centred' design process, where the design process acknowledges the natural and human world as being equal stakeholders to the design outcome or impact. We all want and need access to clean waterways, clean air and clean energy. We want biodiversity in our natural world and to protect our environment. We don't want extreme weather conditions that devastate our communities and wildlife. We all have to work towards a collective good which is for everyone's benefit, and design has a really important part to play in that discussion. Most recently, there has been some inspiring writing that explores what we might learn from living through the pandemic and how we might shift to new ways of working so we can live, study and work within a smaller geographical zone, the 20-mile city for example. How can we create access to safe, quality housing for everyone? How do we protect our public spaces from private interests? How do we encourage communities to grow their own food, slow down our traffic, plant more trees and provide more access to parks and green spaces? All these small, yet crucial moves are fundamental to how we live our lives better in the future and how we create more connected communities.

DL: What advice would you give to a young curator entering the field today? What skill set will the design curator of the future need to have?

FW: I think the most important thing is to be open to opportunities and to approach every project with a curious and critical mind.. Sometimes that requires research and experience and sometimes it's just about asking simple questions such as, what is the contribution? In Australia, curatorial roles in the museum or institution are rare. The upside is that there is a certain freedom in being able to try many different forms of curatorial practice and modes of cultural production. It might be curating a series of talks or a publication, developing a festival, working with a community project or local government, curating a series of digital works or an online programme. During the pandemic, it has been revealing to experience the banality of so many 'talking head' online presentations, which are not very compelling. How can we find more tangible and engaging ways to meet and exchange ideas in digital space? *Design Emergency*, an Instagram Live series founded by design curator, Paola Antonelli with design critic, Alice Rawsthorn, is a really good example of how digital content can be more responsive than a traditional exhibition could ever be. I recently contributed to a series made during lockdown called *Spaced Apart*, created and developed by the creative practice, U_P, which was another good example of a digital programme that was rapidly responsive to current conditions and fostered through shared exchange.

My own experience has taught me that sometimes it is important to take risks and to be independent in order to make a project happen. In 2010, I co-founded an independent gallery called Pin-up Project Space in Collingwood, as part of a larger collective of creative practitioners in a large-scale warehouse space. The space was not funded in any official capacity but, somehow through the generosity of so many collaborators, we managed to make some fantastic projects happen on very little resources. For example, *The Housing Project* focused on the inner-city suburbs of Collingwood and Fitzroy and the rapid gentrification and cultural displacement that was taking place in the area. The project was curated in three parts, as a community-led artwork by Greyspace, featuring interactive architectural models that triggered the sounds of interviews with local residents telling their histories and personal stories. A curated film documented fourteen architect-designed housing projects currently in development, being built or recently completed in the neighbourhood. The project culminated in an open-invitation community debate night to interrogate and reflect upon the pressures of rapid gentrification, densification and access to social, community and affordable housing in the inner-ring suburbs. The Office for the Victorian Government Architecture provided a very modest amount of funding and we were able to invest in the equipment to professionally record the event. We also produced a broadcast programme with ABC radio. Additionally, we made a 'reader' that documented the debate. The publication was produced very rapidly within forty-eight hours using a risograph and spiral-binding process. *The Housing Project* installation, debate and publication captured a moment in time and a conversation with the local community that would have been very difficult for a larger public institution to achieve in the time frame and with the same sense of immediacy. It was a very good example of what can be done with very little resources but with a critical and collaborative team, responsive curatorial ambition and the freedom to take risks.

Wilhelm Finger and
Melita Skamnaki

Directors and Co-founders, Double Decker, London, UK
Interview: 24 September 2020

DONNA LOVEDAY: How did you become curators? How did it all start?

WILHELM FINGER: My background is in communications. After studying communication design at Central Saint Martins, London, in 2001, I worked in various art director roles in the fashion and music industry. I started a publishing company that forecast design trends. My strength has always been in spotting new talent and bringing visual elements together. While I really enjoyed my work and the publications were successful, I reached a point where I wanted to move from purely presenting new talent in print to working with designers and artists on major museum exhibitions. I knew I had the skills to select work but I also realized that curating involves much more than putting objects and images together, so the MA Curating Contemporary Design at Kingston University with the Design Museum offered exactly what I needed at the time to make that change.

MELITA SKAMNAKI: My background is very similar. Following my graduate studies in Art and Design at Camberwell College of Arts, London, in 2000, I became a copywriter and then creative director in an advertising agency, DDB Athens, Upset and Ogilvy Athens. Everything happens so quickly in advertising, by the age of twenty-eight I was a creative director working on award-winning campaigns for TV, radio and print, and also high-profile branding projects. I was confident with concepts. I enjoyed working with film directors and being involved in large-scale productions. It was a very creative environment but I felt that I wanted to do something that had more of an academic base and a different level of sophistication. When I found out about the MA Curating Contemporary Design course in London, I saw this as an opportunity to combine my previous knowledge and experience in storytelling with something more connected to art and design. When I started the course, I hadn't thought about how exactly I wanted to practice curating, but that changed during the course. Once we started working on projects, I started to collaborate with Wilhelm and that was the start of everything.

DL: What was the first exhibition or project you curated?

MS: During our study, we developed a proposal and sent it to the Oscar Niemeyer Museum in Brazil. The museum, which opened in 2002, is considered to be the largest in Latin America and is dedicated to the exhibition of visual arts, architecture, urbanism and design. We already had a strong network of Brazilian artists and designers, and we knew that the museum was open to new ideas. The proposal was based on a publication, *Katalogue XXL*, that Wilhelm had previously curated, and we wanted to realize the publication as an exhibition. We asked artists to respond to the question: What does XXL mean to you? In the publication, the works were presented as unbound, loose sheets in order to allow everyone to set up their own exhibition, whether at home or in the office. It was the first time that the museum had worked with external curators. We went to Brazil, met with the curatorial team and put our programme together. Viewers were guided through a bold, conceptual showcase. Artists represented a range of backgrounds, styles and practices. They took risks in their approach and were ambitious in the execution, whether it was the concept, medium or aesthetic. The exhibition exploded boundaries and was a celebration of fearless new talent in the art world. The resulting show of over eighty works was the most successful at the Oscar Niemeyer Museum since its opening, and the run of the exhibition was extended twice by popular demand.

WF: When I started the course, the term 'curating' had been rather overused in the fashion and design industry in which I worked. It basically stood for a 'special selection of our products', often with no reason or concept to validate it other than to sell. So learning the true meaning of 'curating', how to develop a strong idea, and not just putting it out there with underdeveloped executions and banal slogans, was an eye-opener to me. I learned how to inspire and engage, to develop new audiences and to build memorable experiences. As a curator, you need to convey a strong message or pose a question, or both. At that time in 2008, those in the commercial world we had left behind to study, were engaging with this kind of approach. So to us it was a powerful method and we couldn't wait to put it into action. We would later have the opportunity to apply everything we had learned on the course.

MS: And because we had both come from established careers, we were experienced at putting pitches together. After our studies, we decided that we were going to do something that would be relevant, considered and purposeful. Now we have students from the course working with us and we realize that we often tell them the same things that our tutors said many years ago. I'm not sure that we fully realized the value of what we were learning at the time, but after we graduated and we started the practice, we were like, 'ok, that's it!'

DL: Have certain curators, exhibitions or encounters been decisive for you? What or who influenced your involvement in design?

MS: I always had a special connection with fashion and a particular interest in the connection between fashion and film. I still remember watching *Belle de Jour by* Luis Buñuel over and over. I couldn't get enough of the costumes by Yves Saint Laurent; there was always something new to discover. I first came to London to study when I was eighteen and it was an eye-opener for me. I went to talks about the role of fashion in film, attended exhibitions, discovered more films and the approach behind them. To me, London as a city is very stimulating. The Design Museum in particular has always been a source of inspiration to me. The course brought us closer to the exhibitions and the curators who were involved with them. You had the opportunity to see and hear great designers like Dieter Rams or film directors like Jean-Luc Godard, Alfred Hitchcock or Stanley Kubrick. I think the fact that we were studying in London, were close to the Design Museum and the V&A, and spending time at the ICA, Tate and other independent galleries was extremely important and stimulating. I have always been interested in the Bauhaus movement and during the course we had the opportunity to study it more and in our practice, we still get inspired by it.

WF: For me, my involvement with design is connected to my childhood. My father had a big appreciation for design which, as a child, I never really understood. Our house was a 1960s bungalow with step levels, Ludwig Mies van der Rohe sofas and bold structured chandeliers by Gaetano Sciolari. It was bare and minimal. Our neighbours' houses, by comparison, were very plush with lots of sofas and carpet everywhere. I never really understood when I was a child why our house was like that. But when I bought my first apartment, I was very particular as to the furniture and the artwork I put in there. On my first trip to London in the early 1990s, I came across the Design Museum and it was like, 'wow, the Panton chairs are here. We had those in our dining room – why are they here?' I saw a Krups orange coffee maker that we had in the kitchen and I began to discover the reasons why these things existed. And to think that design was part of my upbringing without even realizing it!

MS:　I think our studies made us more aware of processes we hadn't really considered before. For example: the alarm clock designed for Braun. It was a clock that woke me up every morning but when you see it within the context of a museum, you start to become interested in the process behind it. I then went to a talk at the V&A by its creator, Dieter Rams and I now fully appreciate the design he created.

DL:　Are there any exhibitions that have had a particular influence on each of you?

WF:　We always get drawn to fashion exhibitions, particularly those that communicate the personality behind the work because everybody wants to feel a bit closer to the creator. In 2008 we met Kaat Debo, the director of the Mode Museum (MoMu) in Antwerp. She gave us a private tour of works in the exhibition, *Maison Martin Margiela '20*. We learned about the designer's radically new visual language and how his entire approach is characterized by an exceptional combination of classic tailoring and conceptual thinking, which makes him unique. This exhibition was a perfect example of showing how theory and design go hand in hand. We both also got really inspired by *The House of Victor & Rolf* at the Barbican in 2008. Again it goes back quite a long time but for us it was a new way forward showing how fashion exhibitions can connect with visitors. The theatrical and surreal set-up of the exhibition design was something we had not experienced before. We were totally immersed in the designer's visionary world.

MS:　*Space Shifters* at the Hayward Gallery in 2018, curated by Cliff Lauson, was another exhibition that stands out. It totally reorientated visitors to their surroundings and we found it relevant in connection with our spatial projects. We admired the artists featured in the exhibition and had come across some of them in our work, for example, Alicja Kwade, which made the show even more interesting to us.

WF:　The 2015 Hayward Gallery exhibition, *Decision*, which featured works by Carsten Höller. The exhibition was a series of experimental environments and was completely transformed by immersive scenography. We saw beyond the exhibits. We were plunged into the world of the artist's mind, entering it through a playful approach. This was a great example of bold exhibition curating.

DL:　How would you define your practice as curators? What is the motivation behind your work?

WF: Our practice combines a research-based approach to design with an intense excitement about the experiences it can create. For each of our projects, we want to create a new and unique journey for the audience.

MS: We also want to make art and design accessible, and to find audiences where one wouldn't necessarily expect to find them. We want to stage encounters with design for people in spaces where they wouldn't expect to find them.

WF: The success of the exhibition, *Katalogue XXL*, opened up new possibilities for us. The artists we had commissioned were featured in art and design publications and celebrated as 'a new wave of designers and artists to watch'. A collector then asked us to curate art and design works for his hotel, and Double Decker was born. Both of us are from continental Europe and we had established an international network of designers and artists in our early careers. It felt natural to use and expand that network for projects, and many of these projects were devising collections for the hospitality industry. When we started to work on the exhibition at the Oscar Niemeyer Museum, we realized that we had access to an amazing pool of talent and that we could create the context for bringing their work into public spaces.

DL: Double Decker, as a curating and design practice, occupies a unique space in its field with projects in the cultural, hospitality and communication sectors. You curate artwork collections for leading hotels and cruise liners, you also design visual identities and curate exhibitions and events for high-profile cultural institutions. When you set up the practice, was it your intention to address all of these areas?

WF: While we started with exhibitions, it was always our intention to promote a multidisciplinary form of curating. We knew there were curators working in museums and gallery spaces and curators with specific subject knowledge. We wanted to bring our backgrounds and our communication skills together and set up a multidisciplinary agency which was quite new at the time.

MS: Yes – we knew that we wanted to do something multidisciplinary and multicultural, bringing together artists and designers from all over the world. We didn't know exactly what form this would take. Before we met, applied art, film and photography were really strong in our separate practices. So the merging of these disciplines came naturally and it happened organically.

WF: Our work starts with an overall concept. As curators, whether we are designing signage, a brand identity or an exhibition, we tie it all together through storytelling. It's similar to the experience of visiting a good exhibition; when you enter the space, you encounter signage, you see artwork on the wall, you see a beautiful chair, it all comes together to create a sense of place. We are currently curating artwork collections for hotel brands such as Rosewood, Fairmond, Grand Hyatt and the new Cunard Ocean Liner. At the award-winning PURO Hotel in Gdańsk, Poland, we are fortunate to have creative freedom and the opportunity to explore fresh and inventive ideas (Figure 3.7). Our initial brief was to ensure that a stay at the hotel was 'an experience' rather than simply an overnight sleep in a room. In terms of curatorial approach and storytelling, our inspiration came from the city's location and its iconic shipyard, which was also the birthplace of the Solidarity movement. There are still artist studios within the location, including that of renowned photographer Michal Szlaga. He has dedicated his life to creating a photographic record of the shipyard, and his works now feature at the hotel. Throughout, we sought to capture a distinctive take on Gdańsk, to clearly reference the city, but in a convincingly abstract way. Just as the property brought new elements of hospitality to the region, we also presented an original aesthetic that was progressive and which put the guest at the centre of the experience.

DL: How does curating for a hotel or cruise liner differ from curating for a museum or gallery space? What do you see as the challenges, but also the opportunities?

MS: We are working on a major project for the heritage Ocean Liner company, Cunard which has involved an artistic collaboration with thirty graduates from the Royal College of Art, London, Central Saint Martins, London and Parsons, New York. We have selected work by thirty graduates and asked each of them to take over a specific space on the cruise liner. We wrote a creative brief for

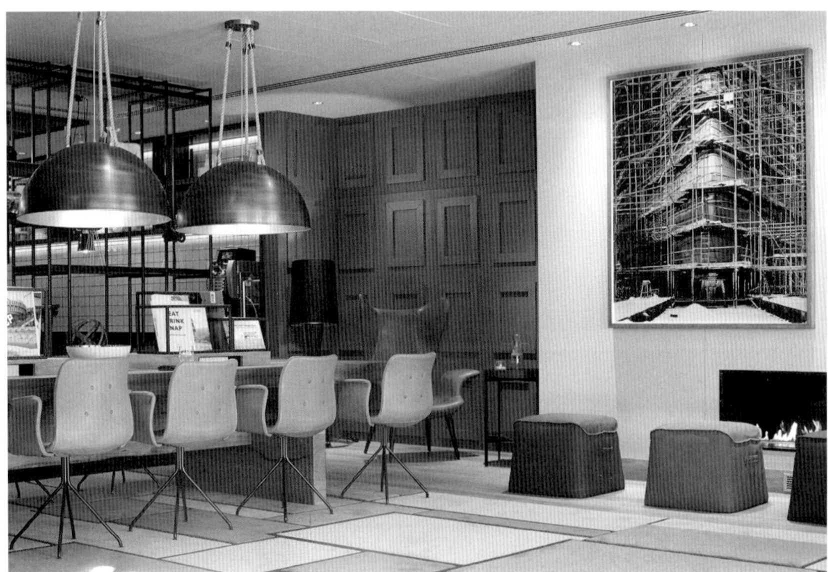

FIGURE 3.7 *Interior view, PURO Hotel, Gdańsk, Poland © Anna Stathaki.*

the graduates but we didn't want to limit them. We followed a research-based approach involving extensive archival research. We selected the graduates who we felt were best able to communicate the overall narrative powerfully and definitively. This process is similar to curating an exhibition, but we had to make sure that the brand's DNA was apparent.

WF: I think the difference in curating for a cruise liner, as opposed to an exhibition in a museum, comes from the fact that we have to respect the client's brief. When you curate an exhibition, there is more opportunity to experiment with different ways of engaging an audience. We have to follow fairly strict guidelines set by the client, so our challenge is to curate unique, previously unseen art and design work while also taking into account the overall ethos of the brand. When we work for an established brand like Cunard, we need to understand what the brand is about and how we need to present the brand, and our background in communications ensures that we are able to do so.

MS: It's the first time such a project has taken place on a cruise liner. We had a really strong case for winning the bid because we could promote the fact that we were curators, rather than advisors. In our pitch we explained we wanted to work with young people and with universities. It's one of the reasons we set up the agency, to foreground young and emerging talent, and this is what we continue to do in our practice.

WF: Curating work in hotels, for example, presents us with a unique opportunity because hotels are places where people come together and expect to see interiors that are different to their own homes. Hospitality settings are often intriguing spaces as they usually present, or imply, a history, a narrative or a set of meanings against which we can work.

DL: You mentioned a research-based approach. Do you spend a lot of time researching a brand?

MS: Cunard have a really incredible archive at Liverpool University. We went many times. We looked at all the visual elements they have collected: the corporate identities, the fixtures and fittings, the evening gowns worn by past guests, the stories of passengers who have travelled on the liners. The chosen graduates also went to the archive to carry out their own research. We gave each university a different subject to work on but they were free to interpret it as they wanted. Everybody responded so well. As a result, we have so many mediums represented: kinetic artwork, photography, tapestry, knitting, weaving. The works are located on the landings of the staircases, which have become vertical gallery spaces.

WF: I think one of the reasons Cunard hired us is because they wanted to broaden their audience. They were keen to engage with a different audience and move away from the traditional image of a cruise ship. They wanted to do something different that had more modernity. The company doesn't operate in the same way as other ocean liners. They have a different approach. They work with interesting interior designers. They also support the idea of working with young artists and this project was a way for them to facilitate that. They also wanted to build up the archives. We didn't just research the 'golden age' of cruise liners in the 1920s and 1930s; we also drew on later material. It would be great if, in a hundred years, the archives refer back to our work.

DL: **Your backgrounds are in advertising and art direction for fashion publishing. How has this influenced your work as curators?**

WF: Recognizing the value and importance of a strong concept and knowing how to put a brief together. It also helped that I had already developed the ability to make selections and identify the right people to work with.

MS: My background in creative advertising has made it easier to hone in on a concept from a plethora of ideas. It's taught me how to put a brief together, how to tell a story, first to the client and then to the viewing audience. Stories should not be overly complicated to discover.

DL: **There have been a plethora of publications on curating but they have mostly focused on the area of fine art curation, with design curation and the role of the design curator remaining largely unexplored. Why do you think the practice of design curating has been so neglected, despite being a growth area over the last twenty years?**

MS: I think that it's a fairly recent shift that people have started to fully appreciate the objects that they use in everyday life. They have started seeing them in museums and exhibitions and understanding more about the process behind them. The most successful and simple design object can often have quite a complicated story behind it.

WF: I think design is a fairly new discipline, because before there was art and craft. Art was always very high-end and craft was considered more inferior in status. There was the V&A but it was more focused on the decorative arts and design really wasn't seen as a subject to be taken seriously. Since the beginnings of the Design Museum in London, design has really started to be more appreciated in the UK.

DL: **So for you the Design Museum has been a really important development in focusing attention on design?**

WF: Definitely. Every design exhibition I have been to has inspired me to further explore the subject, which in turn has been a source of inspiration for developing our concepts for curating. It has expanded my knowledge, not just of design of the eras I naturally feel more inclined towards, but also those that were not so familiar to me. For the Cunard project, I loved being able to research designs from the 1920s onwards.

MS: The Design Museum was one of the first institutions in London to tell the story of design and communicate its impact to a wider audience. We experienced this transition in our first years in London and it has helped us a great deal in our practice.

DL: **What is unique about the practice of curating design? What is distinctive about the role of the design curator?**

WF: We think it's quite simple; it's all about the concept and a narrative. When you go to a design exhibition, a concept and a narrative communicates a message for the overall exhibition. With art exhibitions, the message is often very open. The art curator gives more freedom to the viewer's interpretation. The objects of our everyday lives have some very interesting and deep stories to tell us, which can make people feel more included in the story.

MS: Design is an important force in our lives and the design curator, in many ways, is more involved in the visitor's everyday lives. Curators need to be able to tell an engaging story to help people to feel and understand it. Visitors to exhibitions are viewers, critics and consumers at the same time. The curator has a role in entertaining, educating and ensuring that the visitor has an extraordinary experience.

DL: **What do you feel are the essential components of a good design exhibition?**

MS: A good subject – that's very important. Strong research behind the objects and a strong narrative. The way you combine it all is important. You create an experience so that when people leave an exhibition, they feel inspired. It's similar to when you see a really great movie; you just want to stay with the feeling. I have been to exhibitions that are like that, for example, *ITEMS: Is Fashion Modern?* at MoMA in 2018. The exhibition featured 111 items of clothing and accessories that have had a strong impact on the world in the twentieth- and twenty-first centuries, whether they were made during that time or before, for example, 'the hoodie' or a Sari. It not only explained how items are designed, manufactured and distributed, but also asked questions about the relationships between clothing and functionality, cultural etiquettes, aesthetics, politics, economy and technology. The exhibition also looked ahead by inviting current designers, artists and engineers to respond to some of those indispensable items with new materials, approaches and design techniques. Other exhibitions that come to mind are *The House of Victor and Rolf* at the Barbican (2008), *Yohji Yamamoto* at the V&A (2008) and *Alexander McQueen: Savage Beauty* at the V&A (2015).

DL:　How can design curators and design institutions more successfully interact and engage with their audiences?

MS:　We have found that moving away from traditional exhibition spaces and offering more discursive events such as interactive workshops can really make a difference. In 2016 we curated an exhibition in Greece for the Onassis Cultural Centre. The exhibition, *Strange Cities: Athens*, asked: 'What does it take to capture the essence of a city you have never visited?' We deliberately placed the exhibition in the centre of the city, taking over an old school building very close to the meat market in a deprived, yet busy neighbourhood. We invited twenty-five award-winning visual artists to create new pieces in response to Athens, inspired only by a box of non-visual 'clues' that included a recipe for stuffed tomatoes, a poem and a recording of a popular vintage song. The exhibition was accompanied by thirty wraparound programmes ranging from bicycle tours and city walks to food workshops led by designers and makers. The exhibition cafe offered Greek food inspired by classic Athenian recipes. It was open all the time and accessible to everybody, as we wanted the exhibition to be completely inclusive. It really transformed the character of the area over three months.

WF:　It attracted people of all ages and all backgrounds, from schoolchildren and students to workers, residents and refugees. We believe that the combination of visual and sensory participatory events made it attractive to all those audiences.

MS:　It offered visitors great experiences, for example, on the way out of the exhibition you could take part in a workshop. You were able to create your own still life, take a picture and upload it on Instagram. It was a celebration for everybody. The whole city was talking about the exhibition, people were making repeat visits. It was about Athens from an outsider's perspective, and that's why so many people felt connected to it. It was an exhibition for the city and the people that lived there but it was also for people who hadn't previously visited the city. Local people saw the city from a different perspective and this started really wonderful dialogues. The project has had to stop because of the pandemic but we are planning to continue it in different cities.

DL: **What are the key shifts that have influenced design curating practice over the last two decades?**

MS: Design exhibitions have expanded dramatically. Design is now as collectable as art. Exhibitions have become less didactic, more accessible to wider audiences. Curators often create spectacular experiences in order to tell a story, a fact that audiences enjoy. Design museums around the world are moving away from looking like a furniture store.

WF: What I think has changed is that there is an understanding of the design process. In the past, the object was displayed, there was a label with some information about who designed it and when it was made, and that was about it. Now as much attention is given to explaining the creative process behind an object, or the historical and social context in which the object was created. The overall experience for visitors has become much more engaging. The design of an exhibition has become more participatory. Exhibitions have become more visitor-centred and I think that has been a major shift. Museums are bolder in their approach to reach out to new audiences.

DL: **How have these developments impacted your own practice?**

MS: Museums are more open and this has given us the opportunity as external curators to work with different institutions. Museums have their in-house teams, but we find that when they want something a bit different or want to think about widening their audience, they invite us into the institution.

DL: **What do you feel are the key debates driving design at this moment to which curators must respond?**

WF: We have a lot of pressing environmental problems and the design curator can bring attention to these big issues. If you look back to the introduction of 3D printing, it was very interesting to see new objects created out of recycled material. There is a strong message there. Design curators have the power to heighten awareness.

MS: How to act responsibly as consumers, highlighting the need to ensure that we use the right products to protect ourselves and the planet. Other important issues are accessibility, diversity and inclusivity. It's a good time for design museums to be sharing the message about the importance of these issues. Exhibitions and design objects can present an engaging way to learn about these important issues, instead of only reading depressing articles about them. You can visit an exhibition, learn about the issue in an experiential way, find ways to talk to your children about the issue and discover how to take action. Design has the power to convey a message. If we were starting to work on an exhibition concept now, we would definitely place environmental issues at the top of the agenda … you might have given us an idea!

Curating is everywhere; it now takes place in many different spaces. But the museum is needed to host the experience. We need museums because this is where people source information, they are important educational spaces. Culture needs to be supported by the government. We cannot end up with only consumer spaces. Connecting your children to cultural spaces is important and has a huge impact on them. Dealing with life through culture creates better human beings. And museums offer that.

WF: The museum will get back to where it was before. It's about belonging; it's like going to see a great film in a cinema. This unique experience cannot be taken away. Museums have been very progressive in the last ten years and I think that they will continue to progress, even more so after the pandemic. We have hope!

DL: **What advice would you give to a young curator entering the field today? What skill set will the design curator of the future need to have?**

MS: It is important to have a good idea. Research is very important to back up good ideas. And all the time, be open to new things and stay connected with what's happening around you. We always say that you need to be strict with yourself, otherwise your audience will be. Visitors will remember what didn't go right in a show. Before and during any project, we always ask ourselves; Are we sure about this?

WF: Don't be afraid to be individual. It's really important for a curator to have an identity and a position. Use your work to express what you stand for. Curating has become a very abused word. We have even seen curated crisps! The word was used on the packet and we said, no way! When we pitch to different clients, whether to hotel owners or museum directors, we always talk about our academic background. It's very important for us to have the masters degree to show that we have the academic background to support our practice.

MS: We have created a niche for ourselves, in terms of the clients we work for and the spaces we work in. The design curator at this moment has the ability to define what their practice is. Curating gives you an incredible opportunity to develop new narratives about design and to experiment with new spaces for showing design.

Closing Comments

This book set out to map the key moments that have been pertinent to the development of the practice of curating design. The most important aspect of this development is that, from the 1980s a new type of specialist museum emerged on the global stage focused on the collection, study and exhibition of modern and contemporary design. The new museum of design required creative people to work in this rapidly expanding area of curatorial practice, to interpret and explain design culture. It called for a specialist skill set, to which a proliferation of postgraduate programmes and training courses responded. During the 1990s, the MA History of Design programme at the RCA and the V&A and later, the MA Curating Contemporary Design at Kingston University and the Design Museum, provided important training grounds for those entering the emerging field of design curating.

The design museum, as an institution, has provided a platform for the many different meanings of design communicated through a range of formats: exhibitions and collection displays, learning and public programmes, design awards and residencies. Design is a vast subject. It has come to encompass so many areas in the last few decades – objects but also services, systems, experiences, the virtual and the digital. The role of the design curator is to capture, interpret and communicate this rapidly changing landscape.

With new design museums opening internationally, and existing museums redefining themselves, the design museum looks set to remain a key part of the future of design curating. Design museums make sense of, and interpret, a rapidly changing world and, in so doing, reinforce the distinctiveness of the practice of curating design.

It is clear that the role of the curator has come a long way from its origins as a guardian, overseer or carer of collections. The role has expanded beyond its traditional parameters to become a diverse practice, located within the institution and outside of it. In 2022 the perception of the design curator as primarily the guardian of a collection is no longer accurate, nor is it a useful way of understanding the role. Curating is now articulated as a constantly shifting and adaptive discipline. It is a multifaceted practice that has changed the key constituents of the role.

The interviews with eight curators that form the final section of this book have revealed a fast-moving practice that takes place inside the museum, but that also extends into other spaces such as the commercial gallery, the design festival, the biennial, the public square, digital, publishing, the community project and the small not-for-profit organization. There are a growing number of independent curators working outside public institutions. In these spaces there is a freedom in being able to experiment with many different forms of curatorial practice and cultural production. This might be curating a series of talks or a publication, developing a festival, working with a community project or local government, curating a series of digital works or an online programme. Here the curator is able to be agile and responsive to change, perhaps more so than working within the institutional remit of a museum or larger cultural institution. These spaces offer the curator the possibility of working with new frameworks and processes to create new forms of public engagement.

At this moment, the design curator has the ability to define their practice, develop new narratives about design and experiment with new spaces in which to exhibit design. The curators interviewed for this book connect to earlier debates that were circulating during the 1980s and 1990s, discussed in Part One and Two, but they also signpost future directions for curatorial practice in the field of contemporary design. The findings that have emerged from the individual sections of this book reveal a series of themes that, when taken together, foster an understanding of design curating as a developing practice. They reveal much about the current landscape for contemporary design and its accompanying practice. In addition, the shape of the debate for design museums and design curators for the next decade is already emerging in outline.

In 2020 the world experienced an unprecedented moment of crisis and change. The Covid-19 pandemic had a devastating impact on museums and the cultural sector. National lockdowns in many countries across the world forced museums to close for long periods and to consider how they continued to communicate with their audiences. This period proved to be a transformational eighteen months for the cultural sector, presenting huge challenges but also opportunities for the curator. The pandemic quickly pushed curators and their audiences into virtual spaces. This resulted in a new emphasis on the potential of digital spaces and experiences to connect not only with existing, but also new and underrepresented, audiences.

Many museums are eighteenth- and nineteenth-century institutions that have had to adapt and change to make themselves relevant to twenty-first-century audiences. This struggle is reflected in recent efforts by the International Council of Museums (ICOM) to update their definition of what a museum is. The very public disagreements as to what this new definition should be reflect a wider debate in the cultural sector as to whether museums should be places that exhibit and research artefacts, or ones that actively engage with political and social issues.[1]

In 2020 the Museums Association (MA) launched a new Manifesto for Museum Learning and Engagement. Over twenty years previously, David Anderson's report, *A Common Wealth: Museums in the Learning Age*, had called for learning to be placed at the centre of the development of museums. The new manifesto acknowledged that we now live in a very different world with digital technologies embedded in every aspect of our life and work. The Covid-19 pandemic, the murder of George Floyd and the Black Lives Matter movement have sharply revealed the realities of contemporary inequality, in ways that can no longer be evaded or concealed. The MA acknowledged that museum partnerships, collections, programmes and exhibitions do not represent the diversity of society. The new manifesto calls for museums to play a central role in civic renewal and social change to address the challenges of our time.[2]

Increasingly the design museum has become a space in which to speculate how design can imagine, debate and build a better future. As Professor Don Norman, recipient of the Sir Misha Black 2021 Medal, commented, 'the discipline of design is starting to be recognised for its ability to address core underlying issues facing the world. As a result, we must add both depth and breadth to today's design curricula so that future designers will be leaders in guiding the future of humankind, applying people-centred thinking to the complex issues of the 21st century'.[3] The design curator has a vital role to play in realizing this ambition.

In October 2021 the Design Museum, London, opened a new exhibition that responded to the environmental crisis created by the global 'take, make, waste' economy, *Waste Age: What Can Design Do?* Visitors were immersed in the waste crisis before being shown the transformative potential of new design approaches that are redefining fashion, construction, food, electronics or packaging and the new materials that will help shape a cleaner future. The

---

[1] 'What Is a Museum? A Dispute Erupts over a New Definition', Alex Marshall, *New York Times*, 6 August 2020. Available at: https://www.nytimes.com/2020/08/06/arts/what-is-a-museum/ (accessed 15 August 2020).

[2] Museums Association website. Available at: https://www.museumsassociation.org/campaigns/learning-and-engagement/manifesto/ (accessed 12 September 2020).

[3] Sir Misha Black Awards website. Available at: www.mishablackawards.org.uk (accessed 6 October 2021).

exhibition not only sought to imagine alternative futures, but also to empower the visitor to be part of the solution.

As world leaders convened in Glasgow for the COP26 Climate Change conference in November 2021, the Design Museum launched at the conference a new national programme of research, debate and training, *Future Observatory*. The programme, coordinated by the Design Museum in partnership with the Arts and Humanities Research Council (AHRC) brings together the most important thinkers in academia, industry and culture to define and accelerate how design can find solutions to the most pressing global issues, from building resilience for a post-pandemic world to an ageing population, climate change and the rise of artificial intelligence.[4]

A new curatorial team has been recruited to direct and manage the programme. The new programme demonstrates the potential of the design museum to develop new organizational models and national collaborations for supporting research and innovation across design, architecture and technology. It also provides validation for the role of the design curator in finding innovative ways to communicate the outcomes of the research and to shape public conversation and engagement with design.

In this respect, the curator is no longer in the position of an 'expert' or 'custodian' but one where there is an intent to engage with the contemporary and make sense of global issues and how design might respond to that context. Curator Fleur Watson has underlined the vital role of the curator, given the extreme global challenges the world currently faces, which include climate change, the Covid-19 pandemic, the ongoing impact of colonialism, the rise of nationalistic policies and the 'post-truth' society that has emerged from constant digital connectivity. She argues for a new definition of the curator as 'articulating and responding to the complexity and precariousness of our time, the "new curator" is a hybrid and dexterous practitioner'.[5]

Curators have a duty to reflect on their practice and to think about how they can develop, not only more inclusive ways of working but also how they can give space to more representative narratives and histories that have been overlooked, or deliberately concealed. Design is a great tool for decolonizing. For educator and designer Danah Abdulla, a member of the research group Decolonising Design, 'decoloniality is about shattering the familiar'. Abdulla has written extensively on the colonial systems within which contemporary design operates. She argues that decoloniality is about reimagining something

---

[4]Presentation by Justin McGuirk, Chief Curator, the Design Museum, to MA CCD students at the Design Museum, 27 October 2021.

[5]Fleur Watson, *The New Curator: Exhibiting Architecture and Design*, Oxfordshire: Routledge, 2021: 13.

beyond the current system we exist in.[6] In 2016, a group of museum and heritage professionals formed Museum Detox, a network for people of colour who work in museums, galleries, libraries, archives and the heritage sector. The network aims to champion fair representation and works to deconstruct existing systems of inequality to enable a sector where the workforce and audience is reflective of the UK's twenty-first-century population.[7]

Maura Reilly has suggested that, in the course of their work, curators should ask themselves some key questions: What are my biases? Am I excluding large constituents of people in their selections? Have I favoured male artists over female, white over Black – if so, why? She urges mainstream curators to join the ranks of curatorial activists working worldwide to institute change: 'Don't just sit and wait for change to come: be proactive. Take affirmative action.'[8]

It is for the next generation of design curators to debate and determine the post-pandemic landscape for curating and the new forms of curation that will emerge. As this book has sought to show, curating design in the twenty-first century is complex, challenging, creative and, ultimately, collaborative. It is precisely those aspects that make it such a fascinating and dynamic area of curatorial practice.

---

[6]Anoushka Khandwala, 'What Does It Mean to Decolonize Design?', *Eye on Design*, 5 June 2019. Available at: https://eyeondesign.aiga.org/what-does-it-mean-to-decolonize-design/ (accessed 20 June 2019).
[7]Museum Detox website. Available at: www.museumdetox.org (accessed 20 June 2019).
[8]Maura Reilly, *Curatorial Activism: Towards an Ethics of Curating*, London: Thames & Hudson, 2018: 225.

Bibliography

Antonelli, Paola. *Design and the Elastic Mind*. New York: Museum of Modern Art, 2008.

Antonelli, Paola, and Jamer Hunt (ed.). *Design and Violence*. New York: MoMA, 2015.

Armstrong, Leah, and Felice McDowell (eds.). *Fashioning Identities: Identity and Representation at Work in the Creative Industries*. London: Bloomsbury, 2018.

Balzar, David. *Curationism: How Curating Took Over the Art World and Everything Else*. London: Pluto Press, 2015.

Bayley, Stephen. *Commerce and Culture: From Pre-Industrial Art to Post-Industrial Value*. London: Design Museum, 1989.

Benjamin, Walter. *The Arcades Project*, translated by Howard Eiland and Kevin McLaughlin. Cambridge, MA: Belknap Press of Harvard University Press, 1999.

Benjamin, Walter. *The Work of Art in the Age of Mechanical Reproduction*, translated by J. A. Underwood. London: Penguin Books, 2008.

Bennett, Tony. *The Birth of the Museum: History, Theory, Politics*. London: Routledge, 1995.

Berger, Maurice (ed.). *Museums of Tomorrow: A Virtual Discussion*. Centre for Visual Art and Culture, Baltimore: University of Maryland, 2004.

Bishop, Claire. *Artificial Hells: Participatory Art and the Politics of Spectatorship*. London: Verso Books, 2012.

Black, Graham. *The Engaging Museum: Developing Museums for Visitor Involvement*. London: Routledge, 2005.

Black, Graham. *Transforming Museums in the Twenty-First Century*. London: Routledge, 2011.

Brewer, Christopher, Fiona Fisher and Ghislaine Wood (eds.). *British Design: Tradition and Modernity after 1948*. London: Bloomsbury, 2015.

Bruner, Jerome. *Actual Minds, Possible Worlds*. Cambridge, MA: Harvard University Press, 1986.

Buckley, Cheryl. *Designing Modern Britain*. London: Reaktion Books, 2007.

Burton, Anthony. *Vision & Accident: The Story of the Victoria and Albert Museum*. London: V&A, 1999.

Chaplin, Sarah, and Alexandra Stara (eds). *Curating Architecture and the City*. Oxfordshire: Routledge, 2009.

Charman, Helen. *The Productive Eye: Conceptualising Learning in the Design Museum*. PhD thesis. Institute of Education, University of London, 2011.

Clark, Judith, and Amy De La Haye. *Exhibiting Fashion: Before and After 1971*. New Haven, CT: Yale University Press, 2014.

Conran, Terence. *My Life in Design*. London: Conran Octopus, 2016.

Csikszentmihalyi, Mihaly. *Creativity: Flow and the Psychology of Discovery and Invention*. New York: Harper & Row, 1996.

Dana, John Cotton. *The New Museum: Selected Writings by John Cotton Dana*, edited by W. A. Peniston. Washington, DC: The Newark Museum Association, NJ, 1999.

Dernie, David. *Exhibition Design*. London: Laurence King, 2006.

Dudley, Sandra H. (ed.). *Museum Objects: Experiencing the Properties of Things*. Oxfordshire: Routledge, 2012.

Falk, John H., and Lynn D. Dierking (eds). *The Museum Experience Revisited*. Oxfordshire: Routledge, 2013.

Farrelly, Liz, and Joanna Weddell (eds). *Design Objects and the Museum*. London: Bloomsbury, 2012.

Forty, Adrian. *Objects of Desire: Design and Society since 1750*. London: Thames & Hudson, [1992] 2005.

Fowle, Kate. 'Who Cares? Understanding the Role of the Curator Today', in *Cautionary Tales: Critical Curating*, New York: apexart, 2007.

Gardner, Howard. *Frames of Mind: The Theory of Multiple Intelligences*. New York: Basic Books, 1983.

George, Adrian. *The Curator's Handbook: Museums, Commercial Galleries, Independent Spaces*. London: Thames & Hudson, 2015.

Goodyear, A. Conger. *The Museum of Modern Art: The First Ten Years*. New York: Museum of Modern Art, 1943.

Graham, Beryl, and Sarah Cook. *Rethinking Curating: Art after New Media*. London: Bloomsbury, 2010.

Grau, Oliver. *Virtual Art: From Illusion to Immersion*. Boston, MA: MIT Press, 2003.

Greenberg, Reesa, Bruce W. Ferguson and Sandy Nairne. *Thinking about Exhibitions*. Oxfordshire: Routledge, 1996.

Griffiths, Alison. *Shivers down Your Spine: Cinema, Museums & the Immersive View*. New York: Columbia University Press, 2013.

Hoffmann, Jens (ed.). *The Exhibitionist: Journal on Exhibition Making – the First Six Years 2010–2016*. New York: Artbook, 2017.

Hoffmann, Jens (ed.). *Ten Fundamental Questions of Curating*. Milan: Mousse, 2013.

Hooper-Greenhill, Eilean. *The Educational Role of the Museum*. Oxfordshire: Routledge, 1999.

Hooper-Greenhill, Eilean. *Museums and the Shaping of Knowledge*. Oxfordshire: Routledge, 2015.

Hooper-Greenhill, Eilean. *Museums and Their Visitors*. Oxfordshire: Routledge, 1994.

Hoving, Thomas. *Making the Mummies Dance*. New York: Simon & Schuster, 1993.

Hughes, P. *Exhibition Design*. London: Laurence King, 2010.

Impey, Oliver, and Arthur MacGregor. *The Origins of the Museum: The Cabinet of Curiosities in Sixteenth and Seventeenth Century Europe*. Oxfordshire: Oxford University Press, 1985.

Ince, Catherine. *The World of Charles and Ray Eames*. London: Thames & Hudson, 2015.

Jackson, Andrew. *'From Solving Problems to Selling Products', Designing Britain: 1945–1975*. Available at: https://www.vads.ac.uk/customizations/collection/DCADB/pages/html/crd.html (accessed 12 September 2018).

Jeppsson, Frida (ed.). *In Case of Design – Inject Critical Thinking.* Stockholm: Frida Jeppsson, 2010.

Julier, Guy. *The Culture of Design.* London: Sage, 3rd edition, 2013.

Karch, Fritz, and Rebecca Robertson. *Collected: Living with the Things You Love.* New York: Abrams, 2014.

Kavanagh, G. (ed.). *Making Histories in Museums.* London: Leicester University Press, 2002.

Kirkham, Pat. *Charles and Ray Eames: Designers of the Twentieth Century.* Cambridge, MA: MIT Press, 1995.

Knox, Tim. *Sir John Soane's Museum.* London: Merrell, 2016.

Kolb, David. *Experiential Learning: Experience as the Source of Learning and Development.* New Jersey: Prentice Hall, 1984.

Kotler, Neil G., Philip Kotler and Wendy I. Kotler. *Museum Marketing and Strategy: Designing Missions, Building Audiences, Generating Revenue and Resources.* San Francisco, CA: Jossey-Bass, 2008.

Lang, C., J. Reeve and V. Woollard. *The Responsive Museum.* Hants: Ashgate, 2006.

Macleod, Suzanne, Laura Hourston Hanks and Jonathan Hale (eds). *Museum Making: Narratives, Architectures, Exhibitions.* London: Routledge, 2012.

Marincola, Paula (ed.). *What Makes a Great Exhibition?.* Philadelphia: Philadelphia Exhibitions Press, 2006.

Markopoulos, Leigh (ed.). *Great Expectations: Prospects for the Future of Curatorial Education.* Koln: Koenig Books, 2015.

Martinon, Jean-Paul (ed.). *The Curatorial: A Philosophy of Curating.* London: Bloomsbury, 2013.

McDermott, Catherine. *20th Century Design.* London: Carlton Books, 1997.

Message, Kylie. *Collecting Activism: Archiving Occupy Wall Street.* Oxfordshire: Routledge, 2019.

Message, Kylie. *The Disobedient Museum: Writing at the Edge.* Oxfordshire: Routledge, 2017.

Message, Kylie. *Museums and Racism.* Oxfordshire: Routledge, 2018.

Miller, Daniel. *The Comfort of Things.* Cambridge: Polity Press, 2008.

Morris, Barbara. *Inspiration for Design: The Influence of the Victoria and Albert Museum.* London: Victoria and Albert Museum, 1986.

Newson, Alex, Eleanor Suggett and Deyan Sudjic. *Designer Maker User.* London: Phaidon Press, 2016.

O'Doherty, Brian. *Inside the White Cube: The Ideology of the Gallery Space.* Berkeley: University of California Press, 1976.

O'Neill, Paul. *The Culture of Curating and the Curating of Culture(s).* Cambridge, MA: MIT Press, 2012.

O'Neill, Paul (ed.). *Curating Subjects.* London: Open Editions, 2007.

O'Neill, Paul, and Mick Wilson (eds). *Curating Research.* London: Open Editions, 2015.

O'Neill, Paul, Mick Wilson and Lucy Steeds (eds). *The Curatorial Conundrum: What to Study? What to Research? What to Practice?* London: MIT Press, 2016.

Obrist, Hans Ulrich. *A Brief History of Curating*. Zurich: JRP/Ringier, 2008.

Obrist, Hans Ulrich. *Everything You Always Wanted to Know about Curating*. Berlin: Sternberg Press, 2011.

Palmer, J. A. (ed.). *Fifty Modern Thinkers on Education: From Piaget to the Present*. Oxfordshire: Routledge, 2001.

Pine, B. Joseph, and James H. Gilmore. *The Experience Economy*. Boston, MA: Harvard Business Review Press, 2011.

Raicovich, Laura. *Culture Strike: Art Museums in an Age of Protest*. London: Verso, 2021.

Rand, Steven, and Heather Kouris (eds). *Cautionary Tales: Critical Curating*. New York: apexart, 2007.

Rawsthorn, Alice. *Design as Attitude*. London: JRP Ringier, 2018.

Rawsthorn, Alice. *Hello World: Where Design Meets Life*. London: Hamish Hamilton, 2013.

Read, Herbert. *Art & Industry*. London: Faber and Faber, 1934.

Reilly, Maura. *Curatorial Activism: Towards an Ethics of Curating*. London: Thames & Hudson, 2018.

Richards, Charles R. *Industrial Art and the Museum*. New York: Macmillan, 1927.

Roberts, Lisa C. *From Knowledge to Narrative: Educators and the Changing Museum*. Washington: Smithsonian Institution Press, 1997.

Rogoff, Irit. 'Turning', *e-flux journal*, Issue 00, November 2008. Available at: www.e-flux.com (accessed 15 March 2019).

Rosenbaum, Steven. *Curation Nation: How to Win in a World Where Consumers Are Curators*. New York: McGraw Hill, 2010.

Rugg, Judith, and Michèle Sedgwick (eds). *Issues in Curating Contemporary Art and Performance*. Bristol: Intellect Books, 2007.

Ryan, Zoë (ed.). *As Seen: Exhibitions That Made Architecture and Design History*. London: Yale University Press, 2017.

Sandino, Linda, and Matthew Partington (eds). *Oral History in the Visual Arts*. London: Bloomsbury, 2013.

Schön, Donald A. *The Reflective Practitioner: How Professionals Think in* Action. New York: Basic Books, 1983.

Schubert, Karsten. *The Curator's Egg: The Evolution of the Museum Concept from the French Revolution to the Present Day*. London: One-Off Press, 2000.

Sellers, Libby. *Women Design: Pioneers in Architecture, Industrial, Graphic and Digital Design from the Twentieth Century to the Present Day*. London: Francis Lincoln, 2018.

Serota, Nicholas. *Experience or Interpretation: Dilemma of Museums of Modern Art*. London: Thames & Hudson, 2000.

Simon, Nina. *The Participatory Museum*. Santa Cruz, CA: Museum, 2010.

Smith, Marquard (ed.). *Decolonizing: The Curriculum, the Museum, and the Mind*. Vilnius: Academy of Arts Press, 2020.

Smith, Terry. *Thinking Contemporary Curating*. New York: Independent Curators International, 2012.

Spalding, Julian. *The Poetic Museum*. London: Prestel, 2002.

Sparke, Penny. *Design in Context*. London: Quarto, 1987.

Sparke Penny. *As Long As It's Pink: The Sexual Politics of Taste*. Canada: NSCAD, 2010.

Sparke, Penny, and Deyan Sudjic. *Representing Architecture: New Discussions: Ideologies, Techniques, Curation*. London: Design Museum, 2008.

Sparke, Penny, Brenda Martin and Trevor Keeble (eds.). *The Modern Period Room: The Construction of the Exhibited Interior 1870–1950*. Oxfordshire: Routledge, 2006.

Staniszewski, M. A. *The Power of Display: A History of Exhibition Installation at the Museum of Modern Art*. Cambridge, MA: MIT Press, 1998.

Storrie, Calum. *The Delirious Museum: A Journey from the Louvre to Las Vegas*. London: I. B. Tauris, 2006.

Sudjic, Deyan. *B Is for Bauhaus*. London: Penguin Books, 2014.

Sudjic, Deyan. *The Language of Things*. London: Penguin Books, 2008.

Tallon, Loïc, and Kevin Walker. *Digital Technologies and the Museum Experience: Handheld Guides and Other Media*. Lanham: AltaMira Press, 2008.

Thea, Carolee. *On Curating: Interviews with Ten International Curators*. New York: Distributed Art, 2009.

Twemlow, Alice. *Sifting the Trash: A History of Design Criticism*. Cambridge, MA: MIT Press, 2017.

Vänskä, Annamari, and Hazel Clark (eds). *Fashion Curating: Critical Practice in the Museum and Beyond*. London: Bloomsbury, 2018.

Vergo, Peter (ed.). *The New Museology*. London: Reaktion Books, 1989.

Vest Hansen, Malene, Anne Folke Henningsen and Anne Gregersen (eds). *Curatorial Challenges: Interdisciplinary Perspectives on Contemporary Curating*. Oxfordshire: Routledge, 2019.

von Bismarck, Beatrice, and Benjamin Meyer-Krahmer (eds). *Hospitality: Hosting Relations in Exhibitions*. Berlin: Sternberg Press, 2016.

Walker, Martyn. *The Development of the Mechanics' Institute Movement in Britain and Beyond: Supporting Further Education for the Adult Working Classes*. Oxfordshire: Routledge, 2017.

Watson, Fleur. *The New Curator: Exhibiting Architecture and Design*. Oxfordshire: Routledge, 2021.

Wilk, Christopher. *Creating the British Galleries at the V&A: A Study in Museology*. London: V&A, 2004.

Williams, Gareth. *Design: An Essential Introduction*. London: Goodman Fiell, 2015.

Wilson, Tom (ed.). *Designs of Our Times: 10 Years of Designs of the Year*. London: Design Museum, 2017.

Wilson, Tom. *Imagining Empire: Designing the Commonwealth Institute*. London: Lund Humphries, 2021.

Wilson, Tom. *The Story of the Design Museum*. London: Phaidon Press, 2016.

Index